NO MOUNTAIN TOO HIGH

NO
MOUNTAIN
TOO HIGH

Dr Kumaran Rasappan

WITH JULEEN SHAW

Marshall Cavendish
Editions

Published in 2022 by Marshall Cavendish Editions
An imprint of Marshall Cavendish International

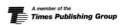

A member of the
Times Publishing Group

The publisher makes no representation or warranties with respect to the contents of this book, and specifically disclaims any implied warranties or merchantability or fitness for any particular purpose, and shall in no event be liable for any loss of profit or any other commercial damage, including but not limited to special, incidental, consequential, or other damages.

Other Marshall Cavendish Offices:
Marshall Cavendish Corporation, 800 Westchester Ave, Suite N-641, Rye Brook, NY 10573, USA • Marshall Cavendish International (Thailand) Co Ltd, 253 Asoke, 16th Floor, Sukhumvit 21 Road, Klongtoey Nua, Wattana, Bangkok 10110, Thailand • Marshall Cavendish (Malaysia) Sdn Bhd, Times Subang, Lot 46, Subang Hi-Tech Industrial Park, Batu Tiga, 40000 Shah Alam, Selangor Darul Ehsan, Malaysia

Marshall Cavendish is a registered trademark of Times Publishing Limited

National Library Board, Singapore Cataloguing-in-Publication Data

Name(s): Rasappan, Kumaran. | Shaw, Juleen, author.
Title: No mountain too high / Dr Kumaran Rasappan with Juleen Shaw.
Description: Singapore : Marshall Cavendish Editions, 2022.
Identifier(s): ISBN 978-981-4828-41-3 (paperback)
Subject(s): LCSH: Rasappan, Kumaran. | Success. | Mountaineering.
Classification: DDC 158.1--dc23

Printed in Singapore

To my wife, Gayathri, whose companionship and dreams drove much of my adventures;

My son, Agillesh, who may one day lead even greater adventures in his life;

My sister, Kumutha, who has always been my greatest pillar of strength;

My mother, Letchimi, whose prayers and immeasurable love kept me safe though my journeys;

And, most importantly, my father, Rasappan, without whom everything that I am today would not have been.

FOREWORD

Not many people can say they have stood on the top of the world. Dr Kumaran Rasappan is one of those select few. This book tells you how this quiet and unassuming doctor came to touch the clouds while keeping firmly grounded to the earth.

Kumaran is a two-time recipient of the SINDA Excellence Award, the highest accolade for top-performing Indian students. He has also been given the Singapore Youth Award and honoured for his contributions to society. Since then, he has continued to motivate youth and inspire Singaporeans and others.

He has an impressive list of accolades to his name. An accomplished orthopaedic surgeon, he has scaled the world's tallest peaks including Mount Everest, and harnessed both experiences to help disadvantaged communities at home and abroad. Now, he is also a published author.

This book is his story — a gripping account of mountaineering feats, but more than that, an inspirational tale of what young people can achieve when they set their hearts and minds to it.

Filled with photographs and vivid descriptions, it brings readers not only to the heights of the starkly beautiful mountains of Nepal but also into the mind of the climber. For this is a story about having a dream and following it. It shows you what it means to cling to hope, to set aside fear, loneliness and exhaustion, to be undeterred by failure, and to have character forged by these experiences.

The chapters document Kumaran's struggles, both physical and mental, and testify to his spirit and resilience. Through his narrative, we see the parallels between his work and his dream of climbing the world's highest mountain.

His trials and tribulations will resonate with people from all walks of life. They also give hope to many, including those in correctional institutions, to whom he regularly gives talks. Some of his staunchest champions today are ex-inmates he inspired at Changi Prison. Encouraging others, in turn, gives him encouragement to keep going.

This is also a story of the people who made his journey possible. Highlighting those who gave advice, help and friendship, Kumaran recounts their impact on his journey and how each played a role in his success.

The story begins with a young Kumaran facing seemingly insurmountable odds — naysayers and broken promises, and rejection after rejection. But at his lowest, he discovers well-wishers from different walks of life, giving him a special perspective on the importance of community, family, sponsors, friends and supporters. His success was not a solo effort, and he is unstinting in his gratitude to those who believed in him.

Kumaran shows what can be achieved when discipline is coupled with passion and conviction. It is for those who struggle that he climbs — raising funds for the Tan Tock Seng Hospital Community Fund, conducting clinics for Sherpas in a remote Himalayan village, delivering donated computer equipment to an impoverished Nepalese school. He carries Singapore's flag high, and when he planted one on the summit of the world, we in Singapore shared vicariously in his triumph.

I hope readers will draw encouragement from Kumaran's book and be inspired to scale and conquer all the mountains you may encounter in your life's journey.

Indranee Rajah
Minister, Prime Minister's Office
Second Minister for Finance and National Development
President, SINDA

Dr Kumaran Rasappan

CHAPTER 1

"The fear of death follows from the fear of life.
A man who lives fully is prepared to die at any time."
Mark Twain

I spent my 27th birthday on a high. Literally.

At 6,400m in Camp 1 of the sixth highest mountain in the world, Turquoise Goddess Cho Oyu, I struggled to suck the thin air, whacking my hands together in an attempt to stoke life back to my fingertips in the withering cold.

At -15°C, with the most protection between the deep freeze and me being a few millimetres of tent nylon, all extremities were painfully exposed to the frigid elements 24/7.

This was not the most comfortable birthday I had ever celebrated. But I was quietly elated.

Sleeping at 6,400m was a personal record for me. And it had been a hard-won badge.

The journey had begun a week ago with a teeth-rattling 100km minivan ride from Kathmandu to the border settlement of Kodari, where we crossed from Nepal into the legendary land of Tibet. Our introduction to Tibet was a narrow road that drunkenly zig zagged its way to Zhangmu, the mountainous Tibetan port of entry, where we obediently submitted our bags to be rifled through, presumably for pro-democracy propaganda. (This, notwithstanding the fact that there was a Sino-Nepal Friendship Bridge a stone's throw away.)

Zhangmu was typical of any utilitarian border town — milling with trucks, massage parlours and a thriving red-light district. We hardly paused. Travelling from Zhangmu on to Nyalam and then to Tingri took us past arid Tibetan villages peppered with colourful stone homes with flat roofs generously insulated with free dung from the family yak.

Despite its remoteness, Tingri would be the last semblance of civilisation I would see for many weeks, and my gaze lingered on the sparse settlement with its ruddy-faced children as we took off again on a bumpy drive to the Cho Oyu Base Camp.

To stay in touch with my family and sponsors, there was no choice but to fork out US$40 for 4 megabytes of data via satellite. A painful sum, but it was the only way I could stay in touch with the outside world from here on. Satellite phones were banned in Tibet at the time.

Here the wheels ended and the footwork began.

My teammates, mostly Americans, two Austrians, a German and an Australian, looked fit and eager to be off. I would get to know them well in the weeks to come.

We were travelling with International Mountain Guides (IMG), an American outfitter with a reputation for leading trekking and mountaineering expeditions around the world from the Alps to the Andes and to the soaring 8,000m peaks of the Himalayas.

Snaking in single file across rivers and rocky moraine from Base Camp (BC) to the Interim Camp was our Cho Oyu team of Sherpas, two Western guides and 11 clients, including myself.

Our ungraceful companions were a couple of hippie-looking hairy yaks helping to transport our expedition supplies.

There wasn't much time to settle into the bright orange tents that would be our portable home and shelter from the elements for the next six weeks or so. One night and we took off again to the Advanced Base Camp (ABC) which, at 5,500m, was only slightly lower than the peak of Kilimanjaro (5,895m), the highest mountain in Africa.

ABC was our base for the next four weeks and, in a classic climbing approach, we planned a series of rotating climbs, up and down to Camp 1 (6,400m), Camp 2 (7,150m) and Camp 3 (7,450m), increasing our altitude by increments in order to acclimate, then returning to ABC to rest and recover.

A host of biological changes ripples through the body at high altitude, and acclimatisation is critical to avoid acute mountain sickness (AMS), a potentially fatal condition.

For a start, fewer oxygen molecules in the lower pressure causes hypoxia, where there is less oxygen in the same volume of air we breathe at sea level. Less oxygen circulating in the body means less oxygen reaching the muscles, with movements becoming laboured. Dehydration, a suppressed appetite, headache, nausea, dizziness and sleeplessness are common, with the worst of the symptoms culminating in cerebral edema, a fatal swelling of the brain.

"Three attributes of a good mountaineer are high pain threshold, bad memory and … I forget the third," goes a favourite joke in mountaineering chat groups.

+++

We arrived at ABC on 1 September. Our plan was to summit Cho Oyu some time between 25 and 30 September during a predicted window of good weather. Standing on the 8,210m summit, we would come face to face with some of the most imposing mountains in the world: Everest (8,848m), Lhotse (8,516m), Chamlang (7,319m), Ama Dablam (6,812m) and a splendid buffet of peaks in the Himalayan Khumbu region.

Two technically demanding sections stood between us and the Cho Oyu summit: An ice cliff between Camp 1 and 2, and a mixed rock wall dubbed the Yellow Band above Camp 3. We would be tackling this with front pointing techniques with our crampons and the use of jumars[1].

In Himalayan expedition custom, we had with us a team of Sherpas to help with load carrying and camp preparation.

The youngest and least experienced of them, a 22-year-old named Kancha, had already summited Everest three times and Cho Oyu twice. The most experienced, 54-year-old Danuru Sherpa, had summited Everest an incredible 11 times.

---

1   Crampons refer to a metal plate with spikes fixed to a boot for walking on ice or rock climbing. A jumar is a clamp with a handle that can move freely up a rope to which it is clipped, but locks when downward pressure is applied. Jumaring is a way climbers ascend a fixed rope.

With Kancha en route from C1 to C2 on Cho Oyu.

Danuru, or Dawa (Thursday) as he was nicknamed in reference to the day of the week he was born, was quiet, hardworking and humble, despite his formidable climbing achievements. I didn't know it then, but this Cho Oyu expedition would be the start of a long friendship between Dawa and me.

Kancha Sherpa, clear-eyed and fresh-faced, was always eager to learn and ready to help. The Nepali base camp manager, Ang Jangbu, had paired us up as we were the two youngest in the group and he figured we would get along.

The dependability of the strong, wiry Sherpas built an invisible bedrock of hope within the team.

Yet it would be foolish to underestimate the wild elements whipping the flanks of an 8,000m massif.

Sherpas themselves acknowledge Nature's sovereignty with a mandatory *puja* (blessing) ceremony before every climb, a plea for the gods to grant safe passage.

As the Sherpas say with hushed reverence: *Mountains create their own weather.*

+++

True enough, the weather took a sharp turn for the worse as soon as our team arrived at ABC. Heavy snow started to fall. And kept falling.

By 6 September, as we approached a 200-metre vertical section of snowdrift just before C1, the weight of the snow we were straining against made every step forward feel like we were in a scrum blocked by an All Blacks prop.

Tread gently, I told myself, *tread gently.* But it was easier said than done. We were carrying all the technical equipment we would need to use above C1 — boots, crampons, harness, ice axe, down suits, sleeping bags, food — all told, my pack weighed more than 20kg. Strain as I might, I was well and truly stuck.

Kancha, who was ahead of me, waded down to relieve me of my pack before I could scramble the rest of the way to C1. Shouldering my pack, Kancha flashed me a good-natured grin before disappearing upwards almost as fast as he came down.

The snow fell even harder as we settled into C1 after a 6½ hour climb, and did not let up for the entire afternoon and night, robbing us of a magnificent view of the mountains from our 6,400m perch.

In everybody's mind was the unspoken question: Can we reach the summit?

Through the crackling of radio frequencies, we heard one expedition team, then another, retreating in the face of the dismal weather, convinced that summiting would not be possible this year. No team had summited last year for the same reasons: relentless snow and avalanche danger.

Despite Cho Oyu enjoying the pleasing reputation of being the easiest 8,000m mountain to climb out of the world's fourteen 8,000ers, in truth, like a wild animal, no mountain is truly safe.

The deadliness of Cho Oyu only hit me when three climbers lost their lives in the space of the time our IMG team was on the mountain.

The first was a man who, for reasons unknown to us, died on the ice cliff above C1. His body, swaying against the blue ice, was left dangling upside down with his feet caught in the ropes.

It was a week before the body was removed by his commercial team, who needed to first contact his family to delicately ask if they would bear the cost of repatriating his body. No sirdar[2] would risk his Sherpas' lives otherwise.

---

2   Head Sherpa responsible for the welfare of the team's guides or porters.

Thankfully, by our next rotation, the unfortunate climber had been removed and I did not have to pass the frozen corpse.

The second death occurred late in the month after a heavy snow storm descended on C1, crushing a sleeping climber in his tent.

The third death was witnessed by all of us from ABC. Two Japanese climbers decided to head to the summit on their own. The first climber was ahead of his counterpart by a large distance, but instead of summiting and then returning, he proceeded to wander up and down the mountain just below the summit for five hours. None of us had any idea why. We suspected he might have been disorientated by cerebral edema. As the sun was setting, we saw him traverse across the west face of the mountain and disappear behind some rocks. He never returned.

His partner made it to Camp 3 (C3) at about 5pm.

I was shocked by these deaths. Despite the cadavers and dead bodies I had encountered as a medical doctor, this was different. This hit too close to home.

But the Sherpas and IMG guides hardly flinched. Deaths on 8,000m peaks are common, they said soberly. If there were no deaths, it would be an unusual year indeed.

Unknown to me, on 7 September, even as I woke up in my tent to a cup of steaming milk tea and the birthday wishes of my teammates, danger was already brewing in the bowels of Cho Oyu.

+++

6pm, 18 September 2011, Camp 1

The snow had finally stopped on our third rotation to C1, and from my perch on a serrated ridge line 6,400m high, a panorama of Olympic proportions swept across the horizon.

Jagged peaks burnished by the setting sun, an infinity of earth and sky — it was a scene as far from anything that a city boy could imagine.

Kancha and I were just settling down for the night in the tent we were sharing.

For maximum comfort and warmth, climbers often strip down to thin, dri-fit long johns and thermal underwear as they zip themselves into snug sleeping bags. Fleece, pants, down suit, cap, goggles, mittens, beanie, socks and boots are tossed aside for the night. Our layers of clothing weigh approximately 8kg in total. It takes almost as much time for us to dress and undress as it takes to cook dinner.

As I lay in my sleeping bag, my mind drifted home to Singapore, where at this time on a Sunday evening, the fierce heat of the day would be softening, the sounds of boisterous children in the playground would be drifting in through the windows of our HDB flat, and piquant smells of *rasam* (an Indian tomato soup) and mutton *briyani* (spiced rice) would be wafting from my mother's kitchen.

My eyes were closing when I felt the tent give a little wobble.

"Thanks," I called out sleepily, believing it was a kind climber outside helping to shake the snow off our tent, as they sometimes did.

But the wobble became a shake, and the shaking grew in violence till the tent was tottering left and right, front and back.

Before Kancha and I could even react, the ground beneath us dropped several centimetres and buckled. My stomach lurched. Our sleeping bags rolled drunkenly towards each other.

"EARTHQUAKE! EARTHQUAKE!" came the shouts of Sherpas in neighbouring tents.

Kancha and I shot up in our sleeping bags, wild eyed.

C1 of Cho Oyu, where tents are lined perilously close to the cliff edge.

Our tent was pitched just 10m from the lip of the ridge, the other side of which dropped abruptly into a black abyss. Each jounce of the earth was inching our tent closer to the edge.

Kancha's wide eyes met mine. We could do nothing to help ourselves. Stripped down to our longjohns and socks, we would have frozen to death had we attempted to leave the tent.

Helplessly, we hung on to the tottering tent, praying it would not plunge off the ridge, dragging us to our deaths.

Panic was rising in my throat and, dimly, I could hear Kancha muttering a Buddhist prayer.

Outside, sounds of chaos crashed around us. In the deepest core of my being, I sensed the ominous rumble of avalanches starting.

Was this the end?

CHAPTER TWO

"As a young boy, Scouting gave me a confidence and camaraderie that is hard to find in modern life."
Bear Grylls

If you had known me as a gangly kid in Naval Base Primary School, you might have voted me "Most *Un*likely to Climb a Mountain".

Nothing in my timid personality, exceedingly average frame, or lackluster PE record (my CCA was library club) gave any indication that my future would include scaling Everest.

In primary school, I nimbly dodged more than one offer to "come and meet my seniors *lah*" (gangspeak for "you are a potential recruit") by saying: "No, cannot *lah*. My mother is waiting for me to go home with her."

(I might have added a regretful tone for dramatic effect.)

My mother was the Tamil teacher in the same school, and the thought of Mrs Rasappan bearing down on them, berating all and sundry in rapid-fire Tamil, may have deterred a gang member or two from trying too hard to recruit her only son.

She was my Tamil teacher for one year and I never knew what to call her in class: *Ma,* or *Aasiriya* ("teacher" in Tamil). The whole year went by without my calling her either, and I was relieved when the year ended.

When I was in Primary Four, my mother decided to sign me up for music classes. For reasons still mysterious to me, the organ was her instrument of choice. Twice a week for two whole years, I obediently attended organ class at our town centre.

I didn't mind. My reward each time was a meal at the fried chicken outlet next door to class. And I would order the whole shebang: Fries, coleslaw, fried chicken or chicken burger and a soft drink.

If my family and teachers noticed that my waistline was increasing in direct proportion to my musical ability, nobody said anything. I myself was blithely clueless.

It was only when we had a psycho-motor sports test in secondary school that I learnt that I was, well, damn fat. Two years in TAF club, when I had to run round the school track during recess while my friends ate chicken rice and played video games, took care of my spare tyres. And, truth be told, the workout turned out to be good preparation for my later, thankfully sportier, years.

Actually my parents suspected that within my soft exterior lurked an iron will. This had revealed itself in a steely determination to own the Big Thing of the Moment: the Sega Mega Drive 16-bit home video console.

In primary school, my best friend from my class was a gregarious fellow named Sreedharan. I spent many a lively afternoon at Sreedharan's house, where the focus, naturally, was his Sega game. Every day, after school, Sreedharan and I would be on the phone for hours discussing game play.

Plead as I might for a Sega console of my own, my father was firm in his objections that it was a waste of good money and a distraction from my schoolwork.

So, determined fellow that I was, I cooked up a plan.

At that time, as an encouragement to me to accumulate my savings, my father would give me $1 for each white hair that I plucked from his head. This ready source of income struck me as a potential means to buying my own Sega. With Sreedharan as an enthusiastic co-conspirator, we plotted for him to help me buy a Sega with my follicular earnings, and hand the Sega to me as a "birthday present" at my upcoming birthday party.

I needed $200 for the Sega, so every evening when my dad was watching TV, I would perch at his shoulder and vigorously rifle through his hair to pluck out the lucrative strands. To my delight, I could earn $10 to $15 every night! Each week at swimming class, I would report to Sreedharan my accumulated earnings as my birthday drew closer. Eventually my enthusiasm raised my dad's suspicions and, despite the fact that his pate was now several patches balder, his amusement at my elaborate plan had him finally buying me a Sega.

My older sister, Kumuthamalar, had been an easy child to raise, and my parents had been under the mistaken impression that all their offspring would be similarly uncomplicated. Instead, as my father bemoaned, raising one kid like me was equivalent to raising 10.

My wilful determination taxed my parents' nerves on many an occasion. But secretly I believe that my stubborn streak contributed in no small way to my making it to the summit of the gruelling mountains I would eventually climb.

+++

As a child, home was a two-room HDB flat in Tanjong Pagar, and later on a five-room maisonette in Yishun.

My mother, Vaiyupuri Muthulatchimi or Letchimi to friends, was a teacher all her life. She was typical of many working class mothers who went to work all week and yet managed to raise her children, keep an orderly house and cook dinner for her family every night, with a more elaborate table on weekends, hers featuring mutton curry, *biryani* (spiced meat and rice), *dosa* (rice flour crepes), spiced cabbage, *iddly* (savoury rice cake) and other traditional treats.

She was an ardent believer in the benefits of a good breakfast and made sure her husband, daughter and son did not leave the house each morning without the fortification of several slices of bread and a hard boiled egg.

My father, Rasappan s/o Karuppa Goundar, was born in the small village of Kavettipatti in Tamil Nadu, and has little recollection of his parents. From what he was told by relatives, his mother had died giving birth to him and his father had followed not long after in a tragic bullock cart accident, leaving him and his older brother, Sellappan, orphaned. My father was just three and his brother, 15. Sellappan stepped up to take on the role of father, mother and brother to his younger sibling.

As a teenager, Sellappan set sail for Singapore in search of a better life. The sea journey took a month. Finding work at a shipyard, he never forgot the younger brother he had left behind and scrupulously saved to bring him over. The reunion finally happened when my father turned 10. Together with a handful of men from the same village, the young boy sailed to Singapore to join his brother.

The group of bachelor immigrants from India took on random jobs while living together in one room over a tea shop where, for subsistence, my father, not yet a teenager, took a job serving tea. Not wanting my father to end up labouring in the same hard shipyard job, my uncle used his earnings to put his brother through school. My father remembers many an evening when the men in the communal lodging put out the lights to sleep, and he would have to creep down to the shophouse to study by lamplight. He was the only educated one in the lot, and was frequently called upon to write letters home for them. He never had the heart to say no.

My uncle's efforts were rewarded when my father steadily progressed to become a teacher and later on a Ministry of Education officer. A lifelong believer in education, my father earned a PhD in Tamil Language and Literature at the age of 62. So we both became doctors within a year of each other.

At my wedding held in a ballroom in Marina Bay Sands, my father gazed up at the chandeliers and down at the plush carpets and softly told my sister and me: "When I think of how my life began in Singapore, I would never, ever have thought my children would be married in a place like this. It is like a dream."

In my growing up years, my family, like many middle-class families in the 1980s and 1990s, was by no means financially comfortable enough to be lavish. It was the aim of many parents, including mine, to get their children a good education so that they would have a stable future. Other than that, spending time with the family was a priority for both my parents.

As children, it did not even occur to my sister and me to peg ourselves to any particular social strata. While we could not afford fancy holidays or fancy meals out ("restaurant" to me meant McDonald's, KFC or Pizza Hut), we were content in knowing that we had a roof over our heads, sufficient food in our bellies, and parents who spent their evenings and weekends at home. The rest was up to us.

With my older sister and parents in a family photo taken in 1990 when I was six years old.

Every once in a while, family life took an exciting turn with a holiday — brief forays to Cameron Highlands, Bali or Koh Samui.

Our most extravagant vacation was a trip to Jaipur, India. That was only possible because my dad was sent on a work conference to New Delhi and, knowing that it was my mother's dearest wish to see the Taj Mahal, paid for his family to join him in Jaipur. It was my first time staying in a hotel and being served at a nice restaurant. I still remember the thrill of riding, goggle-eyed, on an ambling elephant up to the Red Fort.

It was a sweetly simple life, and if you had asked me then if I could foresee a series of big adventures from Africa to China, South America to the Himalayas in my future, I would have thought it a good joke.

+++

When I started secondary school at Raffles Institution, I was determined to make it into a sports team.

By then both my psycho-motor skills and my girth were much improved. But the competition was stiff.

The selection process for each sport was thorough. Hockey, tennis, gymnastics, softball — I tried out for them all. I found myself running, jumping, dribbling and serving with all my might. The no-nonsense gymnastics coach from China stood us in a row, stomach in, chest out, hands behind our back, while he examined our physique to determine who had the most potential.

Eventually I was called up for air rifle and tennis. But I was holding out for hockey or softball, and turned the first two down. Sadly, I was not selected for either. My athleticism, endurance and competitiveness were just not up to par.

What I did get selected for was Scouts.

I was crestfallen. It was the unspoken understanding among the boys that those who were offered uniformed groups were those who did not make it into sports.

Seeking out the different PE heads, I tried my hardest to appeal for a place in sports. While they did not turn me down outright, they gave me variations of: "Why don't you give Scouts a shot? If you don't like it, maybe we can talk."

So I decided to heed their advice. Okay *lah,* I guess I'll try it out, I told myself.

To my interest, I discovered that Scouts ran on a hierarchical system of boys leading boys. Hardly a teacher was present. Many former Scouts of junior college age returned to their alma mater, on their own accord, to invest time in leading, training and inspiring the younger Scouts.

As greenhorn 13-year-olds, fresh out of primary school, we were suitably impressed by these strapping seniors. It appeared to us that when boys crossed over to tertiary institutions, they also crossed some metaphysical portal that transformed squeaky voiced, pimple-prone teenagers into strong, capable, self-assured young men.

This was the first time I caught a glimpse of the beauty of mentoring. At that impressionable age, we saw these seniors as people we could relate to because they were not too distant from us in age, and yet they were clearly role models to whom we could aspire.

In his first speech to us, one of our seniors said wryly: "I know all you guys applied for sports CCAs, right? You didn't get in, and that's why you're looking at Scouts, right?"

A few of us shuffled sheepishly.

"Everyone thinks that Scouts are *wuss-es*," he declared. "Let me show you what Scouts are. See this wood here? This is how we chop wood!"

Expertly, he swung his axe and — *thwack!* — chopped the log clean in half.

"Woahhhhhh," came our awed reaction.

The seniors proceeded to demonstrate an impressive array of skills: building high towers complete with monkey bars and fluttering flags, demonstrating outdoor cooking, tying ropes, executing logsmanship, using a map and compass.

"A Scout is never taken by surprise; he knows exactly what to do when anything unexpected happens," Robert Baden-Powell, founder of the Scout movement, had once pronounced.

Indeed the range of Scouting activities designed to develop leadership, teamwork and discipline in youths at a critical stage of their physical, mental and emotional development is one of the best preparations for adulthood that I can think of.

I was even more impressed to discover that Singapore's founding Prime Minister, Mr Lee Kuan Yew, was a Scout in the 32nd Singapore Scout Troop, which later became the 01 Raffles Scout Group. Former Prime Minister Mr Goh Chok Tong had also been a Scout.

The Singapore Scout Association, established back in 1912, is one of the oldest youth movements in Singapore, with a rich tradition and an illustrious history.

Thus began my deep and enduring relationship with the Scouting movement.

The Scout camps were memorable. My first Scout investiture camp was at the Ministry of Education Punggol site. At my first Investiture camp, we juniors had to pass a series of tests, including starting a fire and repairing various items, in order to be invested. The test for seniors involved backwoodsman cooking using natural resources like mud and bamboo. The Secondary 1 boys helped the Secondary 4 boys start their cooking fire, and in so doing we won our own badge.

Building a brilliant campfire was one of the skills in which Scouts excelled. In the dark of night, under an open sky, the Scouts would sit in a large ring, at the centre of which burned a magnificent flame.

In the light of the flickering campfire, we new Scouts received our scarves, the emblem of a Scout, while senior Scouts received their appointments. Standing at attention, we said our oaths and made the Scouts' promise. It was a solemn moment.

When, in Secondary 3, I received my own appointment as a patrol leader, the appointment letter became a treasured possession. We were called to "discharge your duties far above fear as you are above favour". Even today, I find myself sharing this with my peers and students. It was a valuable reminder to perform to the best of my ability ... *far above fear and favour.*

We were also counselled to "suffer in your own cheerful devotion". This would stay with me when I was in junior college and became a senior Scout. Returning regularly to serve my Scout group as council member and group secretary required sacrifices in my social, family and academic life. (I was not the only Scout alumnus to do this, and many others are doing so today.)

Even medicine, especially in the exhausting houseman and residency years of 30-hour on-call duties and 5am starts, demanded sacrifice and a commitment to stay the course in the face of tough decisions and taxing patients. I was reminded to press on with "cheerful devotion" and commitment.

Being a Scout left a deep impact on my life. From a playful Secondary 1 boy with hardly any leadership potential, I became a patrol leader with responsibilities I took seriously. The awkward kid, who was loath to talk to new people, was forced go knocking on doors and interact with strangers during Job Week.

The wilderness skills I learnt — how to pack for an overnight hike, how to waterproof my backpack, how to start a fire, pitch a tent, or create a simple shelter against the rain — would stand me in good stead when I went to National Service and on my climbing expeditions.

But one of my favourite things about Scouts was the camaraderie. On hiking and caving trips to Malaysia, the seniors had our full attention with their stories of mischievous Scouting exploits: Nearly passing out during treks of 100km over three days without supervision; going to the "lucrative" red-light district during Job Week because scandalised receptionists would hastily stuff money into the hands of the innocent boys just to get us to leave. All of which were, of course, outside of Scouting constitution.

There were tales of life outside Scouting too: Tertiary escapades, National Service adventures, new co-curricular activities offered in university, and especially their experiences with *girls*, a species that was mysteriously alien to us 13-, 14- and 15-year-olds in an all-boys school. If chopping wood had earned our seniors a respectful *"woahhhh"*, their dating experiences elicited even louder expressions of admiration.

Years later, I became a senior Scout, returning to advise the secondary and JC1 Scouts two to three times a month every year, accompanying them on hikes, building fires and forts beside them, joking with them and listening to their teenage worries. I continued with my involvement all the way until my third year of medical school, when mountaineering and third-year clinical rotations required my full attention outside of university.

But my 10 Scouting years with the 01 Raffles Scout Group will always be some of the best years of my life.

When I was presented with the President's Scout Award in 2002, the highest honour of a Singapore Scout, it was the highlight of my young life. To me, this represented the culmination of blood, sweat and dogged commitment.

There were necessary tests required to fulfil the President's Scout Award. Some of the physical requirements were more rigorous than what I experienced later in the army.

Looking back, though, this was the year that I learnt the most and grew the most as a person.

At the Istana, together with the other awardees from Raffles Institution, receiving our honours from the late Mr SR Nathan, the 6th President of Singapore, during the President Scout Award Ceremony 2002.

The award was not the end of my commitment to Scouting, but the beginning of a new chapter in my responsibilities as a senior Scout. I would go on to pioneer a syllabus for working towards the President's Scout Award and coach others in their own bid for the award.

Once or twice, a bright-eyed young man came up to me on the street, saying: "Kumaran, do you remember me? You were my senior in Scouts!" And I would feel a flood of camaraderie.

If I have played a small part in encouraging anyone, it is only because I have been the happy recipient of encouragement myself.

+++

When I summited Everest in 2012, among the bare essentials in my backpack was a carefully folded flag, stamped with the emblems of the 01 Raffles Scout Group and Raffles Institution. I was under no sponsorship obligation. But Scouts had played such a pivotal role in making me who I am, that if I made it to the summit, I wanted my Scouts to be there too.

On 26 May 2012, at 6:55am, I summited Everest. And planted that fluttering flag on its peak.

CHAPTER 3

"I may have been born in another place, but I feel I am from Nepal. The Magic of Nepal has to be felt. "
Avijeet Das

I was 15 years old the first time I set foot in the Himalayas,

My secondary school was organising a trip to Nepal in November and a call went out for interested applicants.

These days, overseas school trips are commonplace. But back in 1999, this was a rare undertaking for a secondary school.

Interest among the boys was not exactly overwhelming. The trip was to a third-world country, which was unfamiliar to us. I easily bagged a spot after a cursory interview along with 18 other boys. Together with four teachers, including a physical education (PE) teacher, a geography teacher and a history teacher, we were a mixed bunch.

The trip was the brainchild of Mr Krishnan Pillay, the history teacher, who had a reputation as a gentle soul with two passions in life: History and community work.

A few years ago, Mr Krishnan had taken a year of no-pay leave and had left for Nepal, where he had taught English at a village secondary school through the auspices of the Singapore International Foundation (SIF).

SIF had despatched him and a volunteer medical doctor to a remote village called Aahale in the highlands of Gorkha. For one year, Mr Krishnan had lived with the villagers, eaten what they ate and waited for infrequent mail delivery to arrive on foot just like they did.

At the end of the year, he had come away from the experience moved by the hardship he had seen and touched by the earnestness of the children.

He wanted us to experience the same.

The school decided to select boys from the Secondary 3 level because we were ostensibly more mature than Sec 1 and 2 boys, but did not have the major 'O' level exams that the Sec 4 boys had.

With the exuberance of youth, we threw ourselves into raising funds for Aahale by selling home-made durian cake, corralling cars at a Teachers' Day carwash, and collecting donated books, clothing and coloured pencils for the children in Nepal.

Training for our four-day hike on a section of the Annapurna Circuit included running at the school track and sweating up and down Bukit Timah Hill. The teachers warned us to anticipate breathlessness while hiking up to the hill station of Poon Hill (3,210m) in Nepal, and advised us to proceed slowly, drink a lot of water and pee frequently.

While all of us nodded sagely, we really had no clue what it all meant. Our sole experience of altitude at the time was limited to Singapore's highest point, Bukit Timah Hill, which stood at a grand 164m.

Copious handouts were distributed by the enthusiastic teachers, including Annapurna Trail maps, a list of common Nepali words, and an animated sequence of calisthenics to help us stay fit.

There was also a packing list that included:
- *good jacket cum windbreaker (for windy, cold temperatures of less than 5C);*
- *undergarments (preferably disposable); and*
- *packed mum's food such as ikan bilis and BBQ pork.*

My dad who, while supportive was not the most sartorially savvy, fulfilled the "jacket cum windbreaker" requirement by going to Mustafa Centre in Little India and buying me the same jacket he had worn to a conference in Chicago in the 1960s — a puffy, brown number for city use.

None of us boys had much travel experience and we turned up in Kathmandu in a colourful array of winterwear totally unsuitable for trekking.

One of Mr Krishnan's objectives for the Namaste Nepal Community Service Project was for us to befriend the youths of Aahale in a cultural exchange that would open our eyes to other corners of the world.

To this end, he devised a penpal programme between his students and the students at Shree Saraswoti Secondary School months before the trip.

Assiduously, we wrote letters about our life in Singapore — swotting for exams, dealing with pesky siblings, facts and figures about the Merlion. And I was delighted to receive a return letter one day with a Nepali postage stamp. It read:

Hi, my name is Ishwar Khadka. I am a Nepali boy. I live in Ghorka at Kattel Danda. There are five members in my family. There are father, mother, two sister and I. My father is a farmer.

I study at Saraswati Secondary School in class g. The subjects I read are Nepali, Maths, English, Geography, Science, Agriculture, Economics, Optional Math. My favourite subject is English.

Every day I wake up at 5 o'clock. I help to carry water and I read my books before I go to school. I like to eat dhaal, bhaat and vegetables. I like to play football.

I hope to receive your reply. Thank you. Hope to meet you soon.

Yours sincerely,
Ishwar Khadka

It was my first glimpse of an adolescent life outside of school tests, Scouts and video games.

Education goes beyond the world of academia, reminded Mr Krishnan, who shared with us a plethora of anecdotes from his time in Nepal.

Many buildings in Kathmandu are half built, he told us, with exposed metal construction rods sticking straight up in upper storeys. Unable to afford constructing the entire building at once, the Nepali build one floor, then years later, when they have saved up enough,

c/o Saraswoti M.V.
prithvi Narayan Municipality.
Word No. 7
Aahale
Gorkha.

Dear friend from Singapore,

My name is Ishwor Khadka. I am a Nepali boy. I live in Gorkha at Thakal Danda. There are five members in my family. There are father, mother, two sister and I. My father is a farmer.

I study at Saraswoti secondary school in class 8. The subjects I read are Nepali, maths, English, Geography, science, Agriculture, Economics, Optional Math. My favourite subject is English.

Every day I wake up at 5 o'clock. I help to carry water and I read my books before I go to school. I like to eat dhaal, bhaat and vegetables. I like to play football.

I hope to receive your reply. Thank you. Hope to meet you soon.

Yours sincerely,
Ishwor Khadka

My pen pal letter from a student from Shree Saraswoti school in Aahale, Gorkha.

build the next floor, and so on until the building is the desired height. Houses can remain uncompleted for decades.

When he had lived in the mountain village three or four years back, the school roof had not yet been properly constructed. Zinc sheets were used as a makeshift substitute, weighed down by rocks to prevent lift-off in inclement weather.

During winter, the students would sometimes arrive at school to find that strong winds had blown the zinc sheets clean away. Too cold to sit in a school without a roof, the students would have their lessons outdoors, where the sun provided a modicum of warmth. Lessons and equations were scratched in the dirt, because there was no blackboard outdoors.

"They would study from the ground — that's how eager they were to learn," Mr Krishnan remarked.

+++

My first ever sighting of Everest was from 9,000m in the air from our Silkair flight to Kathmandu. Before the tragic circumstances of 9/11 set off a series of changes in airline protocol, it was still possible for the odd passenger to enter the cockpit with the pilots' permission.

Like many boys of our generation, some of us had dreams of becoming pilots when we grew up and were thrilled when Mr Krishnan took us to the cockpit in batches. (My best buddy at the time, Sathiyan, did indeed go on to become an airforce pilot in adulthood.)

When it came to my group's turn, we happened to be about an hour from landing, and Everest was just coming into view to the right of our plane.

"See that peak that looks like a three-sided pyramid? That is Everest, the top of the world," pointed out the pilot.

At a distance, just above a thick seam of rolling clouds, Everest rose as an icy shard amidst a crowd of jagged peaks vying for the sky. The brutal hardness of the black massif contrasted curiously with the softness of the snow on its shanks. (I would learn later that snow, when packed together, was not at all soft, but a deadly force.)

I didn't know then that this was just the first of numerous times that I would gaze upon the imposing beauty of Everest. Each view of her would put me in a completely different state of mind.

At 15, my sighting of Everest inspired the adolescent wonder of a student seeing a two-dimensional picture from his Geography textbook materialise before his eyes.

Ten years later, I would be standing at the foot of Everest, ready to trek to Everest Base Camp with the National University of Singapore's mountaineering club, Make it Real (MIR). For an aspiring mountaineer then to be literally touching the earth of Everest was mind blowing.

A scant year later, in 2011, Everest loomed over me as I observed her from her neighbours Cho Oyu and Ama Dablam. That was the year I had made the unprecedented decision to take a gap year after my housemanship to devote myself to climbing seven mountains within 11 months, with a view to summiting Everest at the end.

By then, mountaineering occupied all of my waking moments, and Everest was literally the pinnacle I had set my sights on.

In March 2012, I was finally on my Climb Everest 2012 expedition, gazing upon Everest with the incredible realisation that soon her contours would become intimately familiar to me as I set foot on the infamous Khumbu Icefall and the legendary Hillary Step.

The road ahead, and upward, was incredibly daunting.

Above all, I wondered if I would make it back from Everest alive.

+++

Thirteen 7,000m peaks and sixteen 6,000m peaks make their home in the Annapurna region in north central Nepal, including the notoriously inhospitable Annapurna I (8,091m), which enjoyed the notoriety of having a jaw-dropping 40% death rate — the highest among all 8,000m peaks — at the time.

As a result of this geographical feat, the entire Annapurna region became the first and largest conservation area of Nepal, protected by the Annapurna Conservation Area Project (ACAP).

The Ghorepani Poon Hill trek, as part of the longer Annapurna Circuit, turned out to be an excellent introduction to hiking for our motley group of 15-year-old city boys.

At Nayapul, the start of our four-day trek, we met our Nepali porters for the first time. To our surprise, none of them was more than 1.6 metres tall; many of us at age 15 were taller. But while small in stature, the porters were compact in build, with huge calves (an observation made by our PE teacher).

On their backs, they toted large cone-shaped baskets woven from split bamboo, rattan and rope. To our astonishment, at the sirdar's instruction, the porters proceeded to load four or five boys' heavy haversacks into each basket, and with just the help of a leather headband, hauled the baskets up and nonchalantly set off up the trail. Where we wore waterproof sneakers and winter jackets against the November cold, they wore sandals and shorts.

By the time we reached our rest stop, the porters would not only have beaten us to it, but would also have had our tea boiled. When we left our rest stop to proceed upwards, the porters would still be washing up the cups and packing up the camping equipment. But, again, when we reached our lunch spot, the porters would already have set up a fire and cooked our lunch of *chapathi* (flatbread), *dhal bhat* (lentils and rice), *poori* (fried bread), vegetable curry, and *momo* (dumplings filled with buffalo, goat or chicken).

In the mornings, a hot cup of chai tea and a basin of water with which to wash served as our wake-up call before we gathered at campground tables and benches for a breakfast of toast, butter, jam, omelette and boiled eggs whipped up by the porters.

This was my introduction to the capable and hardy Nepali people.

Having breakfast with my schoolmates enroute to Poon Hill along the Annapurna range in 1999.

My admiration for their stoic tenacity only grew as, in my climbing years, I would get to know the Sherpa race well.

+++

The Poon Hill trek was a novel experience. I loved the cold and could not stop exhaling puffs of "smoke" into the frosty air.

The trail started by winding past small villages of stone huts, rice terraces and fields bright yellow with nodding mustard flowers. A little further up past waterfalls, lush rhododendron bushes and oak forests alive with chirruping birds, we would be overtaken every now and then by sheep on their way to pasture or pack mules delivering food and water to villages further up the trail.

Even higher up, the view opened up to vistas of undulating mountains and the plunging Kali Gandaki Gorge.

Every curve in the path introduced such amazing sights, sounds and smells that we almost forgot about the burning in our calves as we hiked straight up the mountain.

The pristine waters of the rivers, eddying around rocks and boulders, fascinated me. *Ah, water straight from the Himalayan highlands. It can't get any fresher than this!*

At rest breaks, my friend and I would wade into the chilly waters, fill our water bottles and drink deeply. That is, until my PE teacher, who was in charge of security and discipline, happened to catch me in the act and asked suspiciously: "Kumaran, why is your water bottle always full?"

"I fill it up in the rivers, sir!" I said, waving the offensive bottle cheerfully.

Sir, of course, had a fit and ordered us to empty our bottles immediately, scolding us roundly for drinking directly from the rivers. Fortunately our stomachs did not object to the unsterilised water that time.

Each night, we pitched our tents and camped out in the open. Without light pollution, the inky sky was awash with more stars than I had ever imagined possible.

On summit day, our morning call was at 4am. Stumbling out of our tents, we started trekking in the darkness, and finally made it to the peak of Poon Hill. Colourful prayer flags, strung up by pious locals, snapped in the wind as we settled to watch Nature's cosmic light show.

As the sun slowly rose, a finger of gold touched the tips of the mountains, drawing back the cloak of darkness so that, one by one, the peaks revealed themselves in a 360° panorama.

The sheer immensity of the seventh and tenth highest mountains in the world, Dhaulagiri (8,167m) and Annapurna I (8,091m), awed us into silence (which is saying a lot for a bunch of 15-year-old boys).

Catching the dawn from Poon Hill in December 1999, with Annapurna 1 (8,091m) on the left and Annapurna South (7,219m) in the centre.

The mighty Dhaulagiri (8,167m), which I naively thought we were going to climb the next day.

That is, until I broke the silence but enquiring loudly: "Are we going to climb those mountains tomorrow?"

Not tomorrow, replied an amused Mr Krishnan. Those 8,000m mountains require years of dedication to training and months of dangerous climbing to summit, he explained.

How big is this country anyway? was the thought that crossed my mind. We had already hiked for three days and I could see that the trail continued even further. Later on I would realise, of course, that Poon Hill was just a pimple on the face of the great Annapurna range.

Notwithstanding, Poon Hill became my first taste of trekking. And the experience enchanted me so much that I have not stopped since.

+++

The first thing our group ran into when we arrived at Ghorka for our community work was the Maoist Insurgency.

Our parents had been blissfully unaware of the Nepalese civil war when they signed our consent forms.

The civil war, or Maoist Insurgency, started in 1996 when the Communist Party of Nepal (CPN-M) launched a rebellion to overthrow the Nepalese monarchy in favour of a classless People's Republic.

The Maoists, also known as Naxals in India, were politically inspired by the philosophy of China's late Chairman Mao Zedong.

Tragically, the armed rebellion would go on to take the lives of some 17,000 insurgents and civilians and displace thousands, before ending with a peace agreement in 2006.

Fortunately our group of schoolboys witnessed nothing worse than roadblocks, burning tyres and protests.

But, even then, trust me to find trouble.

It was our custom to travel to and from our hotel in a minivan. But during one of the days, a civilian truck was parked in front of the hotel instead. Assuming this to be our alternative transport, I clambered in.

It turned out that the truck was ferrying civilians to a protest.

A few beats passed before I realised that none of my friends had climbed into the truck with me. Instead they were jumping up and down alongside the truck, waving their arms wildly and yelling: *"Kumaran! Kumaran! Get off, get off!"*

I leapt out just as the truck was moving off, and before the teachers caught wind of the latest Kumaran escapade.

+++

The most significant leg of our trip was the final item on our itinerary: A visit to the village of Aahale, Ghorka, around which Mr Krishnan had planned this entire trip.

Much as we had been told about the villagers, they had been told about us, too.

Delighted to have visitors from overseas, the school postponed the examinations in order that its students could line the path into the village to welcome us. The school principal, Mr Netra Mani Kattel, and his students waited two hours for our arrival, ready with garlands composed of flowers plucked from the village.

When we finally showed up, we were cheered all the way in and garlanded like heroes even though we had done nothing to deserve this fine welcome. It was both embarrassing and touching.

Aahale is perched on a Ghorka hillslope and, while the villagers may not have much, what they did have was an extraordinary view of the lush valley of rice terraces and pine forests below, and the soaring mountain peaks above.

A dance performance by the students from Shree Saraswoti school for their Singaporean guests, watched by their families from the "circle seats" on the roof.

The Shree Saraswoti Secondary School, where Mr Krishnan had taught several years ago, was a single-storey, whitewashed, dirt-floored building, devoid of ornamentation. Just as Mr Krishnan had described, metal construction rods were sprouting freely from the top, awaiting the completion of the second storey, if and when funds permitted.

Students of various ages were crammed shoulder to shoulder in a single classroom — boys on one side and girls on the other, sharing long wooden benches. Despite being a secondary school, Saraswoti also had a handful of primary school students. Children from the surrounding villages attended Saraswoti Secondary School as well.

Sathiyan, my best friend, and I were introduced to a cheerful boy of our age, Suboth Kattel[3], in whose home we would stay.

Suboth lived with his parents and sister in a typical two-storey home with walls of hardened mud. There were no chairs or tables, and we ate our meals seated on the ground. The toilet was an outhouse outdoors. Electricity was intermittent; candles and kerosene lamps were more reliable.

The family generously provided us with one of the two bedrooms on the second floor, where the roof was so low I had to crouch to keep from hitting my head.

---

3   Ghorka villagers often take on the name of their home village as their surname. Mr Netra and Suboth were both from Kattel Danda (Kattel village). Many of the students at Saraswoti Secondary School hailed from neighbouring Kattel Danda.

The ground floor of each house was generally left unlocked, but the wooden trapdoor to the second floor could be latched from the top at night when the family went to bed. This I discovered when, in the middle of the night, I had the urgent need to pee and, unable to find the latch to the trapdoor in the dark, resorted to standing at the second-floor window and watering the earth below. (I related this episode to Mr Krishnan years later and he has not let me forget it since.)

The hospitality of our hosts revealed an extraordinary amount of kindness. Although they lived and ate simply, they treated their guests like kings, plying us with *dhal bhat* (lentils and rice), *aloo* (potato) and *sag* (spinach), even slaughtering a chicken in our honour, an event reserved for special occasions.

Suboth and his sister were students at Saraswoti School and their father was the schoolteacher there. In between classes, Mr Kattel could be seen working on his vegetable plot. Many villagers planted millet and maize for subsistence.

Included in Suboth's tour of his village was a visit to the water pump, which the entire village used daily as there was no running water. The pump only worked for one to two hours in the morning and the same length of time in the evening. It was a good 2km walk from some of their homes. Yet not a word of complaint was heard.

In a village that did not have much, the water pump was a facility they were collectively proud of. Without it they could not survive. The other homestay hosts were also showing their guests the water pump, the village tourist attraction. That really had us thinking about things like clean, running water that we took for granted in Singapore.

Children in Aahale had no toys, and even the stubs of pencils were carefully used rather than discarded. Back at his home, Suboth proudly displayed his collection of coloured paper. Coloured and glossy printed material was so rare in the village (photocopiers and printers were unheard of) that any scrap of glossy paper, whether it was a discarded medicine bottle label or an old advertisement, was hoarded and neatly folded.

Although Suboth's family spoke no English and we spoke no Nepali, this proved no obstacle to a good game of marbles, chess or cards. Suboth's father, in particular, enjoyed the card games thoroughly (to his mother's clear disapproval), and when we left him our free packs of glossy airline playing cards, he was delighted.

With my homestay family: Subboth Kattel (2nd from right), with his sister and parents at his home in Kattel Danda.

My schoolmates and I set to work the next day painting the school doors, setting up an index system for the library, and playing riotous games of dog-and-bone with the children. In exchange, the villagers taught us their favourite Bollywood-inspired songs and dances. Few owned television sets, but they would walk to the nearest bazaar for their Bollywood fix.

One of our plans was to create a garden for the school. Since every school in Singapore featured a garden, we figured a garden would be nice for Saraswoti School too.

All day long we turned the soil, dug flower beds and planted seeds and bulbs until blisters popped up on our hands. Looking politely on, the Nepali villagers helpfully dug up their own plants so that we could replant them in the new school garden.

The next day, my friends and I returned to the garden to inspect our pride and joy, only to discover that the cows and goats had eaten up the plants.

On hindsight, the villagers must have been puzzled by our flower beds. After all, the entire village was their garden.

On our final night in Aahale, we planned a great campfire. The entire village turned up and, when the space in front of the campfire became too crowded, mothers pulled their children up to the flat roof of the school and enjoyed the view from their circle seats.

Cultural and games exchanges in the school courtyard.

This was my time to step up. After all, campfires were a Scout specialty. A fellow Scout and I envisioned a beautiful fire in the pit, the whole village singing campfire songs around it on a chilly night. From our shopping list of wood, kerosene, rags and string, we designed a dramatic production where a kerosene fireball would whizz from the first storey into the pit and — *whoosh!* — set the wood aflame.

In our ignorance, we were unaware that wood was expensive and kerosene even more so. But the accommodating villagers brought everything we requested. It was only when we noticed their reluctance to lavishly splash about the kerosene (as we were taught in Scouts) that Mr Krishnan revealed the reason for their frugality. Boy, did we feel sheepish.

The extravagance was not wasted on the older village teenagers however. Somehow they managed to spirit away the jerry can of kerosene, put swigs of kerosene in their mouth and — *phwoo!* — blew out fire with the help of a matchstick, to much amusement all around. That is, until their teacher discovered what they were doing and twisted their ears as punishment.

In the end we did create a fiery spectacle, and the gracious villagers appeared to thoroughly enjoy the campfire singing, despite the fact that the wood and kerosene would have been put to better use in the kitchen.

Singaporean students performing a local dance during the evening of the campfire.

There were many flaws in our grand, but naïve, plans for the village. But the charitable kindness with which the villagers received every single misguided gift was humbling. Charity flows both ways.

From this trip, I learnt my first important lesson in community work: If you want to do good, find out what the beneficiaries *really* need.

+++

Thirteen years later in 2012, directly after I summited Everest, Mr Krishnan, Gayathri (my then girlfriend and now wife) and I returned to Aahale.

We brought with us 20 desktop computers and monitors and 20 UPS units (uninterrupted power supply) for the students of Saraswoti Secondary School.

The main sponsor for my Everest bid was Cerebos, whose product, Brand's, believed in developing the unrealised potential of youths. They envisioned this ethos benefitting schoolchildren in Nepal.

Immediately Saraswoti School sprang to mind.

The creatives at Cerebos launched a Facebook page following my mountaineering exploits and promised to donate S$10,000 if we hit 10,000 likes. Their generous donation would go into buying desktops.

We hit 10k. And Cerebos kept their promise.

Meanwhile, in between preparations for Everest, I had tracked down Mr Krishnan, who by now had left Raffles Institution and was the vice principal of Westgrove Primary School.

Mr Krishnan was elated. He could hardly believe that a young student he had taken to Aahale on a community project 13 years ago had grown up and was now taking *him* back to Aahale on a second-generation community project. It tickled him no end that, not only did I remember *his* school, I was now calling it *our* school.

In a brainwave, Mr Krishnan decided to enlist the help of his old friend, the Saraswoti Secondary School principal, by now ex-principal, Mr Netra Kattel (whom his students respectfully addressed as "Mr Netra Sir"). Mr Netra was now retired and living in Kathmandu with his family.

But, delighted that his former school was about to receive a windfall, he sprang into action. In a flurry of communication with the new headmaster at Aahale, Mr Netra agreed to coordinate the purchase of the desktops. (When I say "flurry", I mean the Himalayan version of flurry — there was no Internet and no e-mail then, so all communication was by snail mail.)

With the $10,000 donated by Cerebos, Mr Netra and Mr Krishnan bought computers which were locally assembled, stretching each dollar so that instead of the two laptops anticipated by the sponsor, they managed to buy 20 laptops and 20 uninterrupted power supply units that would see the desktops through the frequent power cuts.

I was hoping not to have the embarrassing heroes' welcome when we arrived, but there the schoolchildren were again, lining the road, cheering and garlanding us, even though this time there was only Mr Krishnan, Gayathri and myself.

It was with great pleasure that we saw how the school benefitted from the new equipment. Before, in a class of 40 to 50 students, one student would click the mouse, three monitors would display the presentation and the rest of the students would crowd around. Now each pair of students could share a desktop and monitor. We were impressed to discover that the students were not just learning basic word processing, but HTML and Java programming, under the instruction of a computer science teacher.

To encourage a sense of ownership, Mr Netra and the new headmaster encouraged the students' parents to chop wood and build furniture for the new computers. The school staff got into the action, too, by converting their staff room into a computer lab.

By the time we returned to Singapore, Gayathri and I were receiving Facebook friend requests from the Aahale students. And today Shree Saraswoti Secondary School has its own Facebook page.

Back in Aahale for yet another visit some years after this, Mr Krishnan was chatting with a group of villagers about Singaporeans' contributions to the village, including my own. A young man at the back was sitting on his motorbike, listening intently. When Mr Krishnan mentioned my name, the young man piped up: "I know Kumaran! He stayed in my house in 1999!"

That young man was Suboth, all grown up.

For 30 years as an educator, Mr Krishnan had dedicated himself to planting seeds in his students, not knowing how they would eventually turn out. (Mischievous as I was as a kid, I was probably the last one he expected to amount to anything.) In 1999, when I was 15, the seeds he had planted in me were of adventure and community consciousness. That the story had come full circle brought Mr Krishnan deep satisfaction.

In a letter to The Straits Times forum page, after they ran the story "The boy who grew up to climb Everest", Mr Krishnan wrote:

> "Dr Kumaran Rasappan is my former student. The article mentioned his trip to the Nepalese town of Gorkha 13 years ago as a Raffles Institution student. I was there with him. I did not know then that 13 years later, I would go back to the school in Gorkha to witness my former student giving back to society and the community in a big way.
>
> "Every teacher wants his students to aspire to be the best they can be. Every teacher also derives satisfaction when his students give back to society through tangible and intangible ways.
>
> "To witness all this up close is a rare privilege and an honour this teacher will cherish forever."

Mr Krishnan was the first to introduce me to community work (and to the idea that community is global), the first to point out Everest to me (from the cockpit of a plane, no less), and the first to introduce me to trekking — all of which are still a part of my life.

Among the lessons Mr Krishnan taught me was this: We never know how much of an influence we are going to be to the next person. So treat everyone's dreams with respect.

+++

Mr Netra Sir was also a huge influence. A man of character, his strong principles earned him the respect of all the students and villagers. He was someone who approved only of actions that benefitted the greater good, and thought nothing of personal gain.

In 2015, after the devastating 7.8-magnitude earthquake struck Nepal, taking the lives of over 9,000 people and displacing 3.5 million more, Mr Netra and I met briefly in Kathmandu, when I was part of a Mercy Relief medical mission.

The epicentre of the earthquake was Gorkha, where Aahale was located. The damage was widespread.

Concerned, I enquired after Saraswoti School. At that point, Saraswoti, now a double-storey building with concrete floors, had established itself as a reputable regional academic hub.

The school was Mr Netra's baby. He had built it from the ground up, with students he had personally groomed. Yet, to my concerned enquiries about the school, he replied: "Dr Kumaran, the school has received enough from you. Other people need your help more."

Mr Krishnan. Mr Netra. My father and mother. I am immensely grateful for these teachers in my life who have not only taught me, but inspired me.

As French aviator and writer Antoine de Saint-Exupéry says:

"If you want to build a ship, don't drum up people to collect wood and don't assign them tasks and work, but rather teach them to long for the endless immensity of the sea."

Mr Netra Mani Kattel (left) and Mr Krishnan Pillay (right), two educators who have inspired me immensely with their selflessness and far-sightedness.

CHAPTER 4

"Everyone wants to live on top of the mountain, but all the happiness and growth occurs while you're climbing it."
Andy Rooney

Mountaineering is a study of man versus rock.

There are other elements involved, to be sure. Glaciers. Hurricane force winds. Oxygen deprivation. Logistics. Snow conditions. Nerves.

But without the rock, there would be nothing.

Like many mountaineers, my own climbing journey began elementally with rock.

In urban Singapore, this typically started with rock walls.

The rock wall in my junior college was the subject of numerous climbing competitions and inter-house games. Rock climbing looked extremely cool to me — a sport that required little technical equipment, but relied on sheer physical and mental dexterity.

The test of planning moves and executing them precisely is a partnership of brain and brawn, and the challenge appealed to me.

During my first year at the National University of Singapore (NUS), when there was an opportunity to join the competitive rock climbing team, I immediately signed up for selections.

The National University of Singapore Intervarsity climbing team 2005-2006.

Three times a week, our team trained together at the NUS sports and recreation centre, putting in runs, gym work and climbs. On weekends, my batchmates, seniors and I would sometimes attack the bigger walls in Yishun Safra and Climbasia. The intensity of the training and intervarsity competitions against polytechnics, Institute of Technical Education (ITE) and other universities bonded the team quickly and permanently. (We still meet up today.)

My first two years of medical school, when I was also on the intervarsity climbing team, flew by in a blur of lab coats, dissections, exams, barbells, burpees, climbing chalk, too much sweat and too little sleep. This was the life.

A trip to Krabi, Thailand, to scale the limestone rocks with my climbing buddies took the sport to another level for me. Here, in the great outdoors with an expanse of sky above and the rough limestone beneath my palms, it was no longer about competitions, cheers and trophies. It was just me, the rock and the satisfying ache of my muscles.

I loved it.

+++

One of my rock climbing teammates was an adventurous Romanian PhD student by the name of Claudia Szabo.

After a mind-numbing amount of lectures, tutorials and assessments one evening, I was relaxing in front of a computer in my student residence, King Edward VII Hall in NUS.

Logging on to Facebook, my attention was caught by a couple of vivid Flickr photos. I actually thought they were from National Geographic. The craggy peaks of snow-flanked mountains, rising above a bed of thick, rolling clouds, was stunning.

It was when I looked more closely that I realised this was no professional magazine photo. Standing atop a soaring mountain, with a spectacular range of Andean peaks at her feet, was my friend Claudia Szabo.

She was in a bulky, red-and-black snowsuit with heavy boots and gloves, her hood up against the cold and sunglasses to protect against the glare of sun and snow. A mass of ropes snaked around her body. On her face was an exhausted, but totally triumphant, smile.

I was dumbfounded. I knew Claudia as a rock climbing teammate with a similar fitness level as mine. (At that point, I had completed two full Standard Chartered Singapore Marathons, thanks primarily to free fitness training in National Service.)

I was a city boy who had lived all his life at sea level in one of the smallest countries in the world. A mountaineer was as mythical a creature to me as the yeti.

But this was no myth — it was Claudia! Suddenly the walls of my dormitory room and the confines of the humdrum life I was leading fell away. The world was literally within my reach.

Not only had Claudia summited Aconcagua, she had done it alpine style, meaning on her own, with map and compass, lugging her own gear, cooking her own meals and finding her own route up. Impressive. I would later discover that she was not just any climber, she was one of the pioneer female Romanian alpinists of the time.

So I started Googling mountains, searching "the easiest high mountains to climb". Kilimanjaro cropped up.

At 5,895m, Kilimanjaro is Africa's highest mountain and one of the world's tallest free-standing peaks. Technically, ascending Kilimanjaro is a guided hike rather than a climb, as equipment and climbing technique are not required. The oxygen-low

Claudia on an Andean peak.
This inspiring photo set me on
a path to mountaineering and
changed my life..

atmosphere is the biggest challenge and a solid test of endurance for
novice climbers.

By my third year of medical school, in June 2008, I was on a plane
to Kilimanjaro, together with five equally exuberant friends from med
school, my rock climbing team and my residential hall.

+++

Mt Kilimanjaro, with its distinctive flat summit, snow draped over
the top like an unironed white tablecloth, is one of the most iconic
mountains in the world.

It is a dormant volcano consisting of three volcanic cones: Kibo,
Mawenzi and Shira.

Besides being the highest mountain in Africa, Kilimanjaro is a
must-climb for enthusiasts because of its elite status as one of the Seven
Summits[4], every summit being the highest mountain in each of the
seven continents of the world.

---

4 Adventurers who reach the North and South Poles, on top of climbing the Seven Summits, are said to
   have completed the Explorers Grand Slam.

For 1½ months, Claudio Szabo did her best to prepare us for Kili, using Vigilante Drive, a steep slope just behind NUS in Kent Ridge, for our drills.

With youth on our side and a few NAPFA (National Physical Fitness Award/Assessment) tests and IPPT golds (Individual Physical Proficiency Test during National Service) under our belt, my mates and I felt ready to tackle Kili.

It was a thrill to arrive in Tanzania, fabled for such geographical treasures as the game-rich Serengeti savannah, Lake Victoria and Kilimanjaro.

We started off as a bright-eyed, bushy tailed bunch, walking past lowlands inhabited by the local Chagga people who cultivate the land with yams, potatoes and maize.

Above this belt, we moved quickly on the mud trails of the tropical montane forest, a little wilder now and lush with butterflies, bulbul birds and wild flowers unique to Tanzania. Colobus monkeys and nocturnal creatures like the aardvark, badger and civet cat also called this home.

One of the fascinating things about climbing Kilimanjaro is that you go from the tropics to the arctic, passing through five different climate zones before hitting the summit.

Above the montane forests are the moorelands, a boulder-littered landscape where we began to feel the biting cold. Sunrises glowed through daytime mists; nights were blisteringly cold. By the time we reached the alpine deserts between 4,000 and 5,000m, flora and fauna had diminished to insects and moss in the dry air. Striking volcanic lava formations jutted out from the ground.

But we had underestimated Kilimanjaro.

Being impoverished students, my travel mates and I had bought our trekking gear, including boots, from a cheap army supplies store.

Little did we greenhorns know that, at the altitude of 5,000m, temperatures average around freezing point. At the summit, which lies in the glacial zone, temperatures dip to anywhere between -6°C and -20°C. (Better prepared hikers were equipped with fleece, merino wool undergarments, a down jacket for cold nights, a balaclava to block the frost from causing sore throats, and crampons to navigate the ice in the push to the summit.)

My first high-altitude climb on Kilimanjaro with our small team of six.

Stella Point at the crater rim of Kilimanjaro.

Arriving at the arctic zone, a terrain blanketed with snow and ice, our army boots, designed for walking in tropical Asian jungles, had us slipping and sliding so that every step was exhausting.

By the time we arrived at the crater rim, still far from the summit, the local guide was advising us to quit, as the sun was coming up fast in the morning heat, and the melting ice would become dangerously slippery.

According to estimates by park authorities, less than half of trekkers reach the summit. Every year, about 1,000 people are evacuated from the mountain, and approximately 10 deaths are reported, mostly from Acute Mountain Sickness (AMS).

In fact, I was so breathless and coughing so badly that my guide was convinced I had pulmonary edema, a sign of end-stage AMS. He said firmly: "The rock will always be there. Your life is more important."

But the stubborn streak in me pushed me on, one excruciating step at a time. At this point, only my hall mate, Terence, and I had decided to carry on. Each time we asked the guide: *How long more?* he would invariably say: *Two hours.*

When we finally set foot on the summit, there was no one left; all other trekkers had already descended. We were bone-tired and numb to any feeling of accomplishment.

Our descent on the frozen scree was made pretty much on our butts. Without warning, Terence suddenly fell and slid fast down the ice. He would have shot right off the mountain had he not gone past a hole in the ice, which he instinctively grabbed, swinging sideways to a halt.

When we thought things couldn't get any worse, it started raining.

No doubt about it: This was a pretty disastrous first attempt at scaling a mountain.

With the resilience of youth, we signed up for a game safari the next day. Our guide also suggested that we take on another peak that was less intimidating: Ol Doinyo Lengai (2,962m), "Mountain of God" in the Maasai language. Sulphuric fumes rose from the active volcano, the sides of which were slippery with ash. But reaching the top, with the spectacular African Rift Valley spreading below us, was reward enough.

Back in Singapore, as we returned to our humdrum routine, my friends and I incongruously agreed: *That was the most exhilarating adventure EVER.*

My first-ever mountain summit in June 2008: Kilimanjaro (5,895m).

Our reaction was hardly logical. Numerous battle wounds — from battered toes to hacking coughs — attested to our considerable suffering on the mountains. I could have sworn as I struggled to put one foot in front of the other up the mountain that I'd muttered something about never putting myself through this masochism again.

But breaking out of our mundane routines to travel an inordinate distance to a strange and fascinating land in order to push our bodies to the absolute limit … we felt more alive than we had ever been.

It was precisely that moment when my Everest dream was born.

+++

On 25 May 1998, at 8:30am, Outward Bound School instructor Edwin Siew and systems analyst Khoo Swee Chiow[5], together with four Sherpas, successfully summited Everest after an arduous nine-hour ascent that had begun at 11:30pm the previous night.

The two were members of the first Singapore Everest team, comprising 12 people from various walks of life including a doctor, a mechanic, a university undergraduate, and a physical education (PE) teacher.

---

5 Khoo Swee Chiow is a Singaporean adventurer and mountaineer who, in May 2019, became the first Southeast Asian to scale the world's three highest peaks of Mount Everest (8,848m), K2 (8,611m) and Kangchenjunga (8,586m).

In setting the precedence, the team inspired a whole new generation of climbing enthusiasts.

Some of the 1998 Everest teammates, notably defence engineer Robert Goh, and the climbing compatriots from a 2002 Xixapangma (or Shishapangma) Expedition, decided to set up a mountaineering club, Make It Real (MIR), under the auspices of the National University of Singapore. It was their hope that they could pass on their passion and mountaineering skills to Singapore youths.

Cabinet Minister Dr Vivian Balakrishnan became the first patron for MIR, and was a warmly supportive one.

The club made it clear to hopefuls that MIR was not for everyone. Weekly training involved a technical training session, a gym session, a 10km run, a stair training session or a Bukit Timah Hill training session.

The pioneer MIR 1 team set their sights on a 6,000m Himalayan peak, Chulu West (6,419m), by the end of their academic year the following June. The lean team of nine was required to pass stringent assessments in technical competency and physical fitness. (The passing time for running 10km was 50 minutes).

Since then, MIR has groomed over 100 young mountaineers through its Technical Mountaineering Course in New Zealand, and taken its student members on climbing expeditions to the Himalayas, China and Kazakhstan, among other destinations. It also directed the NUS Centennial Everest Expedition in 2005. Two members of the Singapore Women's Everest Expedition in 2009 hailed from MIR.

One of the students on Island Peak (6,189m) took a photo of a note someone had left on the summit. It encapsulated the MIR spirit:

"They say dreamers have their heads in the clouds. As mountaineers, this is a pretty accurate statement."

When I returned from Kilimanjaro, I emailed the president of MIR essentially telling her I hoped to join the club as I had set my sights on Everest.

She might have laughed, I couldn't tell.

A dozen students must have expressed to her lofty dreams of Everest after navigating just one mountain. But, graciously, she replied with a long and encouraging email, welcoming me to join the club in their training and fund-raising activities. And so I joined MIR and the growing number of youths who had their head in the clouds (or at least hoped to one day).

+++

Meanwhile, there was medical school for me to contend with.

Med school was the academic version of mountain climbing: A head-hurting, energy-draining, seemingly never-ending test of endurance, commitment and sacrifice. To top it off, there was a groaning mountain of studying to conquer.

Every now and then a light moment pierced through our brain fog a little.

On one of our general surgery ward rounds, a patient had a lower gastrointestinal bleed. He had not been to the toilet and we could not check his stools for malena (dark, altered blood). The house officer proceeded with a rectal examination. The whole student team, including the consultant, was standing by the bedside, awaiting the results so that we could decide on the management for the patient.

As the house officer withdrew his hand, there was a sigh of relief from the team as there was neither bleeding nor malena. But as the house officer unraveled his rubber gloves, a speck of stool flew from the glove and made a neat landing on the consultant's white shirt. He wasn't aware of this and my fellow students and I did not know how to tell him; we didn't want the house officer to get a shelling. Looking at each other and trying to keep a straight face, we were about to proceed with our rounds when the consultant was called to the surgical theatre for an emergency. I saw the consultant again the next day; but I never saw that shirt again.

Lighter moments aside, many have asked how I managed to balance the punishing medical school workload with commitment-heavy mountaineering. (Between Year 3 and Year 5, I made trips to Mt Kilimanjaro, Island Peak in Nepal, the Siguniang Range in China, and did some ice climbing in Sichuan).

If medical school is all-consuming, working life is even more so. As medical residents, we are required to work, study, do research, give presentations, teach, do administration, clear courses and pass exams. All this while functioning as a human being with basic needs like sleep, food and relationships.

Actually, my passion for mountaineering became my lifeline.

While I could not train and climb as much as my MIR mates (thankfully the club cut me some slack), my sanity was preserved precisely *because* of my passion for climbing.

During breaks from my books, I would recharge and draw energy from reading up about mountains and mountaineering. That medicine and mountains do not have a direct correlation allowed me to step away from one and gain clarity for the other. It was my secret to avoiding burnout.

+++

While in med school, I heard of a Singaporean who was taking people on ice-climbing trips in China.

Lim Kim Boon was one of the 12 climbers in the first Singapore Everest team in 1998 and the base camp manager for the Women's Everest team in 2009.

For 13 years he had been a regular in the Singapore Armed Forces as a commando in the Special Operations Force (SOF). ("I got to run around and jump out of planes. What's not to like?")

When he hung up his army boots, it was to enrol in university in Liverpool, United Kingdom, to study outdoor education and environmental studies. His intention at the time was to teach the same at tertiary level. But he couldn't shake the conviction that outdoor education was not something that could, or should, be taught in a classroom. So instead, he became an Outward Bound School instructor and subsequently the first rock climbing instructor in Singapore.

When MIR was first started by his Everest teammate, Robert Goh, Kim Boon was roped in to train the students for their climbs, and has been involved ever since.

He had started his career with the intention of being a teacher. And, without a doubt, he is. I estimate that three-quarters of Singaporeans who climb have been mentored in one way or another by Kim Boon.

In our small, tightly-knit climbing fraternity, Kim Boon is a rock star. (Pardon the pun.)

When I first approached him about his ice climbing trips and expressed my hope in also climbing a mountain alpine-style, carrying my own load and making my own way without guides, he was measured in his response.

"Come and experience the mountains first, and see how you feel," he said in his reassuringly calm manner.

He told me later that he had actually "prepared a safety net" — pack horses were on standby. (The best teachers never tell you when you are over-ambitious; they allow you to find out for yourself.) He had a knack for being realistic but encouraging at the same time.

In Kim Boon's experience, many novice climbers, while fit, could experience debilitating AMS, some above 3,000m, some even at lower altitudes. Our reactions to altitude are unpredictable, even if we were fine at the same altitude before.

Later on, in my 8,000m climbs, I would realise that we only discover our physical and mental limits when we are so thoroughly wiped out that we hit a metaphorical wall, or when we face a life-or-death situation.

The first time my group came face to face with Kim Boon, who has lived in Wales for the past 20 years, was at the start of the Sichuan trip. He was nothing like any of us had expected. His resume may be hardcore, but he was one of the most amiable men I had ever met, seldom without his trademark smile.

Still, our first trip with him was far from easy.

That year, Sichuan was still devastated by one of the worst earthquakes in China.

In May 2008, a magnitude-8.0 earthquake sheared through Sichuan, toppling buildings and flattening four-fifths of structures in the affected areas. Whole villages and towns were buried under mudslides. Almost 90,000 were believed to be dead or missing. Aftershocks continued months and even years after, including a magnitude 5.0 quake in 2010.

In January 2009, we arrived in Sichuan to discover that the road to the Shuangqiao-kou, where we were headed, had literally disappeared. Landslides triggered by the earthquake had altered the map. Because of

Kim Boon, who has mentored many Singaporean climbers.

Kim Boon's connections with the local people (he had been conducting his ice climbing courses in Chengdu since 2003), we were picked up by his contacts, who took a circuitous route to our destination. What normally took six hours took us two days.

Our group consisted of a random bunch of Singaporeans that included two lawyers, a bartender, a businessman and a documentary producer. My two university friends and I were the youngest in the bunch. Most of them were seasoned trekkers looking to level up their game.

Temperatures were below freezing when we finally arrived at the humble village home that was our accommodation at Shuangqiao-kou. The earthquake had partially destroyed the house, which had a big crack running through the building. Through the damaged ceiling, the sky was visible.

Our eyes were immediately drawn to the charcoal fire pot in the middle of the room, radiating welcome heat in the sub zero temperatures. The eight of us made a beeline for the fire pot to warm our hands.

The homestay was Kim Boon's way of providing an income to villagers. Many of them were farmers who worked hard in the summer months but had no means of earning a living in the winter. He had also trained villagers to assist in his climbs over the years.

Staying in a local home lent the journey a personal warmth lacking in commercially organised trips.

Thick, fatty meat hanging from the kitchen ceiling of the lodge we stayed in, under which we had our daily meals.

The host family served up home-cooked food for our meals. I remember thick noodles in hot oil, fried long beans, and a pork dish that appeared to consist of 90% pork fat and 10% pork skin. The rest eyed this meal dubiously, but everything tasted delicous to me.

The toilet took more getting used to. They were mostly outhouses, which made you think twice about going to the toilet in the night when it was -15°C outside.

A simple shelter with a partition — males on one side and females on the other — you had to squat in order not to see the person on the other side. An open drain carried the sewage along, "flushed" with buckets of water. While I was squatting one day, the owner of the home unceremoniously entered and stood in front of me, asking matter of factly if the poop needed flushing. I was hardly in a position to talk.

Apparently nowadays accommodation in the Siguniang climbing region has been modernised, with heated flooring and nice showers. But, for me, I enjoyed the authentic experience of tradition. There is something beautiful about raw rusticity.

The plan was for us to climb up a few frozen waterfalls in what Kim Boon described as "on-the-job training", learning how to put on crampons, walk on ice, work with ropes and jumars, wear a harness, use ice tools, and rope up to each other.

Ice climbing sounds untenable. Isn't ice slippery, offering no traction? And friable, shattering like glass under heavy weight? But, as Kim Boon told us, while ice climbing is not for the faint hearted, once you know how to use the equipment — crampons, ice axe and screws, harness, ropes — it is not as dangerous as it sounds. In fact, the most dangerous factor is ignorance.

Technique in ice climbing is not as important as in rock climbing; it is a repetition of placing your ice axe, kicking into the ice and repeating, which makes this a sport that anyone with decent cardiovascular fitness can pick up with the right equipment.

A spin-off from mountaineering, ice climbing has been a favourite pursuit of climbers for the last 50 years since Yvon Chouinard, founder of outdoor gear Patagonia, published his book, *Climbing Ice,* in the late 70s.

But the sport has really been around in Europe since the 19th century, developing in tandem with its specialised equipment. In 1908, Oscar Eckenstein developed a claw tooth boot — the first crampon.

In 1932, Laurent Grivel designed a boot with two spikes in the front (which most crampons now feature), allowing climbers to gain more traction and attack steeper inclines. In 1966, Yvon Chouinard designed what is now the modern-day ice axe which, together with crampons, has become standard gear for ice climbers.

Enthusiasts now traverse the globe from China to Canada, Japan to Russia, in search of the next ice climbing challenge. International competitions, including the Ice Climbing World Cup, sees climbers compete in speed, height and difficulty.

Recreational climbers like ourselves usually climb one of two types of ice: Alpine ice (formed from compacted snow) which mountaineers in the Alps and the Himalayas navigate, or cascade ice (from frozen water). Here in the Siguniang range, Kim Boon had us tackling cascade ice from natural waterfalls frozen into haunting crystal sculptures.

Each morning, the eight of us would pile into a van in search of frozen waterfalls. Kim Boon, with his years of experience, could tell which ones were solid enough for climbing. The waterfalls were unlike anything I had ever seen. Water that splashed down rocky mountains in the summer became icy stalactites in the winter, as though they had not had time to race downhill before Father Frost cast his spell over the land.

Slowly we would inch our way up the solid ice: Chop, kick, try to avoid the occasional ice shower from the person above, repeat.

Don Mellor, in his book, *Blue Lines, An Adirondack Ice Climber's Guide*, had this advice to offer: "If you began in the gym or on sport routes, take everything you have been told about falling and leave it at home. Replace the idea with one fact: DON'T."

At one point, I stopped climbing at the elevation of about 3,600m. With my full body weight suspended on the ice, I turned to look back. Behind me there was nothing but silence and an expanse of bitingly cold air. A valley, dotted with hills and homes, spread out thousands of metres below. The view took my breath away.

Each day of climbing ended in the same way: Sitting down together, family style, for dinner. There was plenty of chatter and laughter, likely encouraged by the free flowing local wolfberry alcohol, *sachi*.

Some of us shared the reason we had embarked on this trip. I was too shy to say I had my eye on Everest, and mumbled something about attempting an 8,000m peak one day. One of the climbers, a

Kim Boon teaching us the basics of ice climbing on the frozen waterfalls.

The haunting waterfalls of Shuangqiao-kou, Mt Siguniang National Park, which Kim Boon would pick for us to ice climb.

businessman named Nasser Aljunied, said he wanted to learn from this experience in the mountains to be a better person and a better father.

I can identify. Here in the wild mountains, away from the man-made artifice of city life, you begin to appreciate the small things that you take for granted in efficient Singapore. It is in our human nature to forget to be grateful, until we are taken out of our comfort zone. That's what mountains do for us.

Nasser, whose sincerity became a source of inspiration to me, kindly donated his climbing boots and down suit to me after the climb. Unknown to him, I would go on to wear them on Everest.

+++

On Kim Boon's trips, nobody failed; there was no summit goal. As far as he was concerned, if we picked up new skills, enjoyed experiences that were totally out of the ordinary, and got back home safely with our 10 fingers and 10 toes intact, it was journey enough.

One of his greatest satisfactions, he told me, was seeing people who were afraid of heights approach the ice with trepidation and leave with confidence.

The group parted ways when my two friends and I carried on to climb DaFeng (5,038m), or Big Peak, in the Siguniang range.

From Rilong town, we trekked to the base camp of DaFeng in a straightforward, gentle ascent. Sichuan winters are bitterly cold and the mountain terrain was a barren ice-scape of snow and rock.

Our compact, orange tents offered little protection against the -15°C, -20°C temperatures. When we slept, we would have our hydration packs filled with hot water inside our sleeping bags.

Already bedded down in my sleeping bag one afternoon, I felt a pleasant warmth spreading down my legs.

Hey, this "hot water bottle" really works! I thought to myself.

It turned out that the warm liquid inside the hot water bottle had leaked out. The water soaked my entire sleeping bag and I was drenched.

Draping my sleeping bag on top of my tent to dry, I was wiping myself off when Kim Boon came around to ask what was going on. I related the incident and he immediately asked: "Where's your sleeping bag? Did it get wet?"

When he discovered what I had done with it, he yelled: "Are you crazy? You're going to get yourself killed!"

I gathered this was serious because it was the first time I had seen him lose his cool.

By the time Kim Boon retrieved my sleeping bag, it had frozen as solid as a plank of wood. That had taken all of 20 minutes.

"This kind of thing will get you killed here," he admonished.

Thankfully, he managed to get a porter to warm up the sleeping bag somehow and evaporate the ice so I could sleep in it that night.

We began our summit push the next day, and I experienced my first close shave.

Climbing up a scree of loose rocks, I placed one hand on the edge of a smooth rock the size of a cupboard; I did not expect a rock of that size to be unstable. But as soon as I touched the corner, it tipped over, toppling towards me. My Chinese guide, who did not speak any English while I did not speak any Chinese, had already gone ahead and was oblivious to my cries for help. In the nick of time, I managed to scuttle sideways (not always an easy move on a mountain slope) and the rock rolled past to come to a stop 10 to 15m down. Had I not been able to move away, I would have been crushed.

Climbing is risky business. In Kim Boon's decades of climbing, he has had a few close shaves as well.

In Chamonix, France, a rockfall nearly killed him. The top of a rock formation split off without warning and a rock the size of a car went hurtling down.

"It fell just by my side — *phwoom!* — if I had not moved a split second earlier, I would have died," he said. Rockfall is one of the things that cannot be predicted or prepared for on a mountain.

In Muztagh Ata, Xinjiang, one of the worst nightmares of climbers came to pass for Kim Boon. His team was not roped up, as the Chinese guide had assured them that this flat area was "*meishi-ba*" (no problem).

One moment Kim Boon was standing on solid snow, waiting for the last person on the team to ascend, and the next moment, the ground gave way and he found himself plunging down a deep crevasse.

"It happened so fast that I had no time to think. When I landed, I thought, 'Sh--, I'm in a crevasse'," he said. "When I brushed away the snow from my landing spot, I realised that I had landed on a bridge of ice. If I had fallen just inches to my left or right, I would have missed the bridge and kept on falling. I felt like God had saved me ... put a hand out and held me there.

"I still had my walkie talkie with me, so I got my teammate to lower a rope and pull me up. After that, everybody roped up!"

My close shave with the rolling rock did not deter me from continuing my ascent to the summit of DaFeng. My two friends had turned back because of lateness and tiredness, and Kim Boon suggested that I turn back, too. I was just too damn slow. But that stubborn streak asserted itself once again and, despite my inexperience, the thought of the cut-off time for the summit drove me to push harder.

I made it to the top within 10 minutes of the turnaround cut-off time.

Back at Base Camp, Kim Boon clapped me on the shoulder, congratulated me and said with a smile: "Very good, very good, I didn't think you would make it! I'm surprised by your determination!"

When our group returned to Chengdu, the whole city was in the thick of Chinese New Year festivities. Sim's Cozy Guesthouse, where we stayed, lived up to its name with simple but comfortable two-bed rooms, a rooftop garden and a movie room. With Chinese New Year approaching, big red lanterns swung above the entranceway, welcoming guests. In the alley outside, locals sat drinking tea and playing cards.

The festivities, food and firecrackers inspired an air of joyfulness and high spirits. I tell you, there is nothing that tastes better than *mala* hotpot in the deep freeze of winter.

As much as I was taking photos of everything, the locals were taking photos of me and my Indian friend. In this part of Sichuan, many had never seen Indians before. They assumed we were *feizhou ren* (African).

A side trip to the panda sanctuary in Chengdu made for an amusing end to our journey.

This was my first trip to China, my first experience of winter and the first time I ice climbed. It also became the first time I caught a glimpse of how enjoyable it was to climb with a convivial group of strangers. To this day, I consider this the best trip I have ever taken.

Like many in our small climbing community, I owe Kim Boon a debt of gratitude. Not only has he taken us to spectacular places few are privileged to set foot on, he did it with a grace and patience rare in the rough mountaineering fraternity.

The start of the Mt Chola climb, one of the most stunning mountains I have traversed.

Our refresher course on how to navigate the glacier and how to perform crevasse rescue.

The summit of Mt Chola (6,168m), August 2010.

He was, and is, fully invested in his passion for the outdoors, but equally invested in passing on his fervour and skills to others. I consider him my biggest climbing mentor.

I was to do one more climb with Kim Boon. In August 2010, we took on Mt Chola (6,168m) in a group of 14. I was a house officer by then and only had seven days of annual leave within a four-month posting. Chola required 14 days. So, for some extra days of leave, I devised a qualitative research project where I had to interview every teammate and test if their V02 Max improved after the trip. During the climb, I persuaded my teammates to fill out questionnaires while they rested in their tents. They still won't let me forget what a pest I made of myself.

Chola was stunning. We started out near a mountain lake surrounded by grass and trees, passed tumbling waterfalls, traversed a terrain of glacier and snow, and finally took on a 100m vertical section before arriving at the knife-edge summit. The combination of diverse scenery and different technical challenges, not to mention the great company, made this climb memorable.

Within this group, two of us would go on to summit Everest: Kenneth Koh, whose team had placed second in an ultramarathon in the Gobi Desert in 2008, and myself.

In a 2009 article in The Straits Times, David Lim, expedition leader of the first Singapore Everest team, said: "The media has often taken few pains to educate itself on the sport of mountaineering. Until it educates its reporters that mountaineering excellence has never been defined by an ascent of Everest alone, the sport is truly doomed. Our busy and time-starved public will never be able to fathom anything in mountaineering other than Everest-ing."

He was absolutely right. Like humans, every mountain has its own personality, its own beauty and its own story. Even the same mountain on a different day reveals a different face and mood.

And there's something else: Summiting, while an act of human triumph and a consequence of good fortune, is not necessarily *the* most meaningful part of a climb. This I was about to discover.

CHAPTER 5

"Don't be afraid of the space between your dreams and reality. If you can dream it, you can make it so."
Belva Davis

Why do climbers climb? Many have posed this question, and I have asked it of myself.

Most of the human race tries our hardest to avoid pain and death. Yet for mountaineers, the most tantalising goal lies in climbing the "deathzone mountains". Above 8,000m, oxygen is 34% the concentration it is at sea level, and human habitation is untenable for an extended period of time. In some seasons, mountains like the notorious K2 see death rates of 32%.

Yet mountaineering is not a death wish.

In some weird way, I never felt more alive than when I was in the death zone. Not literally, of course. In the death zone, I was perpetually nauseous, gasping, my limbs moved with frustrating effort and my hypoxic mind was addled.

But in the economy of every movement there was what climber and filmmaker Jimmy Chin calls "a meditation in being present". All of life's artificial noise falls away. And what remains is a keen recognition of human significance that also acknowledges human limitation.

So why do climbers climb? Honestly, it's a rare mountaineer who can answer this question logically. And I'm not one of them.

As climber and investigative journalist, Jon Krakauer, put it in his best-selling book, *Into Thin Air*: "Once Everest was determined to be the highest summit on earth, it was only a matter of time before people decided that Everest needed to be climbed. After the American explorer Robert Peary claimed to have reached the North Pole in 1909 and Roald Amundsen led a Norwegian party to the South Pole in 1911, Everest — the so-called Third Pole — became the most coveted object in the realm of terrestrial exploration."

What compelled me, personally, was not so lofty an ambition. I can only say that once I climbed a mountain, something in my spirit was captivated.

This defies logical explanation as much as falling in love or taking the unpredictable (often unprofitable) path of parenthood.

Mountaineers are not necessarily thrill seekers. As students in the 11th batch of MIR explained in their blog: "Mountaineering is not a sport. It is a lifestyle which encompasses elements of uncertainty and risk, but it is not a blind pursuit of risk for its own sake. Thrill seekers have lots of easier activities to pursue. On the contrary, mountaineering involves detailed planning, preparation and motivation to overcome obstacles and to push the limits of human body further and higher. In the harshest of environments, we truly discover what we are made of. It represents the 'make it real' spirit with brains."

+ + +

By the time I graduated from medical school in 2010, I had chalked up a modest list of treks and climbs including Poon Hill (3,210m), Kilimanjaro (5,895m), Ol Doinyo Lengai (2,962m), DaFeng (5,038m), Island Peak (6,189m), Rinjani (3,726m), Kala Patthar (5,545m), Chola (6,168m) and Everest Base Camp (5,364m). I had also done some ice climbing in Siguniang, China, and in Vatnajokull Glacier, Iceland.

I felt ready to set my sights on Everest.

In preparation, I mapped out a string of mountains I would climb over nine months in 2011-2012, culminating in Everest in May 2012:

- Muztagh Ata, China (7,546m)
- Cho Oyu, Tibet/China (8,201m)

- Ama Dablam, Nepal (6,812m)
- Aconcagua, Argentina (6,962m)
- Ojos del Salado, Argentina/Chile (6,893m)
- Nevado San Francisco, Argentina/Chile (6,018m)
- Lobuche, Nepal (4,940m)
- Everest, Nepal/China (8,848m)

Logistically, as well as physically, this was an intimidating challenge.

At that point, I was a house officer in Tan Tock Seng Hospital, and still under the Ministry of Health bond. Taking a gap year just after medical school was unheard of at the time.

It felt like the biggest risk in my young life, plunging into the deep unknown with this crazy passion. The way ahead was murky. But if I did not follow my Everest dream now, I reasoned, chances were that the window would close forever once I embarked on work, medical board exams, possibly marriage and family.

I was going for it.

+ + +

From the start, my Climb Everest 2012 journey was about following a dream into reality.

I wanted to succeed in my quest for Everest but, even if I failed, I wanted to "succeed in life's most important battle — to defeat the fear of trying"[6].

The giants in our small climbing community were my heroes: Robert Goh and Edwin Siew who launched MIR; Khoo Swee Chiow who was the first Southeast Asian and the fourth person in the world to complete The Explorers Grand Slam; Kim Boon, who trained and led Singapore teams on historic climbs.

When I approached them with my Everest dream, they were generous with their time and advice.

Robert Goh lent me his book, *Xixabangma: An Alpine Ascent of the North Ridge*. That was probably the first mountaineering book I read from cover to cover. Robert eventually became a good friend.

Swee Chiow met up with me at Yakun Kaya Toast in Sengkang Mall and gave me a signed copy of his book, *Journeys to the Ends of the*

6   A quote attributed to evangelist and author Robert Harold Schuller.

Earth. I subsequently had the opportunity to climb Aconcagua, Ojos del Salado and Nevado San Francisco in Argentina with him. He, too, is now a good friend.

David Lim and I were never formally introduced, but I had heard so much about him. He was invited by a youth group to give a talk, and posed this question to the audience: "Why do you think someone would lead the Singapore Everest Expedition?" No one had the answer he was looking for. I raised my hand and ventured: "Because you want to." That was apparently the right answer and he gave me a signed copy of his book, *Mountain to Climb*.

+ + +

As I would be climbing Everest on my own, I had to train on my own. My weekly routine included one to two 20km runs; a 20km walk carrying 25kg weights from my workplace at Tan Tock Seng Hospital to MacRitchie, Mandai and Woodlands; and circuit training at Bukit Timah Hill.

At least twice a week, I would heap my haversack with ankle weights, dumbells, barbells and full water bottles to make 20kg in total weight, and lug the bag to work with me. After my night shift at the emergency department, which started at 10pm and ended at 8am, I would change from my scrubs to physical training (PT) attire, and take a train to Clementi where there were 40-storey blocks of HDB flats. Then it was a good two hours of stair training with my backpack before I finally allowed myself to take the train home to Yishun.

But training was just the tip of the iceberg. It was also necessary for me to find sponsors. Climbing the big mountains is hugely expensive. Some of the things one needs to plan for — even before leaving Singapore — are:
- Government climbing permits;
- Park fees and liaison officers;
- Sherpas and porters;
- Technical climbing equipment, including ropes and tents;
- Bottled oxygen above 8,000 metres;
- Food and communications equipment;
- Medical equipment, doctor's charges and helicopter rescue insurance.

Everest alone takes a minimum of 60 days to climb, including acclimatisation.

Writing letters and sending emails to corporations inviting sponsorship consumed all my hours outside of work.

Liaising with potential sponsors took some manouevering. At the time, I was a medical officer in the emergency department and I was naturally not allowed to pick up phone calls during my eight-hour shift. But if I turned off my phone during office hours, I might miss potential sponsors' calls. Surreptitiously I would excuse myself and duck into the restroom to take their calls.

Rejections piled up. It seemed ludicrous that a house officer who was mountaineering in his spare time, and who had not even made it up a 7,000m mountain could summit the world's highest mountain.

Emotionally, I hit rock bottom. It was not physical fatigue nor rejections that cut the most. It was the scoffers who casually told me: "Even females have summited Everest. Don't waste your time." Some were trusted friends. There were mornings I woke up wondering if my one-year no-pay leave would be a total waste.

But, by nature, moutaineers are determined people. They have to be; there are multiple physical, mental, social, logistical, even political, barriers to overcome before they even start climbing. I was not to be deterred.

+ + +

As a house officer, one of my duties was to keep an eye on patients in the wards and execute a host of duties such as ordering X-rays and blood tests, taking blood, doing cultures, updating patients' relatives and planning patients' discharge.

In the morning the house officers do rounds with the consultants, after which we are in the wards. I began to notice that some patients remain in the wards, not because of medical issues, but social issues. Medical issues tend to get sorted out pretty quickly because the nurses, doctors and allied health workers are focused on them. But social issues are not so easily dealt with.

Some patients do not have anyone to care for them at home; others do not have the means to return to the hospital for follow-up appointments. So they remain stuck in limbo. This is where the medical social workers come in.

They are angels who do their best to take care of the social issues weighing patients down.

As I frequently worked with the medical social workers on discharge matters, I got to know them quite well. One of them, Kelly, went on to play a special role in Climb Everest 2012.

A patient, who was psychotic, was found in his home not eating or drinking. A neighbour noticed his plight and called for an ambulance. The patient was brought to the hospital and his psychosis was managed. He had no income, lived alone and was on welfare. When he was brought to the hospital, he was only wearing a pair of pants. He did not even have the means to return home; he was stuck in the ward for a few days. After Kelly spoke with him, she quietly left and returned with a shirt from a pool of clothes organised by the medical social workers. I saw her reach into her own pocket and pass the patient $20.

"Is this for his cab fare?" I asked her.

"Yeah."

"How often do you do this?"

"I do it when I can."

Kelly and her medical social worker colleagues inspired me to climb Everest not just for myself, but for others, too.

My year-long series of climbs acquired a new campaign tagline: *No Mountain Too High*. As I climbed each mountain, I would be raising funds for the Tan Tock Seng Community Charity Fund to help needy patients overcome their own "mountains".

The TTSH Community Charity Fund, set up in 1995, provides assistance to patients from middle income families who, while able to manage day-to-day expenses, have difficulties coping in the event of family illness. These families are not financially comfortable enough to afford medical bills, yet not so needy that they qualify for public assistance. For chronically ill patients, the fund assists with medical services and treatments, drugs, equipment, assistive devices, home care services and caregiver training.

Despite the fact that the Singapore public healthcare system is robust compared to most developed nations, individual efforts mattered. I hoped to contribute my bit through my passion of climbing. My sponsors were invited to be a part of Climb Everest 2012 via two separate avenues: Donating to the TTSH Community Charity Fund; and/or donating to my personal climb.

I must have written to over 100 companies; 70% did not deign to reply, 20% rejected me outright, and 10% said: "Let's meet up."

Fund raising took me on a rollercoaster of emotions. I had expected some rejection; but the scoffers and promise breakers hurt.

There were days I wondered if Climb Everest 2012 would even take off. But, keeping the faith, I continued training, fund raising and working as a medical officer concurrently.

To my gratification, over $40,000 was eventually raised for the TTSH Community Charity Fund through the generosity and belief of family, friends and sponsors. Climbing for charity gave a new layer of significance to my Everest pursuit.

Sir Edmund Hillary and Tenzing Norgay may be the ones in the history books as the first to summit Everest, but they had massive support from both Sherpas and expedition mates, without whom they may never have made it.

It is the same for most Everest climbers today. And certainly for me.

During my fund-raising, for every naysayer there emerged 10 supporters, many in unexpected ways.

The first donation I received was from Dr Remesh Kunnasegaran. I was just four months into my first posting as a house officer in the orthopaedic department of Tan Tock Seng Hospital. He was a medical officer, my direct senior in the team.

At the time we had only known each other for the four months we were on the same team, as Dr Kunnasegaran had studied in Glasgow, while I had studied in Singapore.

When I had mentioned climbing Everest to him months ago, he'd thought I was joking. Upon seeing me in the hospital library, intent upon drafting my sponsorship proposal, he reached into his pocket and, without hesitation, gave me the $100 he had on him.

I have never forgotten how his belief in me made me feel. His donation represented my very first step on Everest.

It was when I was in Year 4 in medical school that I first heard of Associate Professor Tham Kum Ying, a senior consultant and education director at Tan Tock Seng Hospital, and also the associate dean at the National University of Singapore's Yong Loo Lin School of Medicine at the time. She had a reputation as an excellent educator and has won

Associate Professor Tham Kum Ying, a mentor, teacher and friend.

numerous teaching awards. I emailed her to request her supervision for my Year 4 elective in emergency medicine. She agreed.

Her reputation was well deserved. She turned out to be an excellent mentor, not only for emergency medicine, but later on as a sounding board for Climb Everest 2012. Stern but also approachable, she went through my plans with me, helping me clarify my thought processes. After four agonising months of trying to get my gap year approved by the powers that be, it was Assoc Prof Tham who pointed me to the right authorities and vouched that I would not break my bond but would return to work after Everest. Without her, I might never have obtained approval for the gap year. She became one of my mentors and faithful donors and, in later years, a friend.

Having been an active member of the 01 Raffles Group, I was planning to take the Scout flag with me to the summit of Everest and was confident of the support of my fellow alumni. Invited to their monthly gathering of Gryphons, I waited anxiously as everyone had dinner. Finally it was my turn in the spotlight and one of the alumni, Anand Ragavan, introduced me, whereupon I presented my proposal to the Gryphon group of mostly established professionals and businesspeople, including Eddie Tan, Tang Hock Guan, Chey Chor Wai, Sadanand Barma and Viswa Sathasivam.

The 32nd /2101 Raffles Gryphons Alumni fund-raising event for my Everest expedition at Joan Bowen Café.

To my disappointment, their reaction was disheartening.

Shooting rapid-fire questions at me (some of which, to my mortification, I could not answer), they critically appraised my proposal, sponsorship tiers and donor benefits. I went home demoralised.

Some time later, I was emailing Anand when I expressed my disappointment at how the meeting went. He was surprised.

"We're not critical because we don't support you, we're critical because we want to see you succeed," he said.

It turned out that the alumni had intended to support me all along. The vocal accountants and businesspeople in the group who had torn holes in my proposal did so in order that I could revise and strengthen it so as to attract more corporate sponsors. They went on to organise a gathering of over 50 high-level alumni from the 01 Raffles Group, expressly for the purpose of hearing me share my dream. That evening, the alumni pooled together a cheque for Climb Everest 2012.

Anand would go on to be a personal supporter, both in donations and in moral support, taking it upon himself to update the other alumni on my progress every step of the way. He also remotely introduced me to Santokh Singh, the news editor at The New Paper, who went on to publish the first media article on my being the first medical doctor in Singapore to climb for charity. When the story appeared, people immediately started messaging me.

Climb Everest 2012 was becoming real. There was no turning back.

Sadly, I never saw Mr Singh in person until his funeral. He passed on in 2016 from a heart attack. But, in a quirky twist of fate, his son, Ishwarpal Singh Grewal (a former national hockey player), was to become one of the medical students on Project Aasha ("Hope" in Nepalese), an annual community service project in Nepal organised by my wife, Gayathri, opthalmologist Dr Rupesh Agrawal and me.

In early 2011, just months before my gap year was to begin and I was to leave for my first mountain, I still did not have a major corporate sponsor.

One of the sponsorship appeals I made was to the Lee Foundation, which was known for its generosity towards worthy causes. But, as I heard, they had never funded either an individual or sporting endeavour. Unexpectedly, I received a short call from the Foundation telling me that my two cheques were ready: One for the TTSH Charity Fund and one for my climb.

After my shift in the emergency department one day, I made my way to the OCBC building in Raffles Place, where the Foundation is located. It was all very business-like — a plain envelope was waiting at the reception for me. Thanking the receptionist, I took the elevator down, sat at the iconic bird statue in front of the Singapore River, and opened the envelope. Looking at the cheque, I teared in spite of myself. This was my first breakthrough. I finally had enough to climb my first mountain.

In July 2011, one week after my rotation in emergency medicine ended, I set off for the first peak on my Climb Everest 2012 list: Muztagh Ata (7,546m) in Xinjiang, China.

+ + +

The numbing cycle of cold calls continued throughout the year. Each climb was a gift, the next climb a question mark.

In the nadir of this bleak period, a glimmer of light appeared in the form of two sisters by the names of Anna and Yashodhara Dhoraisingam.

Anna was a physiotherapy patient of my sister's who expressed interest in sponsoring my journey. Yasho was the Law Society president at the time and was also involved in the Hindu Centre's Mitra programme befriending incarcerated youth in the Singapore Prison School. "Mitra" means friend in Sanskrit. And she saw in me someone whom the disenfranchised youths could relate.

So, during the year of mid-2011 to mid-2012, in between the climbs that prepared me for Everest, I would regularly visit the prisons as a volunteer to give talks to the Hindu youths. Sometimes the groups would be new to me, sometimes they were repeat groups with whom I'd already had a connection. They were incarcerated for anything from gang fights and drug offences to rape and murder. One of the groups included offenders housed in Institution A1 of the prison complex, facing life imprisonment. I wondered what I could possibly say to make any difference to them.

My first interaction with the boys was at the Kaki Bukit Center (Prison School) sometime in June before I set off for Mustagh Ata in China.

The boys here were mostly first- or second-time offenders incarcerated for drug consumption and trafficking or petty thefts. Most of them were preparing to take their 'O' level exams at the end of the year. They were studying for the exams but I was told they weren't motivated. Many of them came from low-income, broken families struggling to make ends meet. The boys, disillusioned with life, were lured by easy opportunities to make a quick buck through trafficking and theft.

When they first saw me walking in, they didn't give two hoots about what I had to say. I told them a little about myself and my dream to climb Everest. Their response: Boredom. They had heard enough about other people's dreams that had nothing to do with the reality of their own lives. It was only when I starting speaking about my disappointments that they suddenly sat up — people not believing, not trusting, not supporting — this was something they could relate to.

I was asked to give a second talk after climbing Cho Oyu as the boys were eager to hear about my progress. They could identify with me as a young individual setting a goal and working towards it against seemingly impossible odds.

After Cho Oyu, I returned to this first group of about 12 boys in their new complex at Tanah Merah Prison. My first thought was how, after movitvating them before my climb, I was going to face them after two consecutive failed summit attempts in Mustagh Ata and Cho Oyu. To my astonishment, they seemed to draw strength from my tenacity to carry on.

Apparently news had spread throughout Kaki Bukit Prison about my endeavours and the inmates were rooting for me and trying to follow my progress through whatever media was allowed in prison. Eventually I was giving talks to 350 to 400 inmates at Kaki Bukit Prison. Some of the boys from my previous talks had served their sentence and were released. I heard that a few were interested in meeting up with me for a coffee outside.

Prison staff who noticed the response to my talks to the Hindu youths, invited me to return — this time to Changi Prison to address offenders of all ages and races. I was somewhat nervous as I headed towards the tightly secure Changi Prison block where offenders were serving moderate term sentences of 10 to 25 years. This time, the group comprised 32 inmates with ages ranging from 18 all the way to over 50. It felt odd being a young member of the public discussing values with inmates two to three decades older than I.

Yet the listeners were attentive, the session went well and I was requested to return the following week to deliver another talk, this time at the maximum security prison where inmates were serving full life sentences.

Before I left for Everest, the inmates used their limited writing material to write a poem for me and, together with a song, they wished me safe travels and a victorious return. I was moved beyond words — many did not even write to their families. It still is the most meaningful gift I have ever received and takes pride of place in my showcase at home.

+ + +

Like my newfound friends from the prison, the supporters who saw me through to the end of Climb Everest 2012 came from unexpected quarters.

Mr Shanmugam from Gayathri Restaurant in Race Course Road, a member of the Indian Restaurants Association Singapore, galvanised restaurant owners to raise $20,000.

Mr Pandiyan, vice editor of Tamil Murasu newspaper, featured my story, reporting on every step of my journey up to Everest. Another story followed in The Straits Times. The media exposure added momentum to Climb Everest 2012.

There were many individuals, such as old friends and colleagues at the hospital, who reached into their pockets and pushed their donations into my grateful hands. Often, they donated both to the TTSH Charity Fund as well as my climb.

It did not matter if their promise came in the form of cash or moral support — both were invaluable.

Much of my year-long journey on Climb Everest 2012 was made without the company of a single familiar face. Climbing was often very lonely. But knowing that, many kilometres back home, there were colleagues, community leaders, family members, friends from secondary school, the climbing fraternity, and even my former teachers and their students who were faithfully following my climbing blog and rooting for me, warmed me with the knowledge that they were along on the journey, too.

I was not alone.

CHAPTER 6

"The mountain doesn't say you are black, you are white, you are weak, you are strong. It's one rule for everybody. If you give up, you die."

Nirmal Purja

Muztagh Ata (7,546m), Father of Ice Mountain, rises from a broad, squat base that gives the illusion of a gentle slope to the top. Which may account for the fact that the first person who attempted to summit in 1894 tried to do so on the back of a yak.

The unfortunate yak died and explorer and cartographer, Sven Hedin, attempted to continue to the summit on foot. He failed. In fact his expedition team of experienced climbers (including a 1947 expedition with the reknowned Eric Shipton) was denied the summit a further three times because of plunging temperatures, gale force winds and profound snow. It brought home the fact that there is no 7,000er that is *easy*[7]. Up till 2002, under normal conditions, the summit rate was recorded at only 18%.

In terms of technical difficulty, however, Muztagh Ata is said to be relatively straightforward. So, in June 2011, it became the first mountain on my Climb Everest master plan. The plan was to progress

---

7 The massif was finally summited in 1956 by a Soviet-China team.

A traditional nomadic yurt in the shadow of Mustagh Ata.

from the less difficult mountains to more difficult ones, climaxing in Everest in May 2012.

Situated in the Uygur Autonomous Region of Xinjiang, Muztagh Ata looms over the border of Tajikistan, near Pakistan and Afghanistan. On a good day, she can be seen twice — soaring against a brilliant desert sky, and as a stunning reflection on the alpine Karakol Lake at her feet.

From Urumqi, capital of Xinjiang, we flew over the Tien Shan mountains to Kashgar (for 2,000 years the Silk Route's ancient gateway to central Asia, Tibet, China and India). From there it was another 200km, or five hours by jeep, to Karakol Lake (3,600m) near the Muztagh Ata base camp.

The base camp, at 4,450m, spread beneath the hem of Muztagh Ata's moraine terrace. Even in July, when we arrived, temperatures were a frosty -5°C at night.

Round yurts dotted the arid landscape. The porters and guides were from nomadic tribes who move from place to place with the changing seasons. During the climbing season, they set up yurt camps with whole families in tow. It was not unusual to see yak, goats and children of various ages adding to the liveliness of base camp.

The yurts — sturdy, circular tents covered with animal skins or felt — have been used by the nomadic peoples of Central Asia for thousands of years. They were surprisingly warm even in freezing temperatures, as entire families cook, eat and sleep in the yurts, warmed by the ambient heat of stoves.

There was no running water in our camp and every day the guides took a jeep in search of glacial streams to collect water. A communal generator provided a modest flow of electricity.

I was in the company of friends. Two former MIR teammates, Teng Jie and Sulin, were on the journey with me. This climb was our way of marking MIR's 10th anniversary.

Flora was sparse in the dry Takla Makan desert (our diet was devoid of green vegetables for the duration of our climb). But there was still small desert fauna. While my tentmate, Teng Jie, and I were asleep one night at C1, we heard something scrabbling around our sleeping bags. My first thought was: *Cockroach!*

But we were 5,350m above sea level in freezing temperatures. Surely no cockroaches could subsist here? Alarmed, we sat up and waved our torches around wildly. It was a desert mouse! And it was making a buffet of our snacks. We had to throw out our unwelcome guest.

Our local guides for the climb were Tokte and Abdul who, like many Uyghurs, had the weathered faces and ruddy complexion of the Turkic ethnic group.

Tokte had had six children but, tragically, because of the high child mortality rate in this harsh environment, three of them had died. Of his remaining children, one was in boarding school and his two younger children were at Base Camp with him and his wife.

One morning, Tokte hurried to my tent, desperation written across his normally stoic face. His youngest child, a cherubic three-year-old, had scalded herself badly the evening before. The nearest hospital was in the principal town of Tashkurgan, a day's journey away. If he left the expedition to take his daughter to the hospital in Tashkurgan, he would have to forego a year's income for his family, as there was only one climbing season each year.

On the other hand, three of his children had already died from seemingly minor medical incidents, as the level of hygiene and medical care were poor. He would be risking another child's life if he did not seek help. He had decided to wait it out for a night, but his daughter had been writhing with pain throughout.

Tokte and his family, together with Suling, Teng Jie and me, in their tent at the Mustagh Ata Base Camp.

Uyghur kids at the Mustagh Ata Base Camp occupy themselves as their fathers work on the mountains as guides.

Knowing that I was a doctor, Tokte sought my help. I was, frankly, nonplussed. I had only just finished a year as a house officer and had no experience with paediatric patients.

I examined the little girl and found that her forehead and arm were scalded. Her well-meaning parents had applied toothpaste to her wounds and wrapped them with dirty bandages. There was not much I could do medically. I cleaned the toothpaste off, applied some burn cream on the wounds, dressed them with clean gauze, and gave the child an appropriate dose of analgesia.

By afternoon, she was running around the camp with the other children.

Her father came to me at the dinner tent that evening. The solemnity with which he said "thank you" moved me greatly. In my fledgling medical career, I had never heard thanks that was more sincerely offered.

He and his wife later invited me to their small yurt at BC where we sat and drank salted tea with yak butter. As I was about to leave, his wife presented me with a Kurgys hand-knitted hat. The women in the camp spend the season knitting these traditional hats to sell for about US$50 each. But in gratitude, she gave me the hat which she had spent a month-and-a-half knitting.

Even today, with hours of surgery in operating theatres under my belt, that moment in a windswept desert base camp holds a deep poignancy for me, both as a doctor and a person.

+ + +

The very first step I took on the Muzatagh Ata trail was not just exciting, but symbolic.

When I had first decided to climb Everest, I was just out of medical school, in debt, had a five-year bond with the Ministry of Health, and was about to head into the transitional year residency programme in orthopaedic surgery.

To achieve my Everest dream, I basically had to turn around and go in the opposite direction.

Embarking on the journey meant taking one year of no-pay leave, quitting my transitional year residency programme, and applying to the Ministry of Health to defer the fulfilment of my bond. (This meant six tedious months of official justifications because, locally, no one straight out of medical school had ever done this). Upon my return, I would not be guaranteed a position and would have to reapply for residency again. There were many well-meaning, but discouraging, queries of: "Are you sure about this?"

Four years of planning, one year of training, endless appeals to (and multiple rejections from) sponsors between long shifts at the hospital — the path had seemed interminable. But it had finally brought me to the first of the mountains that would, hopefully, lead me to Everest in nine months.

Actually, I didn't even have enough funds to see me up Everest at this point. But I was counting on my sponsors coming through for me after they saw me summiting one mountain after another in my relentless path to Everest. (At least that was the movie playing in my head.)

For me to set foot on the peak of Muztagh Ata (7,546m), I had first to make numerous acclimatisation rotations past C1 (5,350m), C2 (6,200m) and C3 (6,800m). The most technical part was reputedly between C1 and 2, with its landscape pockmarked with crevasses and a precipitous 50° section 80m long. The plan was to reach the summit on Day 18, on 24 July.

But our plans quickly unravelled.

The snow was thick as our team and I struck out for C1, our heads down against the wind. Adrenaline propelled us at a decent clip. We made it to C1 then came back down to BC to spend the night. But my friends, Teng Jie and Sulin, feeling unwell, were forced to go no further.

It was an inauspicious start. The snowfall was so uncompromising that our guides had to admit that summiting was not likely this year.

My heart sank. Backing down was not a decision I could easily make. The hard truth was: If I could not summit Muztagh Ata, my first and supposedly easiest, mountain, my chances of being sponsored for Everest were practically nil. The dream would be over before it had even begun.

No. I would not give up. Determination had gotten me this far and I was going to press on.

But several incidents would shake me badly over the course of the next few days.

The prolonged bombardment of bad weather at higher camps took its toll on us.

The first happened between C1 and C2. Somehow, at 5,850m, with my feet sinking like lava rocks into the snow with every step, I found myself utterly *lost* in the white-out. The Chinese guides had gone ahead with clipped instructions to follow their footprints, but I felt like Hansel and Gretel, unable to find the trail of breadcrumbs. The relentless snow was covering up their footprints faster than I could make them out. I had no information about where C2 was and no way to communicate with anyone. Every time I spotted a "person" in the snow, my heart lurching with hope, it turned out to be a rock.

After hours of plodding blindly upwards, alternately mumbling prayers and berating myself, I stumbled upon C2. My relief at reuniting with the guides was overwhelming. That was the first time I questioned the wisdom of butting heads with Mother Nature, pushing on blindly against better judgement.

All my life I had heard derision for people who were not determined enough to actualise their goals. But was there such a thing as being *too* determined? It was a question I would face again about 1,000m from the summit a few days later.

In mountaineering there are such immense costs — on time, finances, health, relationships, careers — that turning back is never an easy decision.

Our guides Tokte (left) and Abdul on the slopes of Musatgh Ata.

One of the climbers was climbing in memory of his sister who had died of cancer and was raising funds for a foundation in her name. There had been a fair bit of publicity on him in the British press and there was a lot of public expectation on his shoulders.

Because of Muztagh Ata's broad base, the summit can be seen even from Base Camp. As a result, it tantalises climbers into propelling themselves upwards faster than their body can take the drastic atmospheric changes. The British climber had climbed too far too fast, and was stopped in his tracks by potentially fatal AMS. He was bitterly disappointed at not making it to the summit and threatened to file a lawsuit against his guide when he returned to Britain. He had shared the same Base Camp as us; in mountaineering conditions, that made him a friend of sorts. I could empathise with his frustration. But to see him railing at the guide for not reaching the summit was pretty appalling.

There was another incident. Our team had climbed our way to C2 at 6,200m; it was my personal best at the time. But we were stuck in our tents for days in the face of livid wind and snow. Finally, we decided to make a push for the summit. Fighting the elements one gruelling step at a time, we got up to about 6,400m when, to our surprise, we saw a team of Belgian climbers descending from the summit.

The snow-stacked slopes of Mustagh Ata. Red flags planted strategically indicate a crevasse or cliff.

"Did you make it?" we called out. "Yes, yes," was their curt reply as they hurried on without pausing to acknowledge our congratulations. We knew there was no one else on the summit because of the ferocity of the weather. If this team could make it, couldn't we?

But after a heated discussion, our team made the agonising decision to head back down to Base Camp. It was just too dangerous. I was sorely disappointed.

At Base Camp we received an update on the Belgian team. It seemed that, as they headed down from the summit, the weather had blown in fiercely and they had become lost in the swirling snow. Knowing it would be too dangerous to descend terrain criss-crossed with crevasses in a white-out, they dug a hole in the snow, where they'd spent the night. They had suffered horribly. One of the team members, a physiotherapist by profession, eventually had seven frostbitten fingers that likely required amputation. Through a single decision to push for the summit, he had forever lost the ability to practise his profession.

That cautionary tale completely changed my notions of success and failure. Was reaching the summit my measure of success as a climber, or even as a person?

Nine months later, on the flanks of Everest, I was resting in BC after an acclimatisation cycle when there was a terrifying roar of an avalanche above me.

At BC, we heard that the avalanche drove down like a concrete tidal wave into C1, sweeping one of the sherpas into a crevasse, breaking his ribs and spine. One of my teammates, an American plastic surgeon, was at C1 at the time and witnessed the ghastly devastation. Shortly afterwards, he told the rest of the team that he was done with his Everest bid. He had grown up without a father and did not want to risk the same fate happening to his children.

To turn his back on a long-held dream for a greater good took more courage than continuing.

On 22 May, 2020, Joanne Soo, one of the members of the Singapore Women's Everest Team, wrote in a Facebook post in commemoration of the team's 11th "Everesary":

"The summiting of Mt Everest does not define me … What defines me is how I respond to the constant change of weather; how I respond to that long snow slope that sees no end and that big crevasse right before my eyes. What defines me is how I respond to the routine occurrence of sarcasm and condescending language; how I respond to the good and bad human behaviour. What defines me is how I deal with my own failure, how I deal with the journey that leads to an outcome.

"I am not saying to summit a mountain is not important. Climbing big mountains like Mt Everest requires so much grit in a person, while the summit is the end goal, we must remember the process. We must remind ourselves that it takes more than just luck to stand on the summit."

To reach the summit of a mountain is only to reach the halfway mark – there is still the return journey. In the same way, after the climb, there is still life and love, wisdom to acquire and share, years to grow old in.

On the mountain, it is the sense of the people in your life that steadies you amidst the surges of adrenaline.

After Muztagh Ata, even as I pushed myself towards each summit, I remembered the people who were waiting for me after I got down.

+ + +

During my first few climbs, it was the little things that wore me down — I didn't know how to go to the toilet without soiling my down suit, which pocket to put my hand sanitiser and where to stuff the toilet paper. If I forgot to keep a carabinar or jumar handy, I had to face the frustration of rummaging through my back pack with clumsy gloved fingers.

You quickly learn how to pack your bag optimally — the stuff you won't require till you arrive at camp, like your sleeping bag and down jacket, goes right at the bottom; everything that needs to be used on the climb, like headlamps, food and water, climbing equipment, you keep accessible in the top pouch.

Even the simplest things need planning and consideration. Take peeing, for instance. Picture this: It's the middle of the night. There's a storm outside your tent, the snow is piling up, and you are in your sleeping bag in just your thermal liner, without shoes. At that precise moment, you feel the urge to pee. This can happen three or four times a night if you're acclimatising. You're not about to crawl out of your sleeping bag, tug on layer after layer of clothing and head out into the deep freeze for one minute of peeing.

For this reason, one of our most precious possessions on any expedition is not a memento from our significant other or our family's photo. It is our pee bottle.

A side benefit is that it becomes your hot water bottle after you pee. (Incidentally female climbers use pee bottles too, except theirs includes a funnel.) The key, in the dark, is to remember which bottle contains your pee and which your drinking water. (Eventually you also learn the useful trick of how not to let your pee overflow — it's all in the pitch.)

Pee bottle vs drinking bottle. Both bottles are essential to any mountaineer.

The first time I used the pee bottle, I left it outside my sleeping bag as it seemed unhygienic to be sleeping with pee. In the morning when I woke up, the pee was frozen solid. I couldn't empty it at the toilet tank, and I couldn't abandon my pee bottle because I would need it for the rest of the climb. There was nothing for it but to haul 1 litre of piss up the mountain.

And if you need to take a dump, good luck to you. It is an exercise in strategy and timing. There is hardly time during a climb, so you have to do this at camp. First you have to wait for a sunny day. Then it takes about an hour for the sun to warm your tent enough that you feel able to bare your bum. (Trust me, if the sun disappears behind a cloud, wet wipes turn into panes of ice.) In extremely narrow perches, such as Cho Oyu's C1 or Ama Dablam's C2, you would need to take a rope, secure it to rock, hang your bum over the side of a cliff, check that there's no one unfortunate enough to be below, and do the deed.

Needless to say, grooming on the mountain is not a priority. Dry shampoo occasionally makes an appearance. But by and large the men begin to resemble Hagrid after awhile. Grooming is such a luxury that in my logbook for Mt Cho Oyu, among plans for climbs and technical training, I have an entry for: *Shaving Day.*

As for clothing, you live in the suit you're climbing in, with laundry day taking place once a week. At Base Camp, you have a personal tent for sleeping, but on the mountain, we share tents, sometimes with three or four in one tent, because it is inefficient for the Sherpas to carry excessive loads up the slopes. Fortunately, in the extreme cold, no one smells. Rather, it's your tent mates' snoring that will get you.

Truly, in the wild, both men and women revert to the most elemental versions of themselves.

Meals on an expedition come freeze dried and dehydrated to reduce the carrying load.

+ + +

Remember the earthquake at the beginning of this book? Here's what happened next.

In September 2011, barely eight days in Singapore after Muztagh Ata, I packed up my 45 to 50kg of climbing gear and headed out again. (The excessive load almost always got me into trouble checking in at the airport, so I would end up wearing some of the equipment, most often the ropes, on my body.) This time I was headed for the second peak on my list: Mt Cho Oyu (8,201m).

In many ways this felt like the start of my Climb Everest 2012 bid. Cho Oyu, on the China-Nepal border, was to be my first, *and only*, 8,000m mountain before hitting Everest. It was also the first time I would be using oxygen equipment. While it is the sixth highest mountain on earth, Cho Oyu is said to be the most achievable of the world's fourteen 8,000m peaks, thanks to relatively uncomplicated terrain. It is even dubbed the "mock exam" for Everest.

The expedition began promisingly, with an amiable group of climbers on the IMG team. There were 11 of us — six Americans, two Austrians, an Australian, a German and myself, with two American guides, base camp manager Ang Jangbu and sirdar Ang Pasang.

Max and Craig, the two American guides, were professional and good company. Max and I connected on a fundamental level. He had given up a career in physics for the freedom of the hills. He lived in his car in Boulder, Colorado, and did most of his climbing in the area. Money was not a priority to him at that point, climbing was. We had some cool conversations together — he had a scientific explanation for everything.

Craig and his wife had adopted a child from China whom he doted on. He was brilliant on the guitar and had a good voice, providing us with welcome entertainment in camp. He was an old-school climber who had given his best years to the mountains and repeatedly remarked that Cho Oyu would be his last climb.

At 26, I was the youngest team member on the expedition, and when Craig heard that I had set my sights on Everest even though funding was an issue, he gifted me with his ice axe, saying he wouldn't need it any more and that he hoped it would help me on Everest. Eight months later, I did indeed climb Everest using Craig's ice axe.

Even at ABC the 5,500m altitude was getting to me. The simplest of tasks — going to the toilet, getting to the mess tent for dinner — winded me. But I was otherwise healthy. Five days at ABC were spent on acclimatisation hikes to Lake Camp (6,065m), getting in some

Yaks carrying all our rations and base camp equipment for our two-month expedition on Cho Oyu.

No refrigeration needed — meat used throughout the expedition is hung outside the kitchen tent.

The puja ceremony on Cho Oyu ABC, a Sherpa custom where prayers are offered for safe passage.

Tsampa flour is smeared on the faces of the climbers during the puja ceremony to invite good luck.

A view of Cho Oyu from ABC.

skills training, packing for the climb and getting acquainted with the gamow bag[8].

On Day 6, we struck out for C1.

The route to C1 required negotiation through glacial moraine on a roughly 30° slope. It had snowed every evening since we'd arrived in BC and the there was a steep 200m section of thigh-deep snow just before the camp. The more than 20kg of equipment I was lugging — boots, crampons, harness, ice axe, down suit, sleeping bag and food — was causing me to sink into the snow no matter how gently I tried to tread.

This first rotation to C1 left me exhausted, with my movements becoming increasingly sluggish and the thin air making breathing laborious. It was a relief to spot the camp after 7½ hours.

Relieving ourselves on C1 sometimes meant hanging by a thread off the side of a cliff.

Our yellow tents were spread across a seam of snow at the edge of a cliff. Across was the sheer wall ice that was Nangpai Gosum peak. Visibility was poor and the view hidden, as snow fell unabated.

Last year no one had made it to the peak because of heavy snowfall and avalanche danger. Would we summit this year? Our current weather

---

8 The gamow bag is a portable, pressurised hyperbaric bag that simulates a descent in altitude. It is useful in treating acute mountain sickness.

report predicted a low-pressure zone entering the area. We would have to spend a few days in ABC waiting for a window of good weather.

Sleeping at 6,400m in C1 was my new record. When I woke up, it was my 27th birthday.

Our team trudged back down to ABC, where a special surprise awaited me: The cook had whipped up a delectable chocolate cake complete with "Happy birthday, Kumaran" emblazoned in icing across the top and a bunch of candles he had rustled up from goodness knows where.

As the climbers, guides and porters belted out "Happy birthday" in various accents and with varying degrees of tunefulness, I looked round at their smiling faces and knew this was a birthday I would never forget. To make sure of that, they also presented me with a rock in the shape of Cho Oyu, autographed with each climber's name.

Incidentally, it was also the custom for the camp cooks to produce a celebratory cake at the end of every expedition. After a month or two on the mountain subsisting on rehydrated freeze-dried rations at the higher camps (eating is reduced to mere functionality, as hypoxic climbers lose their appetite), it was oddly satisfying to taste something as decadent as cake.

+ + +

Celebrating my 27th birthday with a chocolate cake baked by Kaji (right), our chief cook.

The entire IMG Cho Oyu Autumn 2011 expedition team.

On 18 September, just 11 days after I turned 27, our team was on our third rotation to C1 when death opened its jaws to swallow me up.

At 6:29pm, Kancha, my young Sherpa guide, and I were settling down for the evening in our tent. It was -15°C and my extremities were freezing. When our tent started to jiggle, Kancha and I initially thought it was a kind soul outside shaking the snow off our tent.

But the shaking was disturbingly peristent. Then, without warning, the earth buckled, tossing us together. Outside our tent, shouts of *EARTHQUAKE! EARTHQUAKE!*

It was already too dark to see, but Kancha and I could sense each other's terror. In panic, we realised that the trembling earth was moving our tent, little by little, towards the cliff edge. Even if we managed to crawl out of our shaking tent, we were stripped down to our thin thermals, without shoes, and would have frozen to death.

"This is it," I thought, my blood turning to ice in my veins. As a mountaineer, you are keenly aware of the life-and-death nature of the game. But I had always imagined that if I did die on the mountain, it would be in an avalanche or a fall. An earthquake did not cross my mind.

Vaguely, I was aware of Kancha muttering a Buddhist prayer. My mind flew to my loved ones thousands of kilometres away.

And then — as instantly as it started — the shaking stopped. Our tent was barely a table length away from the edge. Another 15 seconds and we would have plunged off our 6,400m perch. Scrabbling around for my headlamp, I switched it on, catching sight of Kancha's pale face and bulging eyes. He, too, had never experienced an earthquake at this elevation.

Almost as soon as the shaking stopped, the walkie talkies started howling to life, people checking on each other in panicked shouts. To our relief, we had all survived. Even the climbers further up the mountain were safe. The whole ordeal had lasted maybe 20 seconds but felt like a lifetime.

We braced ourselves for what would come next: Avalanches. It was now pitch dark and we would easily have fallen to our deaths if we tried to make our way down the mountain, especially with the chance of after-shocks and avalanches. There was no choice but to stay huddled in our tent until morning.

All through the long night, we could hear the rolling rumble of avalanches and the crack of massive slabs of ice and snow calving off the mountain. There must have been nine or 10 avalanches; any one of them could have buried us alive. If the slope just infront of us were to give way, we would be swept off the mountain.

When dawn broke, the main slopes were intact. But the avalanches had caused snow and ice to shift and slide in great drifts along many parts of the trail.

The epicentre of the earthquake, which had registered 6.9 on the Richter scale, was at the Sikkim-Nepal border, 300km east of Kathmandu. We heard that at least 111 were killed, including three people in the British embassy in Kathmandu. Its rumblings had also been felt in Bangladesh, Bhutan and across Tibet.

Up on Cho Oyu, after the avalanches, the terrain was stable enough for us to keep climbing. And the group decided to carry on to C2.

Not only was this mentally challenging (we had hardly slept), it turned out to be physically brutal. My inexperience was debilitating. Two ice cliffs and endless knolls took everything out of me. After 7½ hours of torture, I staggered into C2 (7,130m). I had passed the 7,000m barrier without supplemental oxygen, but there was nothing left in me to celebrate.

It took the entire afternoon and evening for me to recuperate. Night saw me tossing and turning in my sleeping bag — it was difficult to rest at 7,000m, where the oxygen content is less than half of what we're used to at sea level. It was a relief when daylight dawned and we could make our way down to ABC again.

+ + +

So my first two weeks as a 27-year-old were anything but boring.

Six days after the earthquake, on 24 September, we mentally prepared ourselves for the first summit push. But the odds weren't good.

The Germans, who had left a day ahead of the main team, sent word that they were stuck in C1 due to a gale. The winds were so fierce that they were simply glad to have survived — all through the long night they had been afraid that their tents would be blown off the ridge.

Only one climber had attempted to ascend above C1 on the 24th. News eventually filtered to us that he had been caught in an avalanche between C2 and C3, losing his ice axe and ski poles in the process. Somehow he had managed to survive and return to ABC.

As we fought our way to C1, we were buffeted by the 100mph winds that the Germans had warned us about. We literally had to duck-walk our way to our tents. As we nervously waited out the night in our tents, the gale was joined by thick snow. Avalanche danger was growing as loose snow swept down the slopes.

This was already our fourth rotation to C1, and I found myself sharing a tent with my IMG teammate Dan, an American-Lebanese urologist. When you are stuck in a shuddering tent on an exposed ridge 6,400m high, trying not to think about all the ways you could die, you tend to bond quickly.

To break the tension, I let Dan in on my plans to propose to my girlfriend, Gayathri, after Everest. "If we make it down this mountain alive," I told him, "you're invited to the wedding!"

Two years later, in 2013, Gayathri and I got married in sunny Singapore, 3,500km from the ice of Cho Oyu. And Dan flew all the way from the United States to attend our wedding.

But that night on Cho Oyu, with our tent straining under the weight of the snow, the wind howling outside and the skies gathering yet more snow, Dan and I were not confident that this expedition would end well. The ill feeling grew the next day, as the weather worsened. Our team of 11 abandoned any attempt at a summit push and slowly made our way back to ABC.

All the commercial groups on the mountain had turned back that day. Some even called it quits and decided to head home after their battle with the elements.

We received news that a climber had died while ascending the first ice cliff on 24 September. His body was left dangling on the ropes, as the storm prevented safe access to him. Climbers who had descended from C2 to C1 could see the body swinging in the gale.

Two days later, the wind and snow had still not abated. The 26th saw a huge snowfall and there was word of another death — a climber from another team suffocated when his tent in C1 collapsed on him under the weight of the snow.

At C2, a few climbers were stuck, unable to descend in the deep snow drifts. I said a quick prayer that they would get a window of opportunity to descend safely. Our guides had exercised extraordinarily good judgement in taking us down to ABC instead of waiting in C1 for a possible window to push for the summit. If they hadn't, we could have been in the same position.

So far only a handful of Koreans had summited. Instead of waiting for the Chinese rope fixers, as was required on Cho Oyu, they had gone ahead to fix their own lines and headed up a week before the rest of us. From the way the weather was going, it looked like they would be the only ones to reach the peak this year.

To add to the dismal news, we heard that a private plane had crashed near Kathmandu on the 25th as a result of the brutal weather. Nineteen international tourists had died on what was simply to have been a scenic flight over the Himalayas.

The odds against summiting this year were mounting. Even if the skies cleared, the snow would be too deep for us to reach the peak, and the avalanche risk too high. Every day we saw more teams pulling out, leaving with yaks loaded with their luggage. Finally the members of our team had a tense discussion and nine out of 11 of us decided to head home.

My morale was at rock bottom. After 1½ months on this expedition, I had only reached C2. This was the second consecutive mountain that I did not summit — first Muztagh Ata, now Cho Oyu. My mind was made up. I would wait out the weather in the hopes of another summit, even though it appeared to be a lost cause. I owed it to my sponsors. And also to myself.

On our 27th day at ABC, I woke up at about 6:35am to ditchwater grey skies. The snow outside was 70cm high and had spilled into the vestibule (the "porch" just outside the inner compartment of the tent) No wonder it was freezing last night. Even my ski poles and crampons were buried six feet under.

Bidding goodbye to the nine departing climbers was one of the most wretched moments of my life. Not only was it wrenching to part from these people who had become friends over the past 1½ months, the sight of them loading up their belongings on the yaks and donkeys, in anticipation of a hot shower, a good meal and the welcome of their loved ones, filled me with self-doubt: *Am I making the wrong decision?*

In ABC, there remained only Max, myself and a Chinese American team member, Patrick, who was in his 60s and who considered this his last chance at summiting an 8,000m mountain. A skeletal crew of Sherpas stayed for support.

Ironically, the day the nine climbers left, the skies cleared and the snow abruptly stopped. For the first time in a month at ABC, we saw the sunset. In Singapore, I had taken for granted every warm, sherbet-coloured sunset. Here, seeing my first sunset after weeks of overcast skies was uplifting.

But if I thought this change in weather was ushering in a change in fortune, I was wrong.

The weather forecast wasn't promising. According to the American weather model used by IMG, jet stream winds were going to hit the mountain on 1 October and linger for a week. The trouble was that the Swiss and international weather models indicated 3 October. The discrepancies had Max frantically making calls back to the United States to try and pin down the correct forecast. An imprecise forecast may be an inconvenience at sea level. But on an 8,000m peak, it would be deadly.

On the morning of the 29th, I was woken up by Max, urging me to pack my bags. All three weather models had miraculously aligned overnight. We were going to make a summit push.

+ + +

The plan was to head out that very day and push for the summit on 2 October, just before the jet streams hit the mountain.

There had been two full days of sunshine at that point. But the ground was still blanketed with heavy snow from the storm on the 26th. This made trekking, even to the Lake Camp, onerous. The scree slope that connected the Lake Camp with C1 was now a slurry of mud and dirt-coloured snow, the combination of which proved easier to negotiate.

But it was when we arrived at C2 that the plan disintegrated.

All the expedition teams were under the impression that the Koreans had summited with fixed ropes[9] all the way to the summit.

9 A fixed rope, customarily used in Himalayan expeditions, is a rope anchored into the terrain so that climbers can advance along it, saving time.

Navigating the first crux of the Cho Oyo climb, the vertical ice cliff that stood between C1 and C2.

The magnificent view of the Tibetan plateau and Gyarag glacier from C1 to C2.

Our teams were expecting to use their ropes in our summit push. But a shock awaited us all.

The experienced Korean team (who at that point had completed 13 out of 14 of the 8,000m peaks in the world) had only laid a thin rope along the segment known as the Yellow Band. This was sufficient for them, skilled as they were. But less experienced climbers from the other commercial expeditions needed fixed lines to reach the summit safely.

The fixed lines were to have been laid out by the Chinese team, to whom we had each paid US$200 to fix the ropes by 1 October. But the Chinese, we discovered, were waiting out the bad weather in Tingri, a Tibetan village at 4,348m. In short, they had reneged on the deal.

The expedition teams were furious.

There at 7,130m, a harried discussion between the team leaders took place to decide which team would employ their Sherpas to lay the fixed lines above C3. The team from Alpine Ascents agreed to leave C2 on the night of the 30th and push all the way to the summit, with their Sherpas laying the fixed lines as their clients moved upwards.

IMG's plan was for its two remaining clients — Patrick and myself — to spend a night at C2, move up to C3 on the 1st, and go for the summit on the 2nd.

But when we woke up on the morning of the 1st, we knew something had gone wrong. The Alpine Ascents team had already returned to C2. They had not reached the summit. The deep freeze had made it dangerous for the Sherpas to lay the fixed lines and they were unwilling to risk life and limb doing so.

Max radioed back to ABC for a tense conversation with Ang Jangbu to decide if the IMG Sherpas should lay the fixed lines. But Jangbu, understandably, did not want to risk his Sherpas' lives either.

There was no choice for it. Max had to pull the plug on IMG's Cho Oyu 2011 autumn expedition.

I was disappointed. But Patrick was devastated. His last chance at a lifelong dream was gone. He broke down weeping.

To our chagrin, we later heard that the Chinese team returned from Tingri a few days later, and with their Sherpas fixing the lines, the entire Chinese team summited on 5 October. This was the first time I was exposed to the politics of climbing.

Sunset from C2 of Cho Oyu.

One other IMG team summited that year. All but two members of the IMG Shishapangma team, who waited out the weather, peaked on 4 October, while another two climbers led by IMG guide, Mike, summited on 12 October after the jet stream had passed. (One of them, Vanessa, would come to be my K2 teammate.)

I was happy for the IMG team with their double success. But the fact that this was the second mountain I didn't summit stung.

As I had just one year to fulfil my Climb Everest 2012 bid, it was necessary to line up my pre-Everest climbs almost back to back. In two weeks I had plans to leave for Ama Dablam. Time was my limiting factor.

If I didn't reach the peak of Ama Dablam — a technically challenging mountain — I would have chalked up the dubious record of having made it only as far as C2 on three different mountains.

So I left Cho Oyu with mixed emotions. On the one hand, the pressure was mounting to prove my mettle to the stakeholders of Climb Everest 2012.

On the other hand, it was exhilarating to have hit my personal record of 7,100m without oxygen, not to mention survived an earthquake at 6,400m.

Weeks later on my expedition to Ama Dablam, I bumped into Kancha, the Sherpa who had survived the Cho Oyu earthquake with me. I had developed photos from Cho Oyu and passed him the photos of our fateful climb. He was grateful for the unexpected gift.

In 2016, my wife, Gayathri, and I crossed paths with Kancha once again. We were on a trekking trip with my orthopaedic department to Everest Base Camp, after which Gayathri and I broke off to head to Island Peak (6,189m). Kancha was guiding a group of trekkers and we bumped into him in the Khumbu hamlet of Chuukung, the last village before the Island Peak BC.

It was a joyful reunion. He was still the same youthful-faced Kancha I remembered, but he had acquired a patina of gravity that came with maturity. He told me he had given up climbing the higher mountains because of the dangers involved. He was delighted to meet Gayathri, the girlfriend I had spoken about on Cho Oyu who was now my wife.

The mates I have climbed with occupy a special place in my memories. Each one of them changed me forever.

CHAPTER 7

"When I have reached a summit, I leave it with great reluctance, unless it is to reach for another higher one."
Gustav Mahler

If there were a beauty contest for mountains, Ama Dablam would be a strong contender for Miss Universe.

Her pleasing symmetry and snowcapped summit make her one of the most comely peaks in the Himalayas. Two long ridges curving from her sides, like arms sheltering a child, put the *Ama* (mother) in her name, while the *dablam* (necklace) refers to a hanging glacier that resembles the double-pendant necklace containing pictures of gods commonly worn by Sherpa women.

Ama Dablam's allure also arises from her audacious challenge.

While this "Matterhorn of the Himalayas" is generally agreed to have one of the most aesthetic climbing routes in the world, the spectacularly exposed ridgelines, colossal towers and vast ice fields make the climb technically demanding — more so than many 8,000m climbs, including Everest. (Edmund Hillary, in fact, had famously declared Ama Dablam "unclimbable".)

Respected mountaineering chronicler Alan Arnette estimates the rock climbing difficulty at 5.7 and ice WF4[10], making ropes, ice axe, crampons, ice screws, cams and jumars as familiar on this climb as our right arm.

I had fallen under Ama Dablam's spell the moment I set eyes on her on my first Everest Base Camp trek with MIR in 2009. For the first four days of the trek, from the village of Lukla (2,850m) to Namche Bazaar (the "capital" of the Sherpas), Everest is mysteriously hidden from view. It is only when you round the bend after Namche Bazaar that you catch your first sight of Everest, the trademark ribbon of cloud streaming from its summit. But then your eye is drawn slightly to the right of Everest to the stunning Ama Dablam (6,856m). I knew I would climb it one day.

My companions on this expedition were Joanne Soo from the Singapore Women's Everest Team (SWET), and ultra marathon runners Joyce and Clarence. The four of us were the first Singaporeans attempting to summit Ama Dablam.

When Joanne Soo summited Everest as a member of Singapore's first all-female expedition team on 22 May 2009, she had been the oldest woman to do so at the age of 39.

I was a big fan of SWET. As their 2009 expedition team was toiling up the slopes of Everest, I was following their every move from Sweden where I was doing my surgical exchange in Karolinska Institutet. In between surgeries of colons and gall bladders, I was going online every day, poring over their website for updates and rooting for the six women from 6,000km away.

It was exhilarating being on the same Ama Dablam expedition as Joanne, who was leading our team. A strong and rational climber, Joanne was well respected in Singapore's climbing community. Today, we still we meet annually for Chinese New Year dinner together with Swee Chiow at the house of our mutual friend, Angie.

Joyce proved to be a quiet companion and a determined climber. Clarence was an adventure racer. On one of our evenings at camp, Clarence had described his wedding, when he and his equally athletic wife decided to make an entrance into the wedding hall on a bicycle. That tickled my imagination and I was inspired to make a unique entrance at my own wedding with Gayathri two years later.

---

10 In climbing disciplines such as rock and ice climbing and mountaineering, climbers may give a grade to describe the technical difficulty and danger of the terrain. This is by nature subjective or by consensus.

Our plan for Ama Dablam was to manouevre our way up the southwest ridge to the summit via the Dablam serac. As was typical in the Himalayas, fixed ropes would be used for taxing stretches en route, including sections of ice ranging from 45° to 70°, steep rock, and a difficult stretch on summit day.

This popular route typically takes climbers through Camps 1, 2 and 3, with C3 tucked under and to the right of the Dablam serac. The logic of placing C3 so precariously was mainly based on the fact that ice calved from the massive serac typically fell to the left and away from the camp.

Tragically, this was not the case in November 2006, when a part of the Dablam serac collapsed into C3, killing three Sherpas and three clients. British expedition guide Tim Mosedale was in Ama Dablam's Base Camp when he was woken at 4:15am by the roar of an avalanche. He recounted in his website:

"I glanced out of my tent to see a huge plume of snow and spindrift floating at the bottom of the mountain. It was obvious that this had been a huge fall."

But C3 was not directly visible from BC, and it was only when Mosedale and his team returned to Kyanjuma, just above Namche Bazaar, that the sun rose and "it was possible to see, even by the naked eye, that a huge area of Camp 3 had basically disappeared … No one stood a chance of surviving what was a huge serac fall and avalanche. The whole of Camp 3 was affected and, indeed, part of Camp 3 fell off the mountain."

Two years later, the Dablam collapsed further, after which some teams chose to bypass C3 altogether, opting for one long and gruelling day from C2 to the summit.

+ + +

Any expedition in the Khumbu mountains, including to Ama Dablam, began with a stomach-churning flight in a tiny propeller aircraft battling winds, and sometimes rain and cloud, to land in what is notoriously dubbed "the world's most dangerous airport".

The Tenzing-Hillary airport runway, at a heart-stopping 527m (many international airport runways are more than 3,000m long), was so short that it was necessarily constructed at an almost 12° incline to slow planes down before the runway abruptly met the side of the mountain. Departing planes had one chance to take off from this 2,860m perch. Once the asphalt ran out, it's a free fall to the valley floor below.

Add to this the fact that several airlines that flew in and out of Tenzing-Hillary airport in Lukla had such appalling safety records that they were blacklisted by the European Commission, and you had the reason mountaineers joke that the most dangerous part of an expedition in the Himalayas was not the climb but the flight landing.

Once in Lukla, the realisation that you had been dropped in the middle of an ocean of mighty Himalayan massifs, their peaks rising and falling like primordial swells of ice and rock, was both humbling and exhilarating.

From Lukla, the 32km hiking trail to Ama Dablam BC weaved its way upwards past Himalayan hamlets where many Sherpas made their home. In the peak climbing months of April to May and September to October, the trails teemed with trekkers and climbers from all over the world.

The teahouses, buzzing with activity, were where everyone spent the night along the trail.

These were often extensions to the homes of the Sherpas living in the Khumbu valley. The private quarters of the Sherpa family would sit to one side of the teahouse, with the public lodging on the other side typically featuring dormitory-style rooms, toilets and a dining room for trekkers. Nowadays it is more common to see teahouses expressly built as lodgings, with the local families living offsite.

For the Khumbu trekker, teahouses were a haven of rest along the trail, where many a vivid conversation with teammates and other trekkers took place, and where we recharged for the night before facing another day of strenuous hiking.

The wood-clad dining room was often warmed by a central stove fuelled by the dung of the family yak or zopkio (a yak-cow hybrid). Every dining room told a story, with walls adorned with family photos, trophies, academic certificates, graduation photos and plenty of climbing pictures of the Sherpas in the family on Everest and other peaks. Trekkers, too, left items of memorabilia in the teahouses, ranging from the flags of their country, to posters of their expeditions signed by the entire team, to graffiti on the walls.

Bedrooms were typically on the floor above, with basic rooms sleeping two. As only the dining room was heated, it was common to sleep in one's sleeping bag on top of the foam mattresses, for both hygiene reasons as well as warmth. Toilets were mostly communal affairs shared by anything from four to 15 rooms. In 2011, hot showers were rarely available and any shower you were brave (or foolhardy) enough to take was with ice-cold water. As a result, most of the time, trekkers' ablutions consisted simply of copious amounts of wet wipes and dry shampoo. Nowadays there are plenty more facilities available — at an extra charge, of course.

+ + +

The Sherpa capital of Namche Bazaar used to be the bare bones of a village. Now it is almost a small town, with postal services, schools, massage parlours, pool halls, bakeries and a police station. As you proceed higher up, the facilities become less "luxurious" by the kilometre.

The porter assigned to me for the hike from Lukla to the Ama Dablam BC was a young fellow who did not speak English. I was alone with him, hurrying to meet the rest of my team. I had had very little time with my family between Cho Oyu and Ama Dablam, and Joanne had encouraged me to spend Deepavali in Singapore with my family before joining the rest on Ama Dablam.

The hike up the stony trail was thirsty work and when the water in my bottle ran out, I asked him with gestures if I could fill my bottle at a free flowing pipe where I saw many of the locals topping up their water containers and washing their clothes.

He gestured what I took to be "no problem", and drank some of the water himself. Filling up my bottle, I chugged the water as we went on our way.

That turned out to be one of the worst mistakes of my life.

I became violently ill with diarrhoea, vomiting and fever for the next two weeks. Even after the fever subsided, the diarrhoea and bloatedness didn't. None of the antibiotics and other medications I carried with me worked.

By the time we arrived at Ama Dablam BC, I was weakened and exhausted. While it was a happy occasion to finally join up with my teammates, weighing on my mind was the real possibility that, with my illness, this could be the third consecutive mountain that I would fail to summit.

There was nothing for it but to push on in a feverish haze.

Base Camp (4,450m) was set up in a spreading meadow watered by a running stream at the terminal moraine of a glacier pouring down from Ama Dablam. Our daily view was of the mountain's west face — 2,500m of rock, snow and ice.

It was late October when we set off from BC for our first rotation. While I had heard that Ama Dablam was a technical climb, I did not imagine it to be this damn difficult. It tested every skill in a mountaineer's inventory. One of our Sherpas, who was on Ama Dablam for the first time, had summited Everest seven times, both from the north and south sides. He readily agreed with our team leader, Joanne, that the level of technical difficulty here beat that of Everest. At that point, I didn't know how hard Everest was. But this sure was one heck of a climb.

Base Camp to the little-used ABC (also known as Yak Camp) and further on to C1 (5,800m), took a 7½-hour trek over an astoundingly long ridge, with the last hour spent scrambling up a boulder field, our senses alert for shifting rocks and slipping slabs. The boulders were just below C1 and marked the start of the fixed ropes. The elevation from BC to C1 was just over 1,000m.

C1 was perched precariously on a ridge so steep and narrow that, for the first time, I saw tents partially floating in mid air — there just wasn't enough flat ground to anchor them completely. Sleep was almost impossible on a bed of uneven rocks locked into the

The Singaporean Autumn 2011 Ama Dablam expedition team. From left to right: Clarence, Joyce, Joanne and me.

Tents perched precariously with random rocks as base fillers in C1 of Ama Dablam.

ice and snow. More than once in the night I found myself sliding towards the end of the tent that precipitated the cliff drop, and had to scramble backwards.

After two weeks of acclimatisation rotations between C1 and BC, we struck out for C2 (6,000m). The primary technical course was between C1 and C3, with sheer slopes up to the summit.

The spectacularly exposed route from C1 to C2 was like nothing I had ever experienced. Knife-edge ridges and tiny, precarious ledges called for mixed climbing techniques of jummaring and traversing along fixed ropes of all types, calibers and ages. Our lives often depended on these ropes, on which we put our whole weight. There were numerous occasions when we came to the end of the rope only to realise with shock how badly frayed some were. Those were the times I thanked the gods for keeping the ropes from snapping.

The infamous Yellow Tower, a vertical segment of unyielding rock over 10m tall, stood between us and C2. At the oxygen-weak altitude of nearly 6,200m, this was *the* technical crux of the route, requiring every bit of physical and mental energy to overcome. It was notorious for turning back many a climber. To scale this behemoth, we needed to weave left across the ridge from C1, and ascend the vertical 15m rock face. The advice from many a seasoned climber was to take the Yellow Tower in one pitch. And to *not look down*.

If the Yellow Tower didn't scare you, C2 would. This camp was a tiny aerie atop a stupendous column of rock, with a footprint barely big enough to tuck in five tents. So incredible a sight it was, that you couldn't help but wonder which joker with a death wish first thought of pitching camp up *there*.

Years ago, it was this jaw dropping picture of C2 — a handful of yellow tents barely able to keep their narrow perch 6,200m above sea level — that lodged in me a burning dream to climb Ama Dablam.

The reality of C2, however, was far different from the dream. Camp 2's nickname was Camp Poo, because you could smell it before you could see it. At precarious points, there was so little space on the rocky perch that, if nature called, we were unable to take even two steps from our tent without plunging off the precipice. To do a number 2, we had to put on a harness, rope up to a fixed line, all the while staying in the tent with just our butt exposed to the elements. Some have been known to clip onto fixed lines while sleeping in their tents for fear of rolling right off the precipice. The result was that the whole place was literally a pile of shit and piss and litter. The smell alone could curl your arm hair.

As we were making our way down the next day, we came across two European men. To our horror, one of them took off his harness to pee, slipped, and disappeared over the edge. His friend was sure he had fallen to his death and started weeping. But the first man returned and they both started crying from relief. Imagine falling to your death just because you took a pee.

C2 of Ama Dablam with tents delicately perched on the top of the rock tower.

The complex tangle of ropes around a single anchor point from previous expeditions.

Straight after C2, the crampons came out. From the first traverse, the view of the eagle's nest that is C2 was stunning. This spot was often where iconic photos of C2 were taken. But there was no time (or space) to rest as the Grey Tower — 60 to 70 metres of 70° degree incline — loomed.

Here we had to front point and jumar all the way up for approximately four hours. Seeing sparks fly off my crampons whenever I missed the ice and hit solid rock was new to me. This was rock climbing on all fours, and the exercise of finding natural nooks and crannies on the rock wall to nimbly place the front spikes of my crampons was enjoyable, but thoroughly taxing. In fact from C1 to C3, there wasn't any flat ground on which to rest. If you needed to take off your backpack to give your back a stretch, you had to clip it on to the fixed lines, leaving it hanging while you caught your breath.

There was a constant traffic jam between ascending and descending climbers on the single fixed line. At best this was annoying, at worst, life threatening. Makeshift lines had to be laid, ropes had to be colour coded and communication among teammates was critical.

The exposure between C2 and C3 was extraordinary. Just when your burning muscles and mental focus couldn't take any more of the Grey Tower, the Mushroom Ridge took over. It was necessary to move in single file on this narrow ridge whose sides plunged down 200 to 400m. More jumaring and flat traversing took us all the way to the Great Couloir near the notorious C3.

C3 (6,450m), in the shadow of the Dablam serac, sat on a bitterly cold snow ridge with room for just three tents. Many climbers avoid it

The narrow, knife edged Mushroom Ridge from C2 to C3.

Tents pitched just below C3 due to the safety concerns of C3. We fondly dubbed this Camp 2.8 as we were almost at C3 but not there yet.

if they could help it, with skilled climbers starting their summit push from C2, and even more rarely, from C1. Temperatures at C2 and C3 were constantly below freezing. Motivating myself here to make the smallest movement was exhausting.

Even though my fever had subsided, my vomiting and chronic diarrhoea had not. It was a miserable thing to have to go to the toilet in the middle of the cold night at every single camp and sometimes even along the climb. (This incident completely changed my gut flora and to this day I have irritable bowel syndrome.)

I could not stomach food either, and had no appetite for even half a bowl of porridge for breakfast and instant noodles for dinner. Each time I tried to eat, everything came back up. By the end of each day, I was left with a cache of uneaten Snickers bars and Kit Kat packed in case of hunger pangs. The diarrhoea and lack of food had me completely drained. Putting one foot infront of the other took all of my focus and determination.

At this point, all that was left between me and my first summit on the Climb Everest 2012 bid was rock and ice at a crazy 70° to 80° incline winding around the hanging glacier.

We started out early on summit day. The oxygen at this altitude was so low that our bodies could only manage 10 steps at a time before we had to stop, gasping for breath. After three hours in -30°C temperatures and a wind that constantly punched the left side of our faces, we rounded the Dablam glacier. Another three hours of excruciatingly slow progress — step-step-step-stop-breathe, step-step-step-stop-breathe — and, incredibly, we hauled ourselves over the crest to the summit on 12 November 2011, 12:30pm.

My reward on the summit, the size of roughly half a badminton court, was a dramatic panorama of some of the most iconic 8,000m peaks of the Himalayas: Everest (8,848m), Lhotse (8,516m), Kangchenjunga (8,586m), Makalu (8,481m), Cho Oyu (8,188m), Shishapangma (8,027m).

Exhilaration doesn't even begin to describe the surge in my heart and head. It was my very first summit in this crazy year-long expedition!

The first thing I did when I set foot on the summit ... was puke. All the pent-up pressure, extreme exertion, not to mention my illness, came spilling out in relief. Actually, that happened to me on a number of other summits. Back in Singapore, people would ask me eagerly:

The summit of Ama Dablam (6,812m) on 12 November 2011. Everest, Nuptse and Lhotse loom in the background.

The entire Everquest Autumn 2011 Ama Dablam team.

A view of C3 while descending from the summit, with clouds shrouding the Khumbu valley below.

So what did you do when you reached the summit? I hardly know how to tell them that the first thing I did was puke.

Our entire team of four made it into the history books as the first Singaporean team to attempt and summit the once-considered "unclimbable" Ama Dablam.

The Singapore and NUS flag were planted proudly on the summit, just as I had promised Teng Jie and the rest of the MIR gang when they came to Changi Airport to send me off.

After the past five months of disappointments and exertion, this moment was incredibly sweet. The odds against my summiting had been immense — I had literally been running on empty during our rough six-day push. By God's grace, the weather had been perfect and there had been no fixed rope problems. There were forces at work here that were entirely beyond my control. I was thankful.

+ + +

Our excellent team of Sherpas from the Everquest climbing company were instrumental in the success of our expedition. They were the ones who went ahead of us every day to set up shelter and anchor the fixed ropes. Our lives had literally been in their hands.

Jamling Bhote navigating the near 70 degree slopes during the summit push.

It was in Ama Dablam, in fact, that I first managed to climb with Jamling Bhote, 34 years old then in 2011. I had heard a great deal about his skill and fitness level from fellow climbers who praised him as a superb climber. He was sought after by many to be their personal Sherpa.

No one had higher praise for Jamling than my friend, Kenneth Koh, who had summited Everest from the north side with Jamling, and had been my teammate at Mt Chola.

Jamling had saved Kenneth's life.

During his Everest summit push, Kenneth had removed his goggles because of an irritation in his eye, and was almost blinded by the extreme sun and wind. The two made it to the summit, where the wind was picking up; they needed to descend quickly. But Kenneth could not see his way well enough to make the dangerous descent. Jamling had held onto Kenneth's feet and painstakingly placed them step by step along the path down from the summit until they reached the lower camps where Kenneth's eyesight recovered.

Jamling was to have been my Sherpa in Cho Oyu, but his plans fell through. Even then, a part of him had gone with me to Cho Oyu. Through a frustrating postal mix-up, the triple-insulated climbing boots necessary for climbing mountains over 8,000m did not arrive in time for my expedition and the big-hearted Jamling had lent me his own boots.

It would be six years before I crossed paths with Jamling again. In June 2017, we would climb Makalu together. By then, he had become one of my dearest friends.

On the journey homeward from Ama Dablam, while trekking back down to Lukla from BC, I wished very much to gaze upon the beauty of Ama Dablam once again. Now that I had seen her from all angles during the climb, I was curious to see if my perspective of her had changed. Sadly, clouds shrouded the mountain on our return journey, and the weather never cleared until we reached Lukla.

+ + +

After the high (literally) of Ama Dablam, coming down to reality in Singapore was a bit of a crash landing.

Elated at having summited Ama Dablam (in many ways my dream mountain), I wore that badge proudly ... only to have people ask: *What is Ama Dablam? Is it foodstuff?*

My Climb Everest 2012 bid had stalled. There was still not enough funds for me to make it to Everest.

By day, I was making endless cold calls for sponsorship for the rest of the expedition, and by night I was a locum at a 24-hour clinic in a bid to earn as much as I could to contribute to the journey. But I knew that, without a title sponsor, it would be impossible for me to set foot on Everest.

One slow night at the clinic, I was on the computer at 2am, feeling less than optimistic about my prospects. My climbing company, IMG, was chasing me to cough up the payment for the scheduled Everest expedition in March to May 2012.

The determined side of me wanted to hold on — give more talks, write more emails, make more calls. But the realistic side of me said: Give up the Everest dream. In this 2011-12 gap year, you've climbed three mountains, with sponsorship enough to climb three more in the South American Andes at the end of the year. *It is enough.*

But was it?

I opened my email to see an unsolicited letter from a certain Cerebos Pacific Ltd. It was my turn to ask: *What is Cerebos? Is it foodstuff?*

In this case, it was.

Cerebos, the Asia Pacific company responsible for Brand's Essence of Chicken and other health and wellness food products, had a vision of being the leading food and beverage company in Asia Pacific by 2020. In their message, they said they saw Everest as a metaphor for the journey on which they were embarking themselves. They had chanced upon my Climb Everest 2012 blog and requested to partner me in my Everest bid.

My head swam. After almost two intense and wearying years of knocking on doors for sponsors, Cerebos was knocking on my door instead. It was an unexpected breakthrough and I admit I shed tears that night, sitting in a lonely clinic at 2am.

Brand's, whose tagline is "Unlocking Greatness", not only came on board as my title sponsor but also as the sponsor of computers and uninterrupted power supply units to the schoolchildren in Aahale, the Nepali village I had visited as a 15-year-old.

The plan was that, directly after my descent from Everest, I would meet up with Gayathri and my old secondary school teacher, Mr Pillay Krishnan, for the trip to Aahale. Mr Krishnan would coordinate this visit, as he had coordinated my first Aahale visit 12 years ago. Together, we would present the computers to the school principal, and his students. No one was more delighted by this upcoming visit than Mr Krishnan, who had volunteered in Aahale (through SIF) in his youth, subsequently guiding 19 teenaged boys there for the benefit of the same experience, and would now return with one of those 15-year-old boys who had taken over the baton. To Mr Krishnan, this was a poignant full circle.

+ + +

2012 began with promise. If the stars aligned, I would be in Everest by April.

To stay in form, I would climb three peaks in Chile and Argentina I had never before tackled: Aconcagua (6,962m), Ojos del Salado (6,893m) and San Francisco (6,018m). The part I most anticipated was taking on the challenge with Swee Chiow.

After Asia, South America is the continent with the highest mountains in the world. The Andean range, with 100 peaks over 6,000m, forms the spine of the continent, stretching from tropical Colombia in the north to the cold, buffeting winds of the Patagonian south.

Aconcagua, the highest peak in South America, and the highest outside of the Himalayas, is one of the mountains in the coveted Seven Summits challenge. Many a mountaineer has dreamt of standing on the peak of the highest mountain of each of the earth's seven continents. Superbly fit, Swee Chiow, a member of Singapore's first Everest expedition in 1998, not only completed the Seven Summits challenge but became the first Southeast Asian and the fourth person in the world to complete the Explorers Grand Slam — the Seven Summits *plus* the North and South poles.

So it was a privilege to be Swee Chiow's climbing mate as he took on one of the Seven Summits.

Cerro Aconcagua, a looming landmark in the heart of the central Andes, lives up to its nickname "Sentinel of Stone". It is said that the mountain was sacred to the ancient Incas, who built shrines and even conducted human sacrifices here, as evidenced by archaeological sites.

Geographically, the mountain is no walk in the park. The UK climbing company, Aconcagua Treks, describes the mighty mountain thus:

"Due to the sheer height of Aconcagua it is often exposed to strong westerly winds (over 5,500m above sea level). Added to the large size of the massif, this creates a unique microclimate and on the summit peaks forms an enormous and infamous 'mushroom' cloud indicative of storms brewing near the peak. This phenomenon can be seen from Plaza de Mulas Base Camp, hanging above the upper part of Aconcagua, creating an incredible spectacle and giving a terrible negative forecast. Even when the weather is good at base camps, this mushroom cloud can be seen as a telling sign that a violent storm is raging higher up and no attempts should be made to continue ascending in these conditions."

Although the normal route up is non-technical, fatalities still happened from altitude sickness. Temperature fluctuations even in summer were notorious in Aconcagua, making it necessary to start a trek in thin clothing and end with down jackets. Even sunburn-inducing heat in the daytime switched to a nighttime temperature of -20°C above 5,000m, dropping further to -30°C on the summit.

On the first three days of our trek in the gentle Vacas valley, the weather was brilliant and hot. On the fourth day, the weather turned and we arrived at the rocky Plaza Argentina BC (4,200m) in a haze of fog and cold, flurries of snow starting to fall even as we set up our tents. By the next morning, the camp had turned white — overnight, we seemed to have skipped two seasons to winter. But within 24 hours, the ground was dry and stony again. Such is the fickleness of Aconcagua.

The trek upwards from C1 to C2 was a struggle against low humidity, low oxygen and deafening winds notorious to Aconcagua. But we arrived at C2, a snowy campsite, on a beautifully clear day. The winds continued to be fierce, and the porters, carrying immense

Our camp along the Polish Traverse Route on Aconcagua.

Our Southeast Asian Aconcagua climbing team comprising Malaysians, Singaporeans and Thais.

loads on their back, had to fight the steep slopes as well as the powerful winds to C3.

Summit day rose with the same clarity — the Andean peaks, tipped with sunlight, now sat below us cushioned in clouds. But on our final push to the summit, past the rocky Canalata, the weather came in grey and freezing, and when we finally stood on the peak of rock and ice, we were in the eye of a total white-out.

Nevertheless, we had reached the highest point of the Western Hemisphere!

Our next mountain: Ojos del Salado (6,893m), meaning "eyes of salt" after the eye-shaped salt lagoons on the slopes around the mountain — is the highest active volcano in the world. Straddling both Argentina and Chile, Ojos has a double summit that can be accessed from each of the countries. Making our way up the volcanic rock took us past the striking ice field of the Penitentes.

At this latitude and altitude, the melting glacier naturally formed a forest of graphic ice sculptures, each as tall as I was, incongruously sitting on dry sand and rock. This climb, though considered a straightforward trek, turned out to be a bigger challenge to me than the higher Aconcagua because of rough conditions from the dry desert winds, a frigid terrain that made progress slow-going, and extremely loose rock near the top.

The weather mimicked desert conditions — extremely dry, with freezing winds at nightfall.

Swee Chiow was so fast that he reached the summit ahead of me and we rejoined at the caldera where I was arguing with our guide who refused to take me further because the winds were picking up. This was not an unfamiliar scenario. But I had been schooled by the mountains.

By this time, I had learnt how to enjoy the checkered journey, with all its unexpected adventures, as much as the patent triumph of setting foot on the summit. More importantly, I was learning to make decisions based on the entire team's well-being rather than prioritising egotistical needs.

It was not an easy balancing act: Climbing necessitates almost single-minded determination. Yet the most mature of climbers, I found, were those who could also face setbacks and temper impediments with good judgement and humanity. I was still learning. But at Ojos del Salado,

I made the decision to capitulate to the warnings of my guide without as much internal wrestling as I would've had a few years ago. Turning our backs to the crater rim at 6,800m — just 100m from the summit — we all headed down to safety.

+ + +

Cerro de San Francisco (6,018m) was next. A rough-hewn, isolated behemoth straddling Argentina and Chile, it is known for its violent, continuous wind and coldness, making it a mountain not to be underestimated. At the same time, it can be climbed in one day, which has earned it a reputation of being the easiest 6,000m summit to achieve in the world. The panoramic view from the slopes of San Francisco included multiple volcanoes in the distance — the active ones belching plumes of smoke high into the clear sky.

On January 27, we stood on the summit in the first Singaporean ascent of San Francisco. The moment marked the completion of our Latino Trilogy. January in South America had flown by in a blur of boots and camps, camaraderie and novel experiences.

The Sherpas and yaks so familiar in the Himalayas were replaced by gauchos and pack mules in this part of the world. It was quite a sight when both the cowboys and the mules galloped in a cloud of dust into the Plaza de Mulas Base Camp. After descending from Aconcagua, a horse ride out of BC through the windswept Horcunas Valley had me feeling a little like a gaucho myself.

Even dusty car rides, as we travelled from place to place in the barren Atacama Desert, was a visual feast of sweeping mountain vistas pockmarked by natural hot springs, as we passed occasional herds of native alpacas foraging in the dry scrub.

Meals at BC were excellent, with traditional *asado*, or barbecues, every night, featuring fat chorizo sausages, pork, chicken and half-kilo beef steaks, washed down with copious amounts of regional red wine. Each mouthwatering slab was bigger than my face.

It was two days overland to the picturesque Argentinian town of Fiambalá, reknowned for its natural hot springs, along the rivers of the Catamarca Province. We stayed in the vineyard home of the hospitable Jonson family.

Khoo Swee Chiow and myself — the first Singaporeans to summit Cerro de San Francisco (6,018m).

Climbing 6,000m volcanoes scattered through the Atacama Desert.

Driving through the barren Atacama Desert towards our climbing objectives.

At Fiambala, Catamarca, with the late Malli Mastan Babu (exteme left) and Swee Chiow (2nd from right).

To climb, we would drive 200km from Fiambalá to the Argentinian border, passing our destination of Ojos, and a further 100km into Chile to get our passports stamped at the immigration checkpoint, before retracing our steps 100km back to Ojos. It was the same when we climbed San Francisco, except without the drive into Chile. Here, driving 200km was like driving to town.

It was also in Fiambalá that Swee Chiow, the first Singaporean to climb the Seven Summits, met the Indian mountaineer who broke a Seven Summits record. Mastan Babu Malli was celebrated for his 2006 world record for climbing the Seven Summits in just 172 days, the fastest time then.

The driven mountaineer told us he would be returning in 2015 to ascend the Nevado Tres Cruces (Three Crosses) massif. In 2015 we heard that indeed he had made it to the mountain. But tragically, he did not leave it alive. Lost in a white-out that prevented rescuers from a search operation, his frozen body was later found.

On my mountaineering travels, I have sadly crossed paths with five climbers who have since died: The Indian record-breaker Malli; Singapore-based Malaysian doctor Dr Chin Wui Kin, who died of his injuries in 2019 after being rescued from Annapurna where he was stranded for two nights; and Icelandic mountaineer John Snorri who in 2017 was the first Icelander to summit K2 but would die on a winter ascent of the same mountain in 2021. Ngima Sherpa, who climbed Ama Dablam with Jamling and me, died not in the mountains but in a tragic motorbike accident. Peter Wittek, an assistant professor at the University of Toronto, who was never found after being caught in an avalanche during an expedition on Mt Trishul, India. He was a PhD student in NUS and was my MIR teammate in 2008.

It is incredibly sad that these experienced mountaineers have perished while an amateur climber like myself am alive to tell my story. It has shown me that, truly, the unpredictable mountains are dangerous to anyone on any given day.

At Fiambalá, we also met a petite climber who was the first woman to climb Monte Pissis (6,795m), an extinct Argentinian volcano, with her two young children. Spending time surrounded by people who heard the siren call of the mountains, as I did, was a rare privilege and great joy. Before we left, Swee Chiow and I left our mark in Fiambalá — a small Singapore flag on which we wrote:

Kumaran Rasappan
Khoo Swee Chiow
Ojos + San Francisco
January 2012

I sometimes wonder if our flag is still in Fiambalá, halfway across the world, together with the flags of all the nations represented by the many who have made their way to this enchanting part of the world.

It was on this leg of my journey that I was reminded of the special relationship between mountains and medicine. There is a frisson of familiarity between people, even strangers, who habitually make life-and-death decisions, the way mountaineers and doctors do.

The cases we encountered in the mountains were far removed, however, from what we are familiar with in the operating theatres of Singapore.

During a 2016 Everest Base Camp trek that Gayathri (by then my wife) and I made with my colleagues from the orthopaedic department, one of these unusual medical events occurred.

Gayathri and I had split off from the group to head to Island Peak for another trek. But this story was told to me by my ortho teammates.

Just 15 or 20 years ago, hot showers on Himalayan treks were a rarity. But by 2016, hot showers were increasingly common, a luxury that one could buy for about US$10 per shower. The quality of the heaters, however, was often questionable — it was not unusual for showers to turn cold midway during a shower, or the hot water to disappear just as you've soaped yourself.

While the team was resting in the village of Lobuche, a woman stepped into the shower and was taking an unusually long time with her ablutions. The water was flowing and no one thought much about it. But after an hour, when the woman still had not emerged and was not responding to the lodge owner's door banging, everyone knew something was wrong. The owner broke down the door and barged in to find the woman lying unconscious on the floor with the shower still running.

My teammates, all doctors, sprang into action. After a prolonged period of warming the woman, applying oxygen and stabilising her vital signs, she was kept alive. But she remained unconscious. Everyone thought that she had suffered AMS, and the lodge owners sent some of the climbing Sherpas to the nearest clinic to obtain AMS medication. The distance to the clinic would have taken a regular trekker one day each way, but these Sherpas made the round trip within three to four hours. From the speed of their return, they might have run the entire distance.

The medication did not seem to help and the woman remained unconscious the whole night. Her vital signs were stable but she was not responsive. Helicopter evacuation was called in, but the bad weather did not allow the pilot to land that evening. The helicopter came at first light the next day and she was transported away safely.

News later came from the Kathmandu hospital that she had suffered carbon monoxide poisoning. The combustible water heater in the lodge was faulty and was producing carbon monoxide as the fuel burnt down to heat the water. In an enclosed space, the unfortunate woman was inhaling carbon monoxide throughout her shower. A few more minutes without assistance and she could have died. The team had rescued her from the edge of death — her pupils were already dilated when they delivered first aid. Happily, she eventually made a full recovery.

As the only doctor on some of my expeditions, I was also sometimes called to practise medicine out in the field. Each time that happened, I was reminded afresh of the crux of medicine — to rescue and restore whomever we can, wherever we can, with whatever we can.

When our Aconcagua team arrived back at BC, some doctorly duties had to be performed. Two of our teammates, Benz and Lucas, had ended up with injured toes. In the course of the rigorous climb, their toenails had turned blue from the pressure build-up of blood beneath the nails. Some anti-bacterial wet wipes and a foldable Swiss army knife, the tip of which I sterilised over a lighter's meagre flame, allowed me to perform nail trephination to relieve the sub ungual haematoma, the bleeding and bruising under the nail.

In the wild, away from the shiny, efficient systems that may not always be necessary but that I had grown accustomed to, the patient once again became the only factor that mattered. Returning to this basic tenet of medicine was centering for me.

After each climb, I found myself returning to work at the hospital with greater energy, empathy and clarity of purpose. That was one of the gifts of the mountains.

The close of the Latin Trilogy was a significant milestone. For almost a year, I had prepared for Everest with almost back-to-back climbs on

- Muztagh Ata, China (7,546m)
- Cho Oyu, Tibet/China (8,201m)
- Ama Dablam, Nepal (6,812m)
- Aconcagua, Argentina (6,962m)
- Ojos del Salado, Argentina/Chile (6,893m)
- Nevado San Francisco, Argentina/Chile (6,018m)

It was pretty incredible that everything had gone according to plan. At any point I could have been sick or injured; there might have been political uprisings or natural impediments from weather or earthquakes (well, one did happen but, thankfully, I walked away unscathed). Everything had miraculously aligned.

When I arrived home, I found that Cerebos had made good on the entire sponsorship sum.

It was finally time to take on the big fella: Everest.

CHAPTER 8

"I feared I was on the way to becoming Tolstoy's stereotype of a doctor, preoccupied with empty formalism, focused on the rote treatment of disease — and utterly missing the larger human significance."
Paul Kalanithi

As Himalayan maps go, the village of Phortse is a nondescript dot in the Khumbu valley, one of many hamlets pockmarked by the tramping boots and thudding poles of trekkers and climbers en route to Everest Base Camp and even higher.

But this rustic mountain community, and home to many a Sherpa guide, turned out to be one of the most memorable points of my Everest journey.

Not least because my future wife, Dr Gayathri Devi Nadarajan, an emergency medicine consultant, and I spent some months in the humble hamlet running the health outpost for the villagers during my Everest bid.

It was in Phortse that the Sherpa people became much more than porters and guides to us. They became some of our closest friends.

+ + +

Gayathri and I had met as gawky 16-year-olds on our first day at junior college. She, a bushy-haired, driven extrovert with dancing eyes, came to Raffles Junior College after 10 years at all-girls' schools. I, a gangly introvert in wire rimmed spectacles, came from four years at an all-boys' secondary school. The opposite sex was still an enigma to us — equal parts bewitching and terrifying.

Apart from the fact that we both came from Indian families, we couldn't have been raised more differently.

Gayathri was an only child of free-spirited and sociable parents who owned a string of backpackers' lodges and took Gayathri on 36-hour bus rides up to Thailand from the age of two. She was that classmate who would have the rest of the class over at her house for drinks, dinner, home movies and birthday celebrations. Home for her, her parents and her extended family (including grandparents, single aunts and uncles), was an HDB flat in Race Course Road, which constantly resounded with laughter and familial warmth.

At her 18th birthday party held at a beach chalet, her lively mother and I shook up the dance floor, to Gayathri's deep mortification and high amusement.

My family was more traditional — irreproachably proper and suitably serious. Childhood, for me, consisted of a rotation of after-school classes: Five years of organ and art, taekwando to the level of black belt, followed by Scouts, and training with the national fencing team. If the idea was to keep me gainfully occupied so that there was no time for me to get up to mischief, I'd say it worked pretty well.

Don't get me wrong, I appreciated the stability and wholesome routine my family provided my sister and me. But I relished the liberating levity of Gayathri's family get-togethers and the refreshing ridiculousness of their conversations. This was a family that didn't take itself too seriously.

Gayathri and I were best friends in junior college, spending long hours sharing notes and joking around in class, after which we would go home and continue yakking on the phone for another three hours. Romance wasn't on our minds yet. At least not to each other.

She was that buddy who would listen to me go on about my many crushes and I trusted her to deliver an honest verdict on which girl was a potential date and which romance was doomed to failure.

Gayathri had dreamt of being a doctor from early primary school, envisioning herself wearing khakis in some rural village treating sick children. Her ambition was sealed when her father suffered a major heart attack when she was 12. By the time he had chest pains and turned cold and clammy in the middle of the night, he was drifting in and out of consciousness. In his mind, he thought: "This is it", as he would tell his family later.

Around the same time, her grandmother suffered a bad fall and ended up in the same hospital. For weeks, the family shuttled between hospital wards. With her PSLE exams looming, and the adults preoccupied, young Gaya took ownership of her studies and buried herself to the eyeballs in textbooks so that she could go on to become the kind of doctor who would heal sick fathers and grandmothers everywhere.

Unlike Gayathri, my own initial motivation to be a doctor was to fulfil my family's ambitions. Having come from humble and hardworking stock, my parents' dream was to have a doctor in the family. (Asian parents can identify.) My older sister, Kumuthamalar, had gone on to be a physiotherapist. So it was up to me to make it to medical school. This was not an unpleasant prospect, and eventually both my best friend and I became med students — Gayathri in St Georges, London, where her paternal great grandmother, granduncle and aunt lived, and I at the National University of Singapore.

Gayathri could only afford her foreign student fees with study loans from family, friends, the Singapore Indian Education Trust (SIET) and good-hearted individuals who barely knew her except for her crazy passion to study medicine. It took her 10 years to pay off all her loans, a strength of character that has earned my great respect till today.

In the midst of our medical school, separated by the 10,800km between London and Singapore, and bolstered by endless long-distance conversations courtesy of a mountain of $10 scratch phone cards (pardon the pun), the both of us came to the astonishing conclusion that we were not just best buds but soulmates. Thus began a long-distance relationship that, in a way, continued long after we reunited in Singapore, as Gayathri came to terms with the fact that having a relationship with me meant there would always be a third party — my beloved mountains.

Raised by her backpacking parents to love adventure and the outdoors, Gayathri was almost as excited as I was when she first heard my grand Everest plan while we were yet undergrads. One of her fondest dreams as a med student was to one day be involved in humanitarian medical work in the communities of the world that lacked basic healthcare.

So while I dreamt of mountain summits, she dreamt of mountain clinics.

And in the year 2012, we managed to make both happen.

+ + +

The Sherpa people are a Tibetan race born and bred on the thin air and rocky earth of some of the harshest mountains in the world. Hardy as alpine shrubs and nimble as gazelles, most are spiritual, family-oriented and generous-hearted.

It may come as a surprise that they do not actually have a mountaineering pedigree. It was only when the early international expeditions grew in number that Sherpas became sought after as guides. After all, they know the Himalayas better than anyone.

In Phortse, a village of less than 400 people, more than 70 have summited Everest, some more than once, earning it fame as the place with the highest concentration of Everest summiters anywhere in the world. Each summiter is awarded a certificate by the government, and the wall of many a Phortse home is decorated with prized certificates. One expedition can earn a guide enough to feed his family for a year.

But the villagers lead hard lives, with danger hovering in the background. Almost every family in Phortse includes a climber, with some families knowing first-hand the grief of losing a son or a father to the mountains.

Khumjung Village, near Phortse, has a school set up by the Edmund Hillary Foundation, relatively reputable in the region. The Foundation also set up the first hospital for the Sherpa community in 1966 — the only medical facility in the Khumbu landscape until late 2000 when four small satellite healthposts sprang up in the surrounding villages of Thame, Monjo, Phortse and Pangboche.

In the beginning, the hospital was run by volunteer doctors from New Zealand or Canada, members of the Foundation who would spend several months ministering to the locals. Villagers were involved as medical assistants, performing the function of nurses, paramedics and radiographers.

Eventually Kami Sherpa, from the village of Thame, proved to be a capable medical assistant, and was identified as a suitable candidate to be trained as a local doctor. So in his late 30s, Kami was sent to medical school in Auckland, New Zealand, where he swotted for exams next to classmates nearly half his age.

By the time he graduated as a medical doctor after 10 years, he was in his 40s. Dr Kami Sherpa made history as the first Sherpa doctor in the whole of Nepal. His son eventually also became a doctor working in Kathmandu. So the Edmund Hillary Foundation changed the fortune of this family and, by providing medical care in the Khumbu valley, the lives of thousands of locals as well.

Something sparked in me when I heard this string of events. I was already raising funds for the Tan Tock Seng Hospital Community Fund through my Everest climb. What if, at the same time, I could also give back to the Sherpa community?

Like many who had climbed in the Himalayas, I had a special relationship with the Sherpa guides who risked their lives to go ahead of us to fix lines on solid rock, place ladders across shifting ice chasms, and haul incredible loads of food and oxygen tanks on their backs from camp to camp.

Few ever gain the kind of acclaim international mountaineers did.

To us, Sherpas are not just porters and guides. They are dream-makers.

I wanted to give something of myself back to my Sherpa friends through my twin passions of climbing and medicine.

From my Cho Oyu climb, when I became friends with some of the Sherpas, I started planning how I could help out at Phortse, the village from which IMG engaged many of their guides. Ang Jangbu, the Nepali IMG head, linked me up with Dr Kami.

So after Ama Dablam, I made a little detour to recce the healthpost at Phortse, population 400 at the time. I discovered random surgical instruments lying around waiting to be taken to Khunde Hospital for autoclaving (sterilisation). There was no running water — the tap and sink did not work. Some antibiotics were at the healthworker's disposal — but unsure of the prescriptions, she left them untouched.

Basic medications were available, but in quantities too small to be effective.

The Phortse healthworker, Lhakpa Yangjee, and Khunde Hospital's Dr Kami, whom I visited on the same trip, had simple requests: Usable medication (by the time medicines donated by foreign donors arrived, they were often near their expiry date), and a lightweight stretcher. Currently it took four people to heft a patient to the clinic over the mountain trails using a heavy, home-made, bamboo-pole stretcher.

Gayathri and I began making plans to spend time in Phortse to refurbish the tiny clinic, offer medical consultations and educational resources to the villagers, and provide additional training to the healthcare workers. A couple of calls and appeals in Singapore produced enough sponsorship for the medical equipment for the task. The hope was to set up a sustainable system that the villagers could trust and run, even after we returned home.

I would manage the Phortse healthpost for a month before Gayathri joined me with fresh supplies and took over the healthpost for the two months that I was on Everest making for the summit.

Unbeknownst to us at the time, our first experience of running a clinic in Nepal together would be far from our last. Today, we are still running Himalayan clinics annually under Project Aahale. This time, as husband and wife.

+ + +

Kathmandu

Chaotic with bustling motorbikes, street vendors and motley groups of tourists on any given day, Kathmandu, the colourful capital of Nepal, becomes mayhem when you're on a time-crunched mission.

I had flown here with 60kg of climbing gear and medical supplies, and there was another 30kg of shipped medical supplies to pick up from the cargo terminal. It took four hours of hustling to get the supplies back to my hotel room, much of the time spent trying to persuade the authorities (without success) to waive the 20% taxation on the supplies which were for charity.

Generic medication had to be purchased from Kathmandu pharmacies, as well as necessities like a 3G device with a data plan. In an attempt to be as prudent with my sponsors' donations as possible, I made all transactions in cold, hard cash. It was rare for businesses to offer credit card transactions, and those that did slapped on an additional 10% fee.

So I was a walking ATM machine, with every pocket from head to toe stuffed with rupee bills.

My hotel room was crazily stacked with boxes of every description. By now my luggage had swollen to 150kg, all of which needed to be at the domestic airport the next morning (where I was charged for 95kg of excess baggage).

No amount of explanation that the medical supplies were for charity made any difference. Dr Kami, the sole doctor serving 8,000 villagers in the Khumbu region where I was headed, related an incident that typified the healthcare situation in Nepal.

An American opthalmologist, having witnessed the lack of medical facilities in the mountains, wanted to donate a slit lamp — an expensive piece of equipment used to examine the retina of an eye. But the device got stuck at Kathmandu customs, where authorities insisted on imposing taxes amounting to more than the cost of the slit lamp. In the end, what was meant to help the locals was stymied by local authorities.

My ridiculously overweight luggage was flown on tiny domestic airplanes into Lukla airport piece by piece. The last piece of baggage did not arrive by noon, when the airport closed for the day. I had no choice but to start on my six-hour uphill trek without it, hoping it would catch up with me during my two-day acclimatisation stay at Namche Bazar.

My companions from Lukla (2,800m) to Namche Bazar (3,440m) were three porters who could not have weighed more than 60kg. They proceeded to haul an astonishing 50kg load each on their backs for the entire 18km journey.

The elevation difference on this six-hour trek would be 640m, and oxygen would drop 6% by the time we arrived at Namche Bazar.

The porters carrying 50kg of medications and medical equipment from Lukla airport to Phortse.

+ + +

Khunde

As soon as my lagging piece of luggage caught up with me, I headed out to the village of Khunde to meet Dr Kami.

The terrain from Namche Bazar to Khunde was uneven and rocky, but the view was faultless, with the Himalayan ranges encircling us in all their raw beauty.

As the three porters and I tramped our way across the meandering valley to meet up with Dr Kami at Khunde Hospital, an amusing recollection made me smile.

Just as we were leaving the Lukla airport, a gentleman with a clipped British accent caught my eye. He had just deplaned. Dressed in rather formal attire, his luggage turned out to be several smart Samsonite suitcases on wheels. He was gobsmacked when the porters began roping up the suitcases to their foreheads as was their custom.

"Couldn't we just roll them along?" he asked, perplexed. I wish I could have seen his face when the poor chap realised the kind of terrain he and his Samsonites would have to navigate up the mountain.

The view of Ama Dablam from Khunde.

Khunde is gifted with a view par excellence — Ama Dablam rises majestically in the distance, its snow-draped peak stretching towards the belly of the heavens. It still stirred wonder in me that I had managed to stand atop its crest.

The hospital was really no more than a large clinic where simple lab work could be done. There was a ward with four to six beds, one X-ray machine, one ultrasound machine, a pharmacy, a consult room, and a delivery room where Dr Kami could do caesarian sections and episiotomies.

Together with the four satellite healthposts run by local health assistants, which were even smaller, the hospital served about 8,000 Sherpa people living in 13 to 14 villages scattered about the mountains, each four to five hours' walk from the other, some even days apart.

To see Dr Kami, a sick patient either had to walk the rugged mountain trail or be carried in on a stretcher hauled by four men. Others were transported on mules, or even carried in a basket strapped to the forehead of a stalwart relative.

The gravely ill, who could not travel, had little choice but to wait out their malaise, which ultimately resulted in one of two courses: Recovery or death.

+ + +

When I arrived at Khunde Hospital bearing medical gifts and ready to train the healthcare workers, Dr Kami was delighted.

There was just one small problem: Two of the healthcare workers, from the villages of Phortse and Monjo, were missing.

Both these female healthworkers had coincidentally become pregnant at the same time, and both had left for Kathmandu, where they had had caesarian sections performed. (Many villagers still preferred to deliver their babies in Kathmandu, much to the chagrin of Dr Kami, who was qualified to perform C-sections and episiotomises.) The ladies had decided to remain in Kathmandu to fully recover before returning. The healthpost in Phortse had been left unattended for six months, much to the consternation of the villagers, who had sacrificed half their school to make space for the clinic.

Khunde Hospital, too, was facing a crisis. There had only been two doctors, each taking turns to be on duty. They would return home

Dr Kami and team unpacking the medical equipment that we delivered.

to their village when they were off-duty. But one of the doctors had resigned without notice, leaving Dr Kami to handle every single shift for the past four months. He was longing to visit his village of Thame, one day's walk from Khunde.

It was with some trepidation that I left Khunde for Phortse, my rustic medical base for the next two weeks.

+ + +

Phortse

The approach to Phortse, a remote settlement at the start of the Gokyo trek, wound past an expanse of gently terraced potato and buckwheat fields which, depending on the season, spread out in swathes of brown or viridescent green.

It was a hamlet so traditional that wood and yak dung were used for fuel until 2003, when electricity via hydroelectric power finally arrived.

Visitors walking to Phortse were easily passed by locals nonchalantly heaving anything from building supplies (including 3m-long planks and bags of concrete), to 20kg bags of rice or potatoes strapped to their foreheads. Such is the hardiness of the Sherpa race.

There was no choice — vehicular traffic was impossible on the

Dawa proudly holding up a plaque presented to him by Sir Edmund Hillary in recognition of his climbing achievements.

rugged paths. Everything that went up the mountains went up by human effort. Incidentally, rice, although a staple in Nepal, does not grow in the thin, sandy soil of Khumbu, so every grain was transported there on somebody's back.

The first person I encountered in Phortse was my friend and lodge owner, Danuru Sherpa, known to the locals as Dawa, who was sleeping wrapped up in blankets when I entered his guesthouse. He was ill but, with true Himalayan hospitality, got up to receive me with a cup of hot milk tea.

Dawa had been my climbing guide on Cho Oyu. An astounding 11-time Everest summiter, he had already chalked up more than 50 expeditions when I met him. Between expeditions, he ran a guest lodge. This was common in Phortse, where any one of the lodge owners could be a star mountaineer. Other reputed climbers became buckwheat or potato farmers during off-seasons. They climbed not for the glory, but simply to feed their families.

I, and later Gayathri, had made arrangements to stay at Dawa's lodge in Phortse while we ran the health post. Proudly he showed us his climbing photos and a plaque on his wall awarded to him by the Edmund Hillary Foundation, signed by Sir Edmund Hillary himself.

Fortunately, in a village that was devoid of electronic communication, word of mouth worked just as effectively as a text message. And almost before I could sweep out the cobwebs in the abandoned clinic, my patients started streaming in.

+ + +

Each day, 18 to 32 people would come for consultation within the space of four hours — some were locals from Phortse, others had made their way here from surrounding villages. Patiently, they squatted in the dust outside the clinic, chatting about farms and families as they waited in line to see the "foreign doctor".

Many of the men were climbers, or had been climbers. The deep lines and profound tan on their faces attested to a life of hard physical labour in harsh elements.

During the popular climbing seasons of spring and autumn, the expeditions would see an exodus of working-age males, leaving Phortse with a sparse population of women, young children and the aged. But it was not yet the peak climbing season.

The absence of the healthcare worker meant that I was left without a translator at the healthpost. Dawa gamely offered to fill the role. Ever enterprising, Sherpas often picked up English, French, German and Japanese through their interaction with international clients. (Later on in Phortse, Gayathri would treat a Japanese man with AMS, and it would be a Sherpa who stepped up as her interpreter.)

The elderly lady who could "see" after my simple act of wiping her spectacle lenses clean.

Not long after I arrived, one of the women in the village came in for consultation. Her eyesight had been deteriorating ever since she got a new pair of spectacles from Kathmandu two years ago, she said. After examining her eyes and not detecting anything amiss, I asked her to show me her spectacles. The lenses were coated with dirt and grime. When I asked her to show me how she cleaned her spectacles, she promptly smeared the thick dirt around with her fingers. Amused, I took the spectacles from her, gave them a thorough, five-minute cleaning with gauze and soapy water, and handed them back.

"I can see!" she exclaimed, thanking me profusely.

My next case was a man who complained of progressive deafness in both ears over the past six years. Thinking it might be an old ear infection, I proceeded to take a look in his ear, but could not insert the autoscope even halfway into the ear canal. Syringing did not work to clear the wax, so I went in with a pair of tweezers. What emerged was a hairy plug of dirt the size of a marble. Even the patient was shocked. It was an accumulation of six years of dirt and wax which, when removed, restored his hearing instantly.

Then there was a young boy with a gash on his hand from an accident while working in the fields with his mother. At my instruction, he washed his hand with the help of a bucket of water we had manually lugged to the clinic as there was no running water. The amount of debris and dirt that fell from the wound was astonishing.

I was beginning to realise that, in a rural clinic, awareness of general hygiene and nutrition might be just as helpful as medical intervention.

Many of the villagers' ailments were particular to their rural, high-altitude lifestyle.

One day, a man in his 50s came to the clinic. He had been guiding on Cho Oyu when he suffered a stroke.

This was not altogether uncommon. Next to oxygen, water — which makes up 60% of our body weight when we are fully hydrated — is the most vital substance for our survival. One of its benefits is to improve the efficiency of red blood cells in collecting oxygen in the lungs. Simply put, we need the help of water to breathe well.

But at high altitudes, dehydration is a nagging problem. Dry, cold air absorbs moisture from the body. Lower oxygen levels, greater activity, the rugged terrain and more weight being carried, combine to cause rapid breathing, which encourages fluid loss.

By the time the man returned to Phortse after his stroke, he was hemiplegic — half his body, the right side, was paralysed. Fortunately, he was still able to walk by dragging his right foot.

In the mountains, if you could not walk, you were as good as non-functioning. Ironically one needed to be mobile even to get to the healthpost; residents of the lower part of the village had to make their way on foot uphill for 20 minutes. It was a challenging prospect for those with arthritis or debilitating injuries.

This former Sherpa guide's wife had left him after his stroke. He was now living alone in the village.

His condition saw the right hand contracting like a claw, a spasticity which caused him all kinds of problems, including not being able to open his hand to wash it or cut his nails, which were digging into his palm. In order to stop his right hand from squeezing shut, he needed something to oppose the contracture.

With Gayathri arriving from Singapore shortly, we hurriedly added a tennis ball to the list of replenishments needed. Grasping it would stop the man's hand from contracting completely.

On another occasion, I paid a home visit to a man who was having tremors in his hands. He could not hold a cup of water or pick up a piece of paper. This had been carrying on for a year.

At the time I had just completed my housemanship and, quite honestly, this was a medical condition that was too advanced for me. But I remembered someone who could help.

When I had embarked on this gap year adventure, one of the senior consultants at Tan Tock Seng Hospital who supported me was Professor Tham Kum Ying. Before I left, she generously told me that, if I ran into problems at the Phortse clinic, I could call her.

Some creative communication was called for. With my phone, I recorded a video of myself conducting a basic examination of the patient. Downsizing the file, I fed the video bit by bit, over a few hours, to Prof Tham over the Internet. With the video in hand, she consulted with a neurologist in Singapore who suggested Propranolol, an oral medication that was routinely used for heart problems and high blood pressure. Again, I had Gayathri bring the medication. Eventually, the tremors improved.

Gayathri and I didn't know it then, but there was a name for what we were doing: Telemedicine.

It was particularly useful in a remote location like Phortse. But telemedicine was even used in Singapore during the COVID-19 pandemic in 2020, when doctors were prohibited from practising in more than one location to minimise the spread of infection.

+ + +

In 2012, however, technology in Phortse was still at its most basic. Legwork — literally — was what was called for.

In some tiny hamlets where the population numbered in two digits, households did not even have phones. And I'm talking about landlines, not mobiles.

My most memorable case in Phortse took three days to unravel. A young man rushed into the clinic one day, asking for painkillers for his father. His 70-year-old father, who lived more than one day's walk away, had woken up with extreme pain in his knee and had taken lame.

The tiny hamlet had no mobile phone reception, or even a landline, and with the old man's condition deteriorating, his wife had walked three hours to the nearest village that had a landline. She left a phone message for her son: *Your father can't walk. Needs medicine.* With that cryptic message, she promptly headed back home.

I was nonplussed. How would I prescribe treatment? The son was walking home to see his father the next day, and I had a lightbulb moment: What if I gave him a list of questions for his father designed to cast light on his condition? So I sent him home with some generic painkillers and a list of questions: *Which part of your knee is hurting? Is there bruising or swelling? What is your range of movement?*

When the son returned to Phortse, I would have the information I needed to make a more informed diagnosis. There was nothing left to do but wait.

But when the son returned after two days, I was none the wiser.

First of all, the pain was not in the knee but in the hip, it seemed. That made my whole list of questions redundant. The old man was also running a low-grade fever.

Fever! Alarm bells rang. Immediately septic arthritis (an infection of the joint space which could potentially destroy the joint if not treated early) came to mind. When I urged the son to take his father to

Khunde Hospital for treatment, he said they did not have the means to transport his father to Khunde, which was a two-day walk from his parents' village.

There was no other way; I had to walk to the old man myself.

Packing all the medications I thought might be important, I set off. In my mind, I was ticking off all the possibilities: Infection of the joints, fracture, appendicitis … he might even need urgent evacuation.

Dawa kindly offered to come along on my somewhat epic house call, and we set off on the Gokyo Trek to the old couple's village. Despite the urgency of our task, the trek, adjacent to the more popular Everest Base Camp trek, lifted our spirits with its sweeping views of the ice-crusted Himalayas.

It was the month of March, and winter was taking its time to ease out. Frozen lakes and waterfalls made an exquisite tableau. Bright orange Brahmin ducks, feathers fluffed up against the cold, stood on one foot on the frozen Gokyo Lake — perhaps it was too frigid to place both feet on the ice?

A glimpse of Cho Oyu made my breath catch and I was flooded with mixed feelings. From this Nepal vantage point, I was awed by the vertical flanks of the mighty massif. I could remember clearly how it felt to toil up its unyielding rock. And the disappointment of turning my back to the summit.

After a day's walk, we made our way to a lodge where we could spend the night. The next day, we walked a further three hours to the old man and his wife.

When we arrived at their little hamlet, Charchung — so small that it didn't feature on any map — we realised that the sum total of the village population was 6.

They were yak herders who lived in three stone-walled homes ringed by meandering rock borders to keep the yaks from wandering. During winter, the population dwindled even further — we were about to see two out of the three residents in the entire village.

The old man and his wife plied Dawa and me with copious amounts of tea in gratitude for our visit. A dark cowshed became my examination room after the buffalo was coaxed out. There was no bed for the man to lie down, so they removed the mat used to cover the leaks in the roof, and laid it down on the ground between the pats of cowdung.

The trek through the Gokyo valley, with snowcapped Cho Oyu in the background, to reach the village of Charchung.

The tiny village of Charchung.

As soon as the old man undressed, his condition was clear.

Turns out … he had shingles. His son had never mentioned a rash, although I had asked. The pain was flaring up over the lumbar 5 nerve root distrubiton, which accounted for the pain in his hip, knee, calf and ankle.

Everything made sense once I saw the lesions. Shingles is a form of reactivated chicken pox triggered when the body is immunocompromised, say, when we are overly tired or sick.

Of all the conditions I had anticipated, this was not one of them and I had not a thing with me that could help.

Relieved as I was that it was not septic arthritis or anything too severe, I kicked myself for not bringing Acyclovir (shingles medication). Instead I had brought the antibiotics Augmentin and Cefalexin — which, for what it was worth, I gave to the old man in case there were secondary skin infections or burst lesions.

Actually, shingles is a self limiting condition — patients usually recover without intervention within about two weeks — so by the time we saw him after one week of to-ing and fro-ing, he was already on the mend!

All we could do was to sheepishly head home.

+ + +

My two weeks in Phortse fell into a pleasant routine. I'd wake up at 8am, have a leisurely breakfast and start out for the clinic at 9:40am. A 10-minute walk uphill, covering a vertical distance of 60 metres, took me to the clinic. I would start seeing the line of patients from 10am.

By 3pm, clouds and cold winds would blow in from the mountains, driving away the patients and signalling time to close the clinic and return to the cosy comfort of the lodge. Just walking up and down the trail between the lodge and the clinic proved to be good pre-climb acclimatisation for me before Everest.

After two weeks, I had seen almost everyone in the village. They came in to have their warts excised, their sprained ankles bandaged, and their musculoskeletal problems examined. I met everyone from guides with spectacular summit records, to a 90-year-old matriarch who was the oldest woman in Phortse, to apple-cheeked babies and children with cheeky smiles despite dirt-streaked faces and well-worn sweaters.

The older the villagers were, the more chronic problems they had. One by one they would come in, have a seat on the rickety wooden chair, and tell me they haven't been able to see properly for the past five years, have had gastric pains for the past 10 years, haven't been able to walk well for 20 years, and did I have medication that could cure everything at once? With no easy access to basic medical care, they had borne their ailments with fortitude. For years.

Of course the "foreign doctor" was a novelty, and some came by just for free medicine and free check-ups. Notwithstanding, I took every complaint seriously — if an 80-year-old had to walk uphill for half an hour just to see me, it was the least I could do.

No matter what their condition, the patients had one thing in common: Gratitude. I actually felt the need to explain that I had limited capabilities. There was no way for me to obtain blood tests, X-rays and MRI scans. Each case was a test of basic clinical acumen.

But patiently they waited for their turn outside the clinic, content to stand in the spring sunshine, with the stunning view of the Himalayas spreading out into the horizon. No one rushed me, no one complained of the long waiting time, allowing me to thoroughly examine each patient. No matter what I could or could not do for them, they thanked me appreciatively, convinced that I had done my best. Despite the primitive conditions, I could not have asked for a more affirming work environment.

The brothers who came to see me in Phortse after almost a full day's walk.

That is, if you discount the bracing temperatures, showers limited to once a week, and one cold bed.

I did make the occasional house call (although none as dramatic as the three-day trek to Charchung), and good-natured family members would turn the occasion into entertainment, often asking for a picture with me. In one photo, crowded with several generations of grinning family members, I was amused to see that even the infirm patient had propped himself up to smile at the camera.

Incidentally, when I was on my way to see the old man with shingles, I had crossed paths with a pair of aged, ruddy-cheeked brothers from another village who were on their way to see me. They had walked for nearly a day and were almost at Phortse, but when they heard I was on my way out and wouldn't be back for three days, they cheerfully said there was no hurry and they would return another day.

Two weeks later, they indeed returned to the clinic, none the worse for wear.

CHAPTER 9

"When there's no place for the scalpel, words are the surgeon's only tool."
Paul Kalanithi

Gayathri joined me at Phortse like the cavalry riding in with reinforcements: 90kg of medications, dressing sets, a pulse oximeter, a blood glucose machine, an oxygen saturation machine, wooden splints, a blood pressure machine … and one tennis ball for my stroke patient.

It was Gayathri's first time in the Khumbu mountains, and when I told her that I would meet her in Lukla, it didn't quite register what that entailed.

She told me later: "The way you casually suggested it, it seemed like you were walking from Orchard Road to Little India to pick me up."

Actually, "picking her up" at Lukla airport required a two-day descent from Phortse to Lukla on foot, and another four-day trek back up.

Living and working in the Khumbu region for two months while I was on my Everest climb would allow Gayathri to experience the Himalayas in a way that bound our dreams together.

I had something else brewing.

Little did Gayathri know that, prior to the trip, while she had been busy rallying donors, I had been busy plotting an Everest marriage proposal.

A lot was riding on my summiting Everest. In a masochistic addition of self-inflicted stress, the plan was to video myself proposing to Gayathri at the summit. So *if* I made it to the top, the occasion would be doubly momentous: It would be a culmination of years of hard work and sacrifice (not only on my part but my loved ones as well), and it would also put me on the road to being a married man.

If she said "yes", that is.

Gayathri was blissfully oblivious to my matrimonial plotting as she went about planning the refurbishment of the health post and producing health materials in the Sherpa language as teaching aids.

Both of us believed that creating awareness of proper first aid and nutrition, as well as providing tips on boosting women's and children's health could improve the lives of the Sherpa families in a sustainable way, long after we returned to Singapore.

Gayathri was not coming alone. With her was a good friend of mine from my Scouting days, Dr Zheng Shuwei.

To Shuwei, I wasn't Dr Kumaran Rasappan, I was just "Maran", as I have been to him since we were skinny secondary schoolboys mad about video games and getting punished with push-ups for being late to Scout meetings. Some of my earliest and best memories of 01 Raffles Scout Group include Shuwei. Now a fellow medical practitioner as an infectious diseases doctor, Shuwei and I were so alike that we had taken parallel paths in life since we were 13, going from Scouts to medical school.

Just two months before I left Singapore, he had decided to give his Scout brother a proper Everest send-off by accompanying me as far as he could go: Everest Base Camp (EBC).

When he was asked why go all the way to EBC, he penned these words which are still on my Climb Everest 2012 blog today:

"I've known Maran as a fellow Scout since we were in Sec 1. He will forever be a close friend and confidante from this closely knit community of Scouts that I appreciate to this day. This journey is about sending my batchmate off, someone with whom I have had the chance to work as a teammate for the many years we were in Scouting together, someone who is bringing the Scout Group's flag up to the peak, someone who has, in his way, sought to make a difference in the lives of many others.

"By comparison, this gesture of mine may not be much, but I hope that together we can send a positive message to all our junior Scouts in 01: that the friendships we cultivate as 01 Scouts will always stay strong, that 01 Scouts will always be there for one another, and that the values inculcated in us through 01 Raffles Scout Group will always bring us through the adversities we face in our lives.

"No amount of words can describe the spirit of 01 that has held batches of Scouts together. Similarly, no amount of words can describe the pride we have in one of our fellow Scout's efforts in taking on the challenge of Everest."

His message moved me greatly.

+ + +

It was April and still snowing when Gayathri and Shuwei arrived in Phortse. The mountain paths were cloaked in white, making our journey to Phortse a little more cumbersome. Especially since we had 90kg of medical supplies to haul uphill.

From the phone conversations we had had in the past two weeks, Gayathri almost felt like she knew the villagers I had described to her at some length.

As I named the villagers I'd seen over the past two weeks, she retorted: "Kumz, you've treated everybody. There's nothing left for me to do!"

But of course this wasn't the case. In fact, she would later realise that we had quite a few "repeat customers" among the residents of Phortse. Some villagers arrived with a different set of problems every day.

The three of us spent two nights in Phortse, where I introduced Gayathri and Shuwei to the villagers, and Gayathri to the home stay hosts and translators with whom she would be working when she ran the healthpost for two months. She was tickled when some of the villagers told her I was not Kumaran, I was "Kumar Sherpa", so comfortably had I integrated with the locals.

Most of our time was spent at the healthpost unpacking and sorting out the new medical supplies. But we also paid home visits to the villagers to whom I had promised special medications or equipment.

It was a humbling moment when we went to the simple home of the stroke patient to give him his new tennis ball. As we watched, he managed to use his left hand to push the tennis ball into his right hand, keeping it from contracting completely. As a result, he was able to perform simple tasks like grasping a doorknob, holding a plastic bag, and even grabbing objects.

How remarkable to see something as mundane as a tennis ball making such a difference to someone.

With each home we visited, it was our hope that our small gestures would make at least a small difference to the Sherpas' lives.

(Top left) With Gayathri, Shuwei and Dr Kami at Khunde hospital.

(Botton left) Restocking the depleted medicines in the Phortse clinic.

(Top right) The tennis ball that was delivered to the elderly Sherpa who had suffered a stroke.

+ + +

Everest

I could hardly believe that the time had come for me to make it up the legendary Chomolungma, Goddess Mother of the World, as the Sherpas call her.

Leading up to this moment were four years of logistics planning, 1½ years of fund-raising, one year of physical training and countless sleepless nights of running everything through my mind in an endless loop. There was an incredible number of moving parts.

When I left for Everest, my close friends and family sent me off. *Don't EverRest* when you're climbing, kidded my friends when they came to see me off at Changi Airport before I left for Kathmandu. Just come back in one piece and don't Rest Forever on the mountain, added my family through quavering smiles. For the first time I saw tears in my dad's eyes, which in turn made me emotional. Friends from the

The send-off at the airport when I left for Everest in March 2012.

climbing community who showed up included Robert Goh and Lulin Reuters, the founders of MIR.

The significance of the moment, the cusp, was not lost on me.

Gayathri and Shuwei were determined to go with me as far as they could go, and so after our two nights at Phortse, the three of us started off on a measured ascent to Everest Base Camp (EBC). We made sure to take it slow — no more than 400 vertical metres each day — it was Shuwei's first time trekking at such a high altitude.

For eight days, we made our way from Phortse to Periche and Lobuche, together taking in the incredible vistas of 6,000m to 7,000m mountains. In the early dawn, the top of the peaks frothed with clouds whipped up by the wind and precipitation.

At times, we literally had our head in the clouds. It was exhilarating. The temperature was well below 0°C at this altitude, even during the day with a bright sun overhead.

The higher we trekked, the more expensive everything became. This was not surprising, considering everything that made its way up was carried up on foot. Food and drink quickly became more expensive than its equivalent in Singapore. A litre of hot water cost S$5. Battery charging cost S$6 per hour. Hot showers were available at S$15 per 20 litres of hot water. A simple meal of dhal bhat and rice cost close to S$10. (And this was in 2012.)

Everest herself would not be visible from the EBC, aside for a tantalising glimpse of its western shoulder

But a side trek to Kala Patthar, near Gorek Shep, three hours' walk from EBC and the last and highest village before the Base Camp, would allow us a sighting of Everest if weather permitted.

By now the peak climbing season had begun and it was difficult booking lodgings at the higher villages. The whole village of Gorek Shep was full or reserved when we arrived, and we settled for a dormitory with no blankets. I was relieved we would be arriving at Base Camp tomorrow, where we could eat, drink and sleep at the IMG camp without worry.

From Gorak Shep, just beneath the south face of Pumori, we set out to catch the sunrise at 5,545m high Kala Patthar ("Black Rock" in Hindi). The view we were rewarded with awed us into reverent silence.

A silver sunrise shimmered through the iron-grey of a sky dominated by Everest. Shuwei and I unfurled the 01 Raffles Scout Group flag and

Shuwei and I with our Raffles and 01 Scout emblem, on the
summit of Kala Patthar (5,545m).

took a photo holding the flag aloft, Everest looming over our shoulder.
We had come a long way together in years as well as distance.

As we made our way to EBC, we passed large numbers of trekkers,
Sherpas and caravans of heavily loaded yaks ambling along to the
melodious clonking of the bells they wore. We were all headed in the
same direction.

From a distance, the animal and human traffic looked like ants
on a snaking trail carrying their precious cargo towards their nest. It
almost felt like we were heading towards a carnival. Gayathri said she
half expected to see balloons, cotton candy and game stands at EBC.

She was not far off the mark.

EBC (5,300m) was dotted with tents of every colour, each one
marking a different trekking company. It sounds odd to describe a
campsite of motley tents as sophisticated, but EBC gave off an air of
civilisation that contrasted with the simplicity of the local hamlets.

The IMG campsite, where we stayed, was impressive with its copious dining tent, shower tent, makeshift toilets complete with toilet seat, communication tent with its satellite dishes and even an entertainment tent where we could watch movies. There was a sense of an international community gathering for a common purpose.

Shuwei left EBC to return to Singapore on the very day we arrived. It was an emotional farewell between old friends who honestly could not be sure they would see each other again. Some who made it even to the summit of Everest had not made it back.

Gayathri and I camped out at EBC for four nights. After being showerless for a week, the yellow bath tent was an oasis, a Himalayan "spa" of sorts — the rocks below the tent trapped the heat from the sun, ingeniously keeping the shower tent comfortably warm. Gayathri's romantic opinion of EBC showers, however, dipped drastically when the bucket ran out of water just after she had soaped up.

Doing her laundry (which meant a good scrub by hand) left her with clothes-shaped ice sculptures the next day. Thawing them out in her tent caused a mini flood.

On the fourth day at EBC, 14 April 2012, which happened to be the Tamil New Year, we joined the Sherpas in the puja ceremony for our IMG team.

Performed before any Himalayan climb at Base Camp, the puja blessing by a lama (holy man) is so essential to the Sherpas that to launch an expedition without it would have been unthinkable.

Food and drink offerings and all manner of climbing equipment — ice axes, boots, crampons, ropes — are leaned against the rocks to be blessed, as the lama chants prayers for a safe passage.

A pole with strings of flags (blue for the sky, white for air, red for fire, green for water, and yellow for earth) is hoisted up. As the wind snaps and swirls the flags inscribed with prayers and poems, the Sherpas believe the prayers are being read out to the gods. The higher the flags, the straighter the path of the prayers to the heavenlies.

To complete the ceremony, *tsampa*, a roasted flour of barley or wheat, is flung into the air three times (an auspicious number) as an offering, with a cry of *lakalu* (victory to the gods)!

I am Hindu by faith, yet I have always felt privileged to take part in this calming ceremony in the shadow of a mountain, shoulder to shoulder with the Sherpas who would be my teammates for the next two months.

To me, the puja is an expression of respect for the sacred mountain, an acknowledgement of forces beyond human control. When you are on the mountain, unable to predict its wild whims, you realise that whether or not you make it down alive is a decision that is not yours to make.

The puja completed, Gayathri and I trekked back to Gorak Shep together. Taking leave of her was one of the hardest farewells of my life. Much later, Gayathri told me that she cried all the way back to Phortse on the two-day walk, not knowing if she would ever see me again. God willing, we would reunite in Phortse in two months after Everest.

Gayathri would descend to Pheriche overnight and be back at Phortse the following day. She had a local porter accompanying her back to Phortse. Like many porters who wore the flimsiest of footwear, sometimes broken ones, he was wearing flip flops on his feet. When she attempted to ask him how he managed the trek to and from EBC in slippers, she realised that he spoke hardly any English, the one English word he knew being: *Okay.*

For two days they made their descent until they arrived at the top of Phortse, whereupon the porter turned to her and asked: "This Phortse?" which struck her as funny since he was her guide.

The day that Gayathri and I parted at the IMG campsite at Everest BC.

And so, on 17 April 2012, on the sixteenth day after Gayathri had arrived in Nepal, she walked into the Phortse healthpost, ready to begin practising rural medicine solo.

+ + +

The Sherpa people, as Gayathri discovered, were some of the warmest and homeliest she would ever meet.

With the climbing season in full swing, most of the young and middle-aged Sherpa males had left for expeditions, although they did occasionally pop by Phortse on their rest days to visit their family.

At the healthpost, Gayathri saw mainly children, women and lamas (monks) from around the region. With the weather warming up, patients were arriving with runny noses, coughs, sore throats and rashes.

While, during my time at the clinic, I had mainly treated the men for body aches and injuries from climbing or carrying heavy loads, Gayathri was busy treating upper respiratory tract infections, dyspepsia (indigestion) and replenishing the villagers' stock of "ninja gel" (diclofenac gel, an anti-inflammatory drug used to reduce cytokinesis that causes inflammation or pain).

Word had travelled that there was a "new foreign doctor" staying at the Namaste Lodge and, on some days, Gayathri would be awoken by a loud banging on her door – usually by porters in search of medicine. The local children were especially captivated by her and, on any given day, several curious small faces would be peeking into

The children of Phortse village.　　　　Gayathri with one of her young patients.

the clinic from the open door. The toddlers who came on the back of their mothers, wore little woollen beanies and tiny down jackets, looking like miniature mountaineers.

Gayathri had planned a two-week visit to the Khunde Hospital where she would help Dr Kami.

The outlying healthposts that radiate from Khunde Hospital function as polyclinics attended by health assistants seeing to simple consultations, health education and family planning. Cases of chronic illnesses such as hypertension or diabetes mellitus were still sent to Khunde Hospital for follow-up care.

The entire staff of the stone-walled, zinc-roofed Khunde Hospital consisted of Dr Kami and a fellow local doctor, a healthcare assistant, a lab technician, a midwife, a cook and a custodian. Simple blood tests, x-rays and basic surgical procedures, such as toilet and sutures, could be administered here. Major surgical cases were flown to Kathmandu on a helicopter, which for the locals could mean blowing a lifetime of savings.

On her very first day at Khunde Hospital, a somewhat alarmed Gayathri saw from afar that a patient who was writhing in pain was being carried to the hospital on a stretcher. The patient had been conveyed in this way, up hill and down dale, for a good two hours from a neighbouring village.

Our donated foldable stretcher from Singapore.

With a thrill, Gayathri saw that the stretcher was the one we had brought from Singapore. It was immensely satisfying to see it being put to good use. As foreign doctors, we knew our impact was temporary and limited; on the other hand, this stretcher and the medical apparatus from Singapore would be of help to the community long after we left for home.

The bad news for Gayathri was that she was the only doctor on duty at the hospital. And it was her first day!

Fortunately the hospital assistants sprang into action, taking the patient's blood pressure and admitting her to the inpatient ward on Gayathri's recommendation. The young woman turned out to have pyelonephritis (a urinary tract infection leading to infection of the kidneys). She eventually recovered well with intravenous antibiotics.

Gayathri was surprised, on another occasion, to see a man arrive with second-degree burns on his face caused by boiling water. In a big city hospital, he would have been rushed to a burns unit. But there was no such luxury in Khunde, and the only treatment that could be administered was using burns dressings to prevent infection and analgesia for pain relief.

The bonus for anyone hospitalised at Khunde Hospital was that the hospital windows framed a stunning view of the most dramatic peaks in the world. The spectacle alone was restorative.

+ + +

When Gayathri returned to Phortse, she had a pleasant surprise. The healthcare worker, Lhakpa Yangjee, had returned from her prolonged maternity leave in Kathmandu, where she had had an emergency caesarean section.

The result was a rosy, plump dumpling of a baby girl, Pasang Doma, who henceforth became something of a mascot at the village clinic.

When the days were sunny, Gayathri would usher everyone out of the clinic to an outdoor clearing with a priceless view of the surrounding peaks. With the men mostly away on expeditions, she took the opportunity to hold talks for the women on female health issues, antenatal care, potential complications during childbirth, postnatal care, contraception and childcare.

Gayathri conducting healthcare education sessions for the Phortse mothers.

Up to 50% of deliveries were still done at home by the husband and mother of the pregnant woman – home delivery was so common that the husband was even given a sterile set with which to cut the umbilical cord.

The good-natured local mothers told Gayathri that the way it usually went was: When the mother "pops", the father "catches". Even breech deliveries (where a foot presents itself before the head) often took place at home.

The turnout for the health education talks was unexpectedly good. Most of the village women showed up, many with rosy-cheeked babes and toddlers in tow, peering at the pictures in Gayathri's laptop, giggling shyly at posters of delivery positions, and gamely sharing their personal experiences.

Lhakpa helped to translate, making the women chortle when she used her own baby as a visual aid. It was an opportunity for them to socialise in the fresh air and sunshine in between household chores.

+ + +

After Phortse, Pangboche was next on Gayathri's itinerary.

She made a special friendship during her two weeks in Pangboche. The villagers of Phortse and Pangboche were closely related, with many an in-law hailing from one village or the other.

Jima, 65, was the owner of Gomba Lodge, the Pangboche guesthouse where Gayathri stayed.

From the pictures on the walls of the lodge, Gayathri had the impression that Jima's husband, Namkha Sherpa, had been well regarded in the community. He'd been a Himalayan Rescue Association medical assistant for over 20 years. Taking pride of place on the walls of the lodge were multiple certificates of appreciation and photos of happy times with friends and family members. Jima's life with her husband, with whom she had three children, appeared rich and colourful.

But he passed away a year ago and she now ran the lodge alone, accompanied by her youthful helper, Kanji.

With no other lodgers at the guesthouse, Gayathri ended up in the cosy kitchen with Jima and Kanji every night. They hardly spoke any English, while Gayathri didn't speak the Sherpa language. Yet the two Nepali women showed hospitality in ways that needed no words.

They shared their food with Gayathri, most often potato in various forms. In turn, Gayathri showed them photos of her parents on her laptop, eliciting an *"Aww, good people!"* from Jima.

That the three of them could not hold a full conversation had comical results, but the warmth and cheerfulness of Jima and Kanji were irresistible. In halting words, Jima told Gayathri that her husband had been "very smart" — he could speak both English and Japanese, while she couldn't even speak English. To which Gayathri laughingly replied that Jima's English was way better than her Nepalese.

The women learnt a great deal about each other, sharing their lives over *tsampa* tea and *dhal bat* despite not having a common language.

One evening, Jima produced a plastic bag filled with wires and a small laptop which someone had gifted her husband. When Gayathri got the laptop working, she discovered an array of pictures, documentaries, American dramas and cartoons already loaded.

Thus began the women's after-dinner "movie" ritual.

Discovering *Family Guy* in the laptop, Gayathri showed an episode to the Sherpa women — what could be more entertaining than a cartoon? Only it happened to be the episode where Meg stripped to her undergarments to seduce Bryan. The horrified look on the Nepali women's faces had Gayathri swearing never to play *Family Guy* again.

From then on, the "channel" of choice was BBC Planet documentaries. Kanji and Jima *ooh-ed* and *aah-ed* at the sights and

Gayathri with Jima from Gomba Lodge, Pangboche.

sounds of the jungles, oceans, snow, desert — all of which opened up new worlds to them. They watched at least two documentaries every night, inviting a different friend over each time, including the local monk, Lama Penju.

When Gayathri left Pangboche after two weeks, Jima had a gift for her — a *katar*, the traditional white scarf presented by the Sherpa people to convey respect and appreciation.

The parting was tearful. Gayathri had made her way to Pangboche alone, but thanks to Jima's warmth and simple kindness, she had never felt alone. It was the first time that the naturally garrulous Gayathri saw that affection needed no words.

+ + +

While Gayathri did not share the language of the locals, one thing she did share with them was their worry and prayers for loved ones who were on expeditions.

From the Namaste Lodge, where Gayathri stayed in Phortse, she would frequently see helicopters flying by. The sight of the yellow choppers struck fear, because they were often on rescue missions. Gayathri had witnessed a few rescues and was even involved in one when she helped to transport a patient from a helicopter to Khunde Hospital.

On 6 May, the Phortse villagers received news that three Sherpas had died so far in this 2012 Mt Everest expedition season. The first had premorbidities, possibly liver cirrhosis. The cause of death was presumed to be altitude sickness. The second fell. The third died recently in a Kathmandu hospital.

This third death hit close to home as the young man was from Phortse. While Gayathri was at the clinic, news came that a Phortse Sherpa was being rescued from Everest by helicopter to be transferred to the intensive care unit in a Kathmandu hospital.

Tension built up in the village throughout the day. Though she didn't know the Sherpa language enough to fully understand the anxious chatter, the distress of the villagers spoke volumes. A few hours later, she saw a helter skelter of people rushing by with the grim report that the man had passed away in Kathmandu.

A deep gloom settled over the village. Although Gayathri had never met the young man, she felt an overwhelming sorrow when she heard that he was between 30 and 40 years of age, and had two young children. She had, in fact, treated his four-year-old son at the clinic for a cough and runny nose.

With almost every Phortse home seeing a son, husband or father go off on expeditions every year, there was a baseline level of anxiety that hummed through the village during the climbing season.

While I was navigating Everest with IMG, the Sherpa family Gayathri stayed with had a son on the same team.

They, too, struck up a warm friendship with Gayathri. Every morning, Lhakpa, the owner of Namaste Lodge, accompanied Gayathri to the clinic. He became her translator and, as they saw patients together, he went to great lengths to fill her in on the patients' family background so that she could understand their complaints better and manage their cases accordingly.

Lhakpa's daughter worked in the library just in front of the clinic. At lunchtime, the young lady would meet up with Lhakpa and Gayathri and the three of them would walk back to the lodge together for lunch.

Gayathri became a family friend, and they made sure to warn her of weather changes if she planned to go on a trek, waved "hello" to her parents when she Skyped home, and had dinner with her in the evenings.

Their shared circumstance, waiting for a loved one to return safely from Everest, made Gayathri someone they could relate to.

Despite the language and cultural barrier, the Sherpas and the Singapore girl found themselves praying in one voice for our safe return.

CHAPTER 10

"The Khumbu is probably the most dangerous single place in the climbing world. You can just sit at base camp during the day and watch avalanches roar down right over the climbing route. It scares everyone."

Conrad Anker

On Everest, people don't just die. They vanish.

In 1924, British mountaineer George Mallory made his third attempt at summiting Everest with climbing partner Andrew "Sandy" Irvine, a 21-year-old Oxford undergraduate. On 8 June, they were spotted by teammate Noel Odell at 26,000 ft (7,010m) "moving expeditiously" toward the summit. It was the last time the pair was ever seen alive. It took 75 years before Mallory's body was discovered. Irvine vanished and was never found.

In 1974, the deputy mayor of Chamonix, Gerard Devouassoux led a team of 19 climbers up Everest's West Ridge. During the night, monsoons triggered an avalanche that bore down on the camp and buried Devouassoux and five Sherpas as they slept. Their bodies were never found. For the next five years climbers avoided the West Ridge.

In one of the worst accidents in the history of Everest, 16 Sherpas were killed in the notorious Khumbu Icefall in 2014 when an ice chunk the size of a 10-storey building sheared off the west shoulder of the mountain, triggering a massive avalanche. The Sherpas were swept into the jaws of yawning crevasses, or buried under tons of snow that turned to concrete when it settled. A huge rescue operation followed. Three of the bodies were never found.

So when I produced a piece of paper with the heading: *Body Disposal Election Form*, and asked my dad, "*Appa*, what is your preference?", he was aghast.

The form served to indicate which option I pre-chose in the event that I die on expedition: *A) Left on mountain, B) Cremation, or C) Repatriation.*

There were caveats:

"If you die on the mountain, your body will be put in a crevasse or buried in a respectful manner by your Expedition team members, unless you specify otherwise, and it is feasible to do otherwise at the discretion of the Expedition Leader.

"If you die down low, it might be possible to get your body down where it could be cremated by Buddhist monks from the local monastery. This would cost well in excess of several thousand dollars, including the cost of recovery labor, transport, body preparation, wood, and appropriate donations to the local monastery.

"If you die down low, it might be possible to get your body down for repatriation. If you elect repatriation of the body, it would be via Kathmandu and would be quite complicated and expensive (tens of thousands of dollars, probably) and might take several weeks."

(For the record, my parents picked 'C', a choice more emotional than practical, if you ask me.)

Machismo — of which the sport of extreme climbing has no lack — dictates that the entire Everest ordeal is downplayed.

"Everest is basically hiking up a ski slope. But with a 2,000-pound elephant on your chest and head," said legendary American alpinist Conrad Anker.

But while adventure technology has produced mountaineering gear that has improved performance, in the process doubling the summit success rate in the past 30 years, roughly 1 in 100 people who attempt Everest still die trying.

Mountaineers are tragically familiar with death and grief. Conrad Anker himself lost some of the people he was closest to to the mountains, including his mentor and his best friend.

As evidence of the extreme sport's capriciousness, 2018 saw a record 800 successful Everest summits from both sides of the mountain, a result of an unprecedented weather window. Records were set, including Kami Rita Sherpa who, at age 48, chalked up the most Everest summits when he peaked for the 22nd time. Lhakpa Sherpa, 44, broke her own female record with her ninth summit. And in an incredible feat of both physicality and spirit, 70-year-old Xia Boyu, a double amputee from China, summited after he won an appeal to the Nepal Supreme Court to overturn a ban against double amputees climbing Nepal's mountains.

But the very next year, 2019, would go down in history for an appalling 11 Everest deaths in one of the deadliest years on the mountain. They died of the usual suspects — falls, avalanches, hypothermia, storms, pulmonary edema, stroke — under a range of circumstances that included inclement weather, inexperience and even politics.

So every mountaineer will tell you: When you gun for an 8,000m peak, you have to be prepared to not return.

This alone gives poignancy and purchase to every Everest journey.

+ + +

21 April: Lobuche

We spend our whole lives trying to achieve comfort — a kind of middling point, with "perfect" being not too hot, not too cold, not too hungry, not too full, not too stressed, not too free — that it comes as an immense shock to the system when you find yourself stretched to the very perimetre of harsh extremes.

Everest would show me exactly what that felt like.

Lobuche was to be our first acclimatisation peak, leading up to Everest. From Lobuche peak (6,119m), Mt Everest, Pumori, Ama Dablam and Lhotse could be seen rising as imposing turrets on fortresses of rock and ice.

There were two expedition companies at Lobuche Base Camp at the time: One was characterised by the green tents of Russell Brice's Himalayan Experience team. On the other side of Awi Peak were the yellow tents of our company, IMG.

The first time I trekked with my teammates was when we took a long detour to the other side of Lobuche to reach our campsite. We quick marched without rest for four hours from EBC to Lobuche Base Camp.

My teammates were *fast*.

I had hoped that my one-month acclimatisation in Phortse would get me up to speed, but these fellows were of a different calibre.

The IMG climbers were split into three groups: The hybrid team, the classic team, and the Lhotse/Lobuche climbers who were banded together with EBC trekkers.

I was part of the 15-member classic team, overseen by two American guides, with a personal Sherpa attached to each climber for the duration of the expedition. The hybrid team would also have one Sherpa attached to each climber, and on top of that, have the luxury of one American guide overseeing every four climbers.

With this many climbers and trekkers, we had to be split into three groups, flown into Lukla at staggered intervals to avoid overcrowding at the lodges.

The international clients from the IMG classic team on the Everest Spring 2012 expedition.

I was put in the second group, together with Olga and Vadim, an amiable Latvian couple; Amin, an uber fit American of Middle Eastern origin; Heidi, a German ultra marathoner and mother who had also been on my Cho Oyu expedition; Brad, a Colorado native, who had a neverending supply of good-humoured quips; and Lars, a cool Norwegian man. We were quite the United Nations.

Dawa Finjhok Sherpa, a wiry young man who only came up to my shoulder, was introduced to me as my personal Sherpa. At just 24 years of age, Dawa had already summited Everest twice and Kanchenjunga once.

Kanchenjunga (8,586m), the world's third highest mountain, was notoriously bruising, trailing only behind Annapurna and K2 in difficulty level. Ang Jangbu, who had decades of experience pairing Sherpas up with clients, figured we would get along as we were of a similar age — Dawa was 24 to my 27. A good pairing was imperative. In the weeks to come, our lives would be in each other's hands.

There was one teammate I didn't care for. He was one of the guides on his first Everest expedition — a loud fellow whose favourite topic of conversation was himself. We had first met in a Namche lodge, when I was spending some final moments with my friends Shuwei and Gayathri before joining the climbing group. I was feeling a little under the weather that day, coughing and sneezing. When I spotted the group that was to be my Everest team for the next two months, I naturally went over to introduce myself.

"Don't shake my hand," the guide immediately retorted. "That's how people get sick. When I saw you sitting in the corner coughing away, I was thinking: *Who is this guy who's going to spread his germs to the rest?* If I had known you were in my group, I would have told you to leave."

I was taken aback by his brusqueness. This was my guide? In the next two months, I was to discover that he had a knack for offending his teammates.

+ + +

Our team's first acclimatisation climb took us to the east peak of Lobuche (6,119m). The rocky triangle of its East face rose over the mottled moraine skirt of the Khumbu Glacier.

Our time at Lobuche High Camp was a short one. By 2:45am, we were up and preparing to make for the Lobuche summit. The route was cold and pitch black until the sun made a timid appearance at 5am, gradually revealing the vertical vastness of the mountain. Our crampons came on at 4am while it was still dark and, from there on, it was jummaring up the fixed lines all the way to the top.

It took me 5 hours to reach the Lobuche summit. The fastest members in my team made it up in less than 4 hours.

While making my dogged way up, I crossed paths with a female climber. I didn't know who she was then, but when you are straining towards a 6,000m peak and you pass a woman strutting down without breaking a sweat and without any safety lines, you can't help but do a double-take. As she passed me by, she threw some advice over her shoulder: "Take smaller steps. It'll save you energy."

It was only later that Dawa told me with reverence that this was Gerlinde Kaltenbrunner, the Austrian mountaineer listed in the Britannica Encyclopedia as one of the first women to climb all 14 of the world's 8,000ers, and the first woman to do so without the use of supplemental oxygen. This included a daring ascent on the notorious north face of K2.

If I hadn't already been inspired by watching her stroll down a 6,000m mountain, I was inspired now.

Incidentally, I met two more familiar faces on the way up — my Aconcagua teammate, Khoo Swee Chiow, and Jamling Bhote. They were also headed for the Lobuche peak.

After weeks spent with strangers, it was heartening to see their grinning faces. They might have felt the same way, because we all stopped in our tracks and had a quick conversation at 5,900m (much to the annoyance of the climbers who were trying to pass us). This exchange among friends, brief as it was, gave me the emotional fuel to continue upwards with a lighter step.

The air was clear and cold as diamonds as we summited Lobuche. The view we were rewarded with glittered far into the horizon. We could see the pointed crests of nearly all the mountains of the Khumbu valley except Cho Oyu which was blocked by the true summit of Lobuche. Even though this was just an acclimatisation climb, summiting amongst these legendary peaks felt like an accomplishment in itself.

From here we could see Everest's jet stream frothing down from her summit.

Chomolungma — a giant among giants.

How could I possibly stand at that pinnacle in a few weeks? The end seemed impossible, the journey immense.

It was an effort to pull my mind back to the present, to focus on putting one foot in front of the other and remember that even the greatest feat is paved with individual steps. Even a small stumble forward counted.

When we finally got back to the EBC, the entire team was keyed up. Tomorrow we would start making our rotation up to C1 and C2 on Everest.

With Dawa Finjhok on the summit of Lobuche East (6,119m), the Everest Lhotse complex rises in the background.

There was just one thing that stood between us and the upper camps: The ominous Khumbu Icefall.

+ + +

It was the legendary alpinist and veteran leader of the North Face climbing team, Conrad Anker, who said in an interview with *Outside*

Magazine that "the Khumbu is probably the most dangerous single place in the climbing world. You can just sit at base camp during the day and watch avalanches roar down right over the climbing route. It scares everyone."

Confronting Everest climbers almost from the start, Khumbu Icefall is a dramatic stretch of broken ice, varying in size from boulders to buildings, that sits at the head of the Khumbu Glacier and the foot of the Western Cwm.

American Alan Arnette, who has made four expeditions to Everest and was described by *Outside Magazine* as "one of the world's most respected chroniclers of Everest", described Khumbu this way: "As with all glaciers, the Khumbu moves as much as 1 metre a day in the center while barely moving at the edges due to friction against rock walls. The top of the glacier moves faster than the bottom due to friction against the earth. It is this dynamic of fast and slow moving sections plus the precipitous drop that create the deep crevasses, some over 45m deep and towering ice seracs over 9m high."

This was the terrifying physics of what we were forced to cross in order to get up to the higher camps.

Within a single expedition, this initially well placed ladder has moved so much that it is now suspended in mid air, due to the constantly moving ice.

From 1953 to 2016 alone, there were 44 fatalities in the 4km-long Icefall, 14% of whom fell into crevasses while crossing, 21% from parts of the Icefall collapsing, and 66% from avalanches, reported Arnette from data gathered from the Himalayan Database.

In 2014, one of the most tragic days in Everest history, 16 Sherpas were swept to their deaths by an avalanche triggered by the collapse of a hanging serac while ferrying loads to the higher camps.

The prospect of avalanches and the collapse of giant seracs added to the dangerous dynamic.

In response to the unstable ice, some elite local guides are appointed as Ice Doctors each season. Their job: To secure a safe route through the criss-crossing crevasses and precarious seracs of the Khumbu Icefall.

They are well named. Like any doctor, they examine the subject, diagnose its condition and, in some cases, administer restorative treatment. In real terms, this means waking up at 2am before the rest of the climbers to check the ladders over the crevasses, and to pick the most secure route through the season's avalanche debris and unstable snow. No summit would even be possible without the Ice Doctors.

I had first seen the Khumbu Icefall from base camp in 2009 when the NUS MIR 8 team made our Island Peak and EBC expedition. It was surreal to be stepping on the Icefall now.

This was just a dry run — the team's plan was to walk into the Icefall for about two hours before turning back, taking on four ladders (out of the total 21) by way of practice.

Sounded simple enough, but the Icefall proved to be more challenging than I'd expected. From afar it appeared relatively flat, but there were multiple steep sections requiring fixed lines and jummaring.

Then there were the ladders. Teetering in boots and crampons on the rungs of two or three lightweight aluminum ladders lashed together and placed across the jaws of plunging crevasses was one of the most harrowing experiences of my life.

It didn't help that this was my first time on the ladders. Since I had arrived later than the rest of my team, I had missed out on the critical ladder practice at Base Camp. Dawa's patient efforts to ensure my safety were reassuring. But the tightrope act was tricky, and the tinkle of crampons on the aluminium ladders was an unnerving reminder of just how flimsy the contraption was.

Navigating the complex system of ladders and crevasses in the Khumbu Ice Falls.

The guide ropes I was clipped to shook from my nervous hands. Dawa, on the other hand, astonished me by taking the rungs two at a time, despite his legs being far shorter than mine.

At one point, he was pointing my video camera into the distance. "What are you recording?" I was curious. It turned out that, as I was on one ladder, a climber on another ladder had overbalanced and tumbled into a crevasse. He was dangling by the safety ropes and a frantic rescue operation was taking place.

We finished our dry run without mishap. A few days later, we would graduate to the real deal, crossing the 21 ladders that stood between us and C1.

+ + +

29 April: Rotations to Everest Camp 2

The palpable danger in the Icefall field proved to be more than anyone on the team had expected.

Sleeping in my tent each night, I would be woken up by the rumble of avalanches around us. The hybrid team had already set off and had made it to C2.

As we proceeded deeper into the Icefall, navigating in pitch darkness, the pace started picking up.

The dead of night was the best time to cross the Icefall. In the day, sunlight melted the ice, rendering it unstable. Frigid night temperatures kept the ice solid, maximising our chances of making it through the Icefall with less likelihood of a serac breaking off and triggering an avalanche. But it was a balancing act between moving carefully and moving quickly. The average climber took four to six hours to traverse the Icefall — there was no way to predict the shifting dynamics of the glacier churning in minute degrees beneath the glassy surface.

The Sherpas, who knew well the dangers of the Icefall, turned jittery as they hurried us along the dangerous segments where seracs the size of houses hung over our route. It was only a matter of time before these seracs collapsed, and we could only pray that it would not happen while we were walking underneath.

After the aptly named "popcorn field" of scattered ice blocks was the "football field", a relatively flat section of ice where we felt safe enough to pause for a break.

News had reached us that part of the seracs on Lho La peak had collapsed over the Icefall, wiping out the fixed lines on a segment spanning more than 50 vertical metres. We were to climb over the collapsed ice without any fixed lines.

Once a serac collapses, the surrounding area becomes unstable and prone to further collapses. I could hear Dawa muttering Tibetan Buddhist prayers as he fixed my safety line onto his harness. Roped together, we hurried through the freshly fallen tumble of ice, navigating the naked segment of unfixed lines as fast as we could. Looking up, we could see the half collapsed Lho La ice seracs perched precariously, ready to collapse once more.

Glancing back, I could see the other climbers trailing along for 200m, gingerly making their way across the avalanche area.

Breathlessly trying to keep up with Dawa, I was relieved to pass the seracs. Traffic was sometimes a concern when teams going up and down the Khumbu jammed up against each other in narrow sections.

Ladder crossings were vertical as well as horizontal. Up and down glacial faces and through narrow segments of ice we climbed and jummared, our Sherpas drilling into us to: 1) Always be clipped into the fixed ropes, even on ladders, 2) don't linger in one spot, 3) move as fast as you possibly can.

Some of the ladders had broken rungs, hardly inspiring confidence.

There was one particularly harrowing ladder segment. Dawa had repeatedly pointed this out as being the spot of "the accident".

Just two days ago, a Sherpa had plunged into the crevasse when he had failed to clip in his safety line. It was a fatal mistake. His body had to be long roped on a helicopter and flown back to his village down the Khumbu valley.

When I peered over to the far end of the crevasse where the top of my ladder rested, I could see blood splotches on the ice and his backpack lodged deep in the crevasse.

The Go-Pro mounted on my helmet — sponsored by Cerebos — captured this ladder crossing, my audible breathlessness a result of both low oxygen levels and the terror of stepping out over the black chasm. I was betting my life on two thin ropes in mid air that I was clipped to, and a flimsy ladder perched on a shifting glacier at one end and a thin tower of blue ice on the other.

It took me by surprise that, as a doctor who had encountered multiple deaths in a hospital setting, the death of a climber could shake me so. But this felt different. It felt personal. The false sense of control in a hospital, surrounded by medical technology, was stripped away here on Nature's equalising field.

It was disconcerting.

The cold was also a creature I had underestimated.

Temperatures were far below zero every night. Everything froze — water bottles, contact lens solution, pee inside the pee bottle. Even the water in our water bottles zipped inside our jackets. My fingers ached with the constant cold. I had anticipated that frost bite would be a concern during summit day, but I was unprepared for frostbite so early in the climb.

As soon as we arrived at C1, I stuck my hands as close as I could to the stove set up by the Sherpas in the kitchen tent.

It had taken me five hours from EBC to C1. Inside, I silently worried about how I was going to manage further up the mountain when I was already struggling down in the low camps. My only consolation was that there was one more acclimatisation cycle.

We stayed in C1 for two nights. The view from my tent was of the lofty Lhotse face and the entire stretch of the Western Cwm. A 1½-hour acclimatisation walk towards C2 (6,400m) on the second day rewarded us with our first glimpse of the summit of Everest from the Western Cwm.

The slope here was gentle, but the altitude still made the going frustratingly slow. The faces of Nuptse and Lhotse and the western shoulder of Everest reflected the sunlight into the Western Cwm, heating the area with a microwave oven effect.

+ + +

The second cycle got us to C1 and, after 3½ hours, to C2. Spread out under massive frozen seracs, C2 was sometimes dubbed the Advanced Base Camp of the south side.

With almost as many tents as EBC, C2 turned out to be such a sprawling area that it took us 40 minutes just to get through the camp to the IMG tents near the top.

Seeing the Lhotse face up close was more intimidating than ever. It was 1½ vertical kilometers of solid ice, at a 60° angle, standing sentinel between C2 and the South Col (C4). That was the face we had to scale on our next rotation. If a chunk of ice broke off this face and started rolling down towards us at speed, we would be shoved off the mountain to our death.

The rope team started fixing the lines on the Lhotse face that same day. Even this experienced team reported the route as tough going.

That evening, the IMG teams at C2 gathered for dinner in a large tent set up by the Sherpas who dished up sizzling chicken on a hot plate and spaghetti bolognese, trying to perk up our waning appetites. What a luxury to perch on camp chairs in the rocky ground and sit at a table together, a bunch of Michelin men in our layers of down clothing, boots and head gear.

Near the dining tent, I could see dozens of oxygen cylinders waiting to be hauled up to the higher camps. It was precious cargo that could mean the difference between life and death.

+ + +

Conrad Anker told *Outside* magazine: "I'm always amped. Total ADHD. But the heart is the one muscle that can't fail. So, it's about realising where you are in life and knowing your limits."

I second that. As a medical doctor I have seen the difference that even small precautions make.

I had started taking Aspirin from about a month ago. Stroke, deep vein thrombosis and central retinal vein obstruction were some of the common blood disorders at high altitude. The over-production of red blood cells (polycythemia) as a result of the low-oxygen environment (hypoxia), and dehydration during exertion, meant there was a greater chance of blood stasis and clotting. The danger was when these clots dislodged from the blood vessels and travel to different parts of the body.

Aspirin thins the blood and is commonly taken by patients of previous strokes and heart disease. These blood disorders were not uncommon here and a good proportion of climbers and Sherpas, including famed ones, have suffered strokes.

While there is no conclusive scientific evidence of Aspirin working, most mountaineers don't take the chance.

I also took Omeprazole to prevent gastric stress ulcers, a condition which had left some of my friends with melena (black, tarry stools).

There was one other benefit from taking Aspirin. On such a long expedition, trekking day after cold day, it was easy to lose track of time and the day of the week. The back of Aspirin packets were conveniently printed with the days of the week, and every morning when I popped a pill from the packet, I kept track of the days. The passage of time spoke of encouraging progress.

+ + +

In the multiple rotations up and down during acclimatisation climbs, I always found the descent more dangerous than the ascent.

It is a fact backed up by statistics. Most fatalities on mountains occur during descent. It might be the sheer exhaustion that prompts a drop in concentration.

Naturally every iota of energy is used to get to the summit, and psychologically as well as physically, it is easy to drift off afterward. A single lapse of judgement is all it takes for a fatal misstep.

By this time, I knew what profound exhaustion felt like. We were no higher than C2, but already I had little to give physically after trying to keep up with Dawa. He was moving down the Icefall at a rapid pace to avoid lagging at the danger points.

On an early morning descent, in an unfocused instant, my crampons caught on each other and I tripped, tumbling forward. The tiny clip attached to the safety line gave a jerk and arrested my fall.

That jolted me from my stupor.

The moment we arrived back at BC, a long rumble rolled down the mountain. We would later discover that a huge avalanche had occurred between C1 and C2. One of the giant seracs hanging off Nuptse had broken off and rolled down into the valley, sending a huge gust of wind and ice onto the floor of the Western Cwm.

A Sherpa from another team was swept into a crevasse and broke a few of his ribs and vertebrae. He had to be heli-evacuated back to Kathmandu for treatment. The avalanche took out a few camps in C1. But IMG's climbers at C1 and the Western Cwm were unharmed.

We had one more rotation on the Icefall before the summit push.

Everest, Lhotse, Nuptse and the Khumbu glacier as seen from the high camp of Pumori during one of our acclimatisation hikes.

Meanwhile, we would stay at Base Camp, gathering energy and waiting for the high altitude jet stream winds to shift to the south of Everest before heading back out on our second rotation to C3.

It felt good to be back resting in the relatively warmer conditions of EBC, with its savoury, cooked meals. Already my mind was making a list of the hawker food I would make a beeline for when I arrived home.

If I arrived home.

+ + +

14 May: Rotations complete

If I thought I knew what to anticipate by now, I was wrong. The C3 rotation proved to be more exacting than I'd expected.

The original route was abruptly altered by a heavy rockfall that had injured eight climbers. The new route saw us veering to the right of the Lhotse face, picking our way on a snow ramp that zigzagged its way up to a vertical ice face. IMG's plan for this second rotation had been for us to spend a night at C3 before returning to C2. But on the day we left for C3, the winds accelerated to 100km/h, pushing us back just before the ice face, about a quarter way up to C3.

Exhausted from battling the winds and being pelted by snow, we collapsed in our C2 tents. We would attempt the route again the next day.

Miraculously, the weather held the next day and, this time, we managed to reach the lower C3. Even though we didn't spend the night at C3, the 7,100m point was the highest elevation I had ever reached.

Our acclimatisation was now complete. The next time we struck out, it would be all the way to the summit.

+ + +

We had a few rest days before the final push and, like many of the IMG climbers who chose to spend their time down in the lower Khumbu valley where the air was thicker with oxygen, I headed for the village of Pangboche.

Gayathri and I had an emotional reunion here. There was a great feeling of wellbeing as I rested and listened to her recount her past weeks at Phortse and Khunde Hospital. Gayathri's chatter felt like a return to a world both familiar and distant.

She had not only run clinics, she had also been conducting mass talks on women and children's healthcare, much to the delight of the villagers who seized the opportunity to turn the meetings into social occasions.

For five days, we slept till noon, took leisurely walks, watched movies and went back to sleep. On one of those days we walked to the village of Tengboche, where scores of climbers visited the famous Lama

Receiving blessings from the late Lama Geshe in Pangboche during my rest cycle.

Geshe for blessings before their expeditions. Here on Everest, so close to the heavens, spirituality was a significant part of life.

It was not easy saying goodbye after five days of bliss. But the time had come to gun for the summit of Everest.

+ + +

Everest is not just a physical feat. The psychological and emotional challenge takes it toll too.

I was about to reach C1 during my second rotation when I heard over the walkie-talkie that a climber was calling it quits.

He'd seen an avalanche in the Khumbu Icefalls and the sight had stunned him. The crossfit fanatic was in good physical shape and he'd heard that Everest was an easy commercial enterprise. He had totally underestimated the real dangers that still lurked on Everest. A deep-seated misgiving convinced him it was time to head home and propose to his waiting fiance. I never saw him again.

When we returned to BC, another climber announced he was turning back. Amin, the American plastic surgeon, was on a different rotation than I was and had been at C1 when he'd witnessed the devastation wrought by the avalanche whose roar we had heard in BC.

He told the team: "I have been very lucky so far. I have seen what I had only read about in books and in documentaries my whole life. That is already a gift. My ego wants me to reach the summit, but I know I've got more to lose by doing so. I know what it is like to grow up without a father and I don't want the same thing to happen to my five-month-old child. For me, this is it."

The thought of my worried family back home was weighing on me too. I was drained mentally, physically and emotionally.

It was not the first time I questioned being here, and it wouldn't be the last. To be here meant we were in the best physical condition of our lives. Yet each of us was vulnerable in unseen ways. The cracks were forming at the edges of our psyche.

At that moment, staying the course was a hard decision.

Yet I respected Amin's decision to turn back because of his commitment to his personal priorities. An Everest expedition requires such an incredible amount of investment and sacrifice, that at some point it seems like you have passed the point of no return. There are some who have died for this conviction.

They could not turn back.

There were more surprises to come. IMG and Himalayan Experience (Himex) were the biggest companies on Everest at that point, each with about 40 clients. In a shock move, Russell Brice, who headed Himax, announced that his whole company was pulling out of the expedition this season. We didn't hear from Brice himself, but the speculation was that he had pulled out due to the bad weather this season which had left the Icefall in a precarious state. I didn't envy him the task of breaking the news to his 40 clients.

Yet his caution was not without reason. To date, there had already been four deaths on Everest this season. One Sherpa had plunged to his death while crossing a ladder over a crevasse in the Khumbu Icefall, another Sherpa had died from AMS before his expedition had even begun. An Indian climber had suffered a massive stroke. And another Sherpa had had a stroke that had caused him to fall into a crevasse between C1 and C2.

News reached us of other injuries that called for evacuation. In our tents, sleep was constantly interrupted by two sounds: the *whoosh* and rumble of frequent avalanches around Base Camp, and the *whop-whop-whop* of helicopters flying in for emergency evacuations.

In our own IMG team, five climbers had already left the expedition — some from dangerous medical conditions later diagnosed in Kathmandu as high-altitude pulmonary edema or deep vein thrombosis, and some because they were convinced that the bad weather made summiting unlikely this year.

A big team meeting was called in our IMG camp. The leaders wanted to check in on us, find out what was going through our minds and if the rest of us wanted to carry on. Himex was a large and experienced outfitter and their pulling out left us shaken and unsure if it was safe to go on. But collectively, we made a decision: We would carry on.

The fixed lines had only been established up to the South Col so far. The ill weather hampered any attempts at fixing the lines all the way to the summit. The Sherpas were kept busy ferrying loads up to the South Col, stashing food and oxygen there to wait for the right time to transport them further up Everest.

My expected summit day of 15 May was now pushed back to the third week of May.

Would there be a good window of weather to get the ropes fixed to the summit? Would it even be possible to summit? Questions were swirling around my exhausted mind. We were headed to Base Camp today to rest and wait for the magic weather window of clear skies and low winds to appear, and when it did, I had to trust that all my training would be enough to push me to the summit.

And come back down again.

+ + +

19 May: Base Camp

The mood was quietly jubilant at Base Camp.

The fixed lines had finally been laid all the way to the summit and IMG had our first summiteers — our rope-laying Sherpas! The harsh weather had severely delayed the rope laying. Now the teams could finally push on all the way up.

IMG's hybrid team, along with almost 250 climbers from various companies, had positioned themselves strategically at the higher camps, ready to push off for the summit during the narrow weather window on the 19th and 20th. Excitedly, we heard of some of the first summits of the season.

The plan was that the IMG classic team, including myself, would wait for the second weather window due to open up on the 25th. I was to leave on the 21st for my summit push.

The mood at camp was expectant as we waited for departure day.

Apart from a brief period when I had a bout of vomiting — which worried my teammates as it was just a few days from our summit push — I was feeling well acclimatised, with no headaches and no difficulty sleeping. Did I mention I love my sleep? When the sun went down at 6pm, I nipped straight into my sleeping bag after dinner and would sleep till the banging of the pots and pans from the kitchen tent woke me up for breakfast the next morning.

Base Camp life had its little quirks and perks. An expedition is not just full-on climbing. If it were, I doubt many of us would have survived till the end. There were rest days at camp too — and, after the exertion of climbing days, the more mundane camp life was, the better.

Base Camp life was pretty much like an extreme camping trip with a bunch of strangers of all personality types. It was amusing to catch different accents and try to guess where everyone hailed from.

Despite the limited facilities and supplies, the ingenious camp cooks managed to plate up fries, corn, kidney beans, *chapatti*, coleslaw, chicken steaks, noodles and Nepali *momo*. I even had *sushi* once, don't ask me how the kitchen staff managed that. A cacophonous gong beckoned us to the dining tent at mealtimes (8am, noon and 6pm). Lunch and dinner were eaten communally at long tables. When food and drink flowed, the camaraderie flowed too.

Going from efficient, high-rise Singapore to a colony of makeshift tents took some getting used to. On days we didn't have short treks, oxygen clinics, food packing sessions or medical talks, it was common to see climbers enjoying the sun on a camp chair, book in one hand and iPod in the other. Some tents would be colourfully draped with laundry — sleeping bags or down jackets being given a good airing.

We had personal tents to sleep in, but the life of the camp was really found in the communal tents. The climbers customarily hung out in the dining tent which, while we were far from home, was a convivial substitute for our family kitchen.

Then there was the capacious kitchen tent, where all the food preparation by the camp cooks happened. This was often a busy, merry place piled with great aluminium cooking pots, towers of egg cartons, sacks of condiments, baskets of potatoes and crates of rice and flour, where the Sherpas relaxed and congregated. It was in this homey tent that I was often found, hanging out with the easy-going Sherpas.

The large, cylindrical medical tent was efficiently run by Dr Luanne Freer, who basically set up an Everest ER unit in response to the number of mortalities and casualties on Everest. She and local doctor, Dr Ashish, were members of the Himalayan Rescue Association (HRA) team, a voluntary non-profit organisation set up in 1973 to provide emergency support to villagers and trekkers at high altitude via emergency health posts at Pheriche, Everest Base Camp and Manang.

On our earlier trip to Base Camp together, Gayathri and I had some long chats with them about the specifics of mountain medicine. They inspired me so much, in fact, that I returned six years later to take the qualifications for the DiMM (Diploma in Mountain Medicine), the only accredited mountain, wilderness and rescue medicine course in the world. I hoped that one day I could return as an HRA volunteer.

The communication tent, where we sent and received emails and charged our mobile devices, was our one link to home and civilisation, which made it the second most important tent after the kitchen tent. After lunch, this tent, run on solar power and a generator, would turn into a camp cinema, with movies playing on laptops, iPads and iPhones. My prodigious stash of pirated videos earned me the moniker Pirate King.

Our oxygen clinic, where we familiarised ourselves with using the oxygen cylinder and tried out our full summit gear, was also held here in the comms tent.

The cosy IMG kitchen tent with our head cook, Kaji (right).

At the Everest ER tent in 2012 with (left to right) Dr Luanne Freer, Gayathri, myself and Dr Ashish.

The insulated sitting toilet seat at Everest BC.

The IMG campsite on Everest BC.

The outdoor toilets, set a distance from the tents, featured toilet seats perched on carefully constructed platforms of glacial rock and ice. At EBC they were in covered tents. At other mountain camps, they might be partitioned for males on one side and females on the other. Some were roofless, so if you were tall, let's just say you got too much information about the next person when you stood up.

Water for daily use was heated creatively by manually filling a barrel at the top of a rocky incline where it could get warmed by the sun. Gravity got the water down to us via a pipe, where it was further heated with the help of a propane gas tank. That was the water we used for laundry, washing, shaving and showers.

Laundry was a pain, done by hand in a tin basin. More often than not, the clothes froze over before they could be dried by the sun.

Speaking of laundry, if you're wondering what we wore to keep from freezing in sub-zero temperatures, this was a typical mountaineer's gear: Thermal underwear, dri-fit base layer, fleece, down suit, goggles/sunglasses, beanie, balaclava, base layer gloves, mittens, all of which weighed in at about 8kg. On a climb, add to that a headlamp, backpack, boots, ice axe, harness with jumar and caribinars, crampons, helmet and oxygen cylinder. Lugging about 20kg up the mountain on top of our body weight was par for the course.

You can imagine what a complicated production it was just to go to the toilet.

The shower tents were always a welcome sight — at first. Once I was happily lathered in soap when the water in the tank completely ran out. Only after 10 minutes of yelling in the withering cold did someone trot over to fill up the tank again. The luxury of a "hot water" shower was courtesy of the propane gas cylinder used both for cooking and heating water. I say "hot water" because it was more like hot-icecold-hot-icecold as the gas sputtered — it was not unusual to hear yelping and cursing coming from the shower tents. After a few of these schizophrenic showers, that tent lost its appeal.

But once we left Base Camp to start climbing, even those temperamental weekly showers were missed. One of the best moments after any expedition is that first shower in a civilised guest house after subsisting on wet wipes for one to two months on the mountain. After shaving and sloughing off all the sunburnt patches on your face, you take a shower so hot and so long that steam radiates from your body as you walk around.

To our surprise, one day at Base Camp, in strolled a celebrity in the mountaineering community: Conrad Anker. Described by National Geographic as someone "who has been pushing the cutting edge of alpinism for the past three decades", Anker had summited Everest without supplemental oxygen as a member of a National Geographic expedition celebrating the 50th anniversary of the first American ascent.

The veteran North Face alpinist was here to lead a team up Everest's West Ridge, a route seldom visited. Hearing this legend talk about his work to raise funds for the Khumbu Climbing Centre for Sherpas was an unexpected highlight.

In the communication tent on 19 May, I typed out my last blog post before my summit push. Before each cycle I tried to keep sponsors, friends and family updated. If I was lucky, I'd also manage to patch through a quick call to Gayathri, after which she would wait anxiously for about a week until my next communication.

Being in the Khumbu Valley, and living among many families who also had loved ones on expeditions, Gayathri often received firsthand news quicker than I could convey — some of which (accidents, mishaps, weather changes) inspired more anxiety than peace. She was the closest person to home I had here, and just hearing her voice stirred a jumble of emotions within.

Everyone on the team was getting twitchy and impatient to get going. It had been too long since we had seen home. If all went well, summit day would dawn on either 25 or 26 May.

What had started out as an arbitrary, almost ridiculous, dream in 2008 after taking on Kilimanjaro, was now moments away from being realised after four arduous years in the planning. Gratitude washed over me for family, friends and sponsors for believing in the dream of a random doctor who had the slimmest of mountaineering pedigrees.

Whether I summited, or I didn't, this remarkable journey had already been a tremendous gift to a Yishun boy from the Little Red Dot.

"See you guys on the other side," I tapped out on my laptop, and closed it.

Whatever God willed, would be.

CHAPTER 11

*"I never wanted to be here. In the death zone,
surrounded by ghosts. But it's so strangely beautiful.
I can't make myself leave."*
Renan Ozturk

26 May: The roof of the world

At 2am, my alarm clock buzzed. This would be the last time I would be
rousing myself this early at Base Camp, I thought, my stomach jittery
from nerves.

We were finally on our last cycle, our summit push. Breakfast, gear
up, a farewell to everyone remaining at Base Camp … we had performed
this routine several times now on our acclimatisation rotations. But this
time, the mood was sombre. There would be summits and there would
be disappointments, we knew. What we didn't know was whether, at
the end, we would see everyone again.

As the sun started to rise, we could tell that the ice was less stable
than a few weeks ago, as the season drew to a close. Crossing the
Khumbu Icefall, multiple mini avalanches sent ice drifts spinning past.

In an alarming instant, part of the western shoulder gave a crack and
broke off right infront of us, sending us all ducking from the debris.
As we stilled ourselves for a few seconds, waiting for the wind to settle,

we knew this had been a small avalanche, but it still scared the wits out of us. Clearly this was our last chance at a summit attempt this season.

After a quick rest in C1, we were already on our way to C2 by the late morning. Whether from adrenaline or training, I clocked my fastest time yet to C2. But there was no time to celebrate — the route was sprawled with dangers we hadn't experienced on earlier rotations.

The rapidly warming weather saw ice from both sides of the Western Cwm starting to break off from Nuptse and Everest's western shoulder. This made the section prone to avalanches, with enormous blocks of ice and rock spewed all across the cwm. A few small avalanches gave us pause, and then a huge one which had us kneeling just to avoid the spindrift. Parts of the straightforward route had to be modified as gaping crevasses had formed very close to the main route. Would the way be even more precarious when we made our return a few days from now?

Just when I thought I had arrived at C2, I remembered that the IMG camp was the furthest and highest amongst the rest. I had another 40 minutes of trekking to do before I could stop. There was close to nothing left in my tank, after climbing for a full day straight through from BC to C2.

We made it to C2 in a daze. A quick and early breakfast the next morning and we were up the Lhotse face by sunrise via a new route, just to the right of the old one, in an attempt to avoid rockfall.

Clip, jumar, stab the ice with crampons, one foot, then the other. Step by slow step, limbs feeling as heavy as wet sand, we made it to the first tents of C3 by 2pm. Hold the relief. The IMG C3 camp was still 1½ hours away.

When we finally collapsed in our bright orange Eureka tents at C3, we were handed a gift: Bottled oxygen. Slapping on our O2 masks, we set the regulator at 0.5L/minute and finally settled down to rest.

My appetite was almost zero. Whatever our favourite foods were barely palatable at this altitude. Whatever we disliked made us puke just at the sight of it. So we brought whatever we thought we could keep down — chocolate, chips, *bak kwa* (BBQ pork). I was swallowing M&Ms with mashed potato, trying not to gag.

The view from the open flap of our tent was celestial. Islands of massive mountain peaks rose from an immense, roiling sea of clouds filling the Western Cwm. As far as the eye could see, there was sky, cloud and rock.

Looking down over the Western Cwm from C3 on the Lhotse face.

This was as much nutrition as I could swallow at C3: M&Ms with mashed potato mixed with warm water.

I understood now the reverence of the Sherpas for Everest. This was the view that Chomolungma, Goddess Mother of the World, has gazed upon from time immemorial.

With O2 pumping into my body, I could feel myself being recharged faster, especially when I took care to keep well hydrated, nourished and warm in my sleeping bag. But I had forgotten from my Cho Oyu days how uncomfortable sleeping with O2 was. As you breathe, moisture condenses inside the mask, with water pooling and dripping into your nose. Sometimes the valve freezes and you feel as though you are choking. It was hard to take a deep breath.

As I drifted in and out of sleep, my anticipation for the next day's climb was hard to contain.

We had an early 5am start as soon as the sun hit the Lhotse face. For the first time on this expedition, I was climbing with O2 — the difference was immense. Strength returned to my bones and had me moving faster than the days before.

An hour later, we were scrambling up the Yellow Band — a vertical 30m segment of rock so solid that our crampons sparked and screeched as we hauled ourselves up. I could see a queue of climbers behind us, waiting to clear the segment.

Crossing the Yellow Band after C3.

Past the Yellow Band was the Geneva Spur, where the trail branched for those headed for Lhotse. We carried on west towards the South Col. On and on, step by heavy step, and then, to my relief, I caught a glimpse of C4 perched amongst the ragged debris of old expeditions on the spectacular South Col (7,900m).

The climb from C3 to C4 had taken no more than 3½ hours.

C4 was a dry, isolated place with dead bodies hidden amongst the ruins of shredded tents, plastic and used oxygen (O2) tanks from 60 years of past expeditions.

After a month-and-a-half of pain and endurance, the glimpse of our finish line squeezed hope into my heart. The end seemed so near, just possible by wringing out one last bit of energy. But when we arrived at C4, my resolve plummeted.

A massive rock loomed in front of our eyes. Through the fog of my brain I despaired of making it up that one vertical kilometre snaking up to the sky. I had nothing left to give.

The despair was overwhelming. Self-doubt washed over me-

Collapsing into the tent, I was too spent to even react to the rantings of the unpleasant guide who happened to be my tentmate in C4. But an amusing incident brought some comic relief.

The South Col of Everest.

At 7,900m, it took a great deal of effort to even go to the toilet. Typically we would go as far from our tent as possible — away from the dead bodies, the detritus of broken tents and spent oxygen cylinders. Even squatting made me breathless. The wind would whip around and toilet paper needed to be held down by rocks. When I returned to the tent, the guide, who had not stopped talking about hygiene during the entire expedition, demanded to know if I had washed my hands: *Show me your hands!*

The tent flap was not fully zipped up. And right on cue, as he was ranting about hygiene, the swirling wind blew in a square of used toilet paper (who knew who that belonged to) that slapped him right in the face.

Not mine! I said, throwing up my hands innocently. His swears and curses reverberated around the tent as I tried to swallow my laughter.

My rest from noon till 8pm was fragmented. Despite the oxygen cylinder, the breathlessness was constant. I thought to myself: This is what a soldier on the cusp of war must feel like — a tense jumble of anxiety, excitement, apprehension and anticipation. My mind raced with an unending reel of worries, prayers and fears, chief of which was the question: *Would I make it back alive? Or die on this mountain, far from home and family?*

At 8pm of the same day, we were off again.

With the O2 set at 1.5L/minute now, I was fast. We climbed past the triangular rock face and, there and then, I had my first close-up encounter with a dead climber.

On 19 May, during the first summit window, over 200 climbers were vying for the summit. The subsequent traffic jam saw many climbers, their O2 tanks running low, being urged to turn back. Some did. Some were determined to push on against all reason. Four climbers who clawed their way to the summit died in the descent when their oxygen ran out. Sometimes cheap outfitters cut corners by providing just enough oxygen for a smooth climb. The problem was, there was no guarantee of a smooth climb, and if climbers got stuck in a traffic jam queueing up or down the summit, running out of oxygen was inevitable.

As I passed the body lying still in the snow, I had initially thought he was resting. But when he lay motionless for the next 10 minutes even as I walked past, it occurred to me that this was one of the climbers who had died on the 19th.

I encountered three out of four of those who died. We were forced to walk around and cross them as they were lying across our path.

I couldn't help but be reminded of my own mortality. I was treading the path these very men had tread just a week ago. Would it be my cold body on someone's path next week?

There were other bodies. One of them was draped with a Canadian flag. An older corpse had a glove off, the hand mummified in the dryness and cold, the head half buried in the snow.

I had to shake myself out of my morbid fear and regain focus. Distraction was dangerous in the death zone.

At 8,400m, on the Balcony, we had our first O2 tank change. My mask was off for about five minutes, and even in this brief time, my fingers and toes started seizing up in the -40°C air. I was panting hard. In the death zone, O2 levels dropped to one-third the level at sea level.

The boost of O2 from the portable oxygen tanks not only gave us the breath of life, it also got our blood circulating, which raised our body temperature. This was the main reason Sherpas used the tanks, I suspect — it was not that they could not make it up to the summit without them, but to keep warmer with them. Did the oxygen make me warmer? Maybe. Did I feel warm? Hardly.

The new tank was a relief. Both physically and psychologically, it provided the surge of energy I needed to tackle the rest of the southeast ridge.

It seemed like a good idea for the sake of my freezing extremities to place one of those hand warmer packets in my boots. They worked by activating in a slow release and I hoped that would make some difference to my cold feet. What I did not anticipate was that there was too little oxygen at this altitude to activate the packets. To my dismay, not only did the packets not warm up, they seized up in the cold, becoming rocks in my boots that chafed against my toes painfully.

There was no way to remove them during the climb, and after two hours, I could not feel my toes even when I was kicking my crampons hard into the ice. It was now 10pm and we were climbing in pitch darkness, the intense cold asserting itself into the fog of my consciousness.

There was a difficult decision to be made: I had to set a time limit for my endurance. If I didn't, I would be putting myself in jeopardy.

Four hours. If something did not change in the next four hours, I would turn back, I told myself. A picture flashed before my eyes of the Belgian climber in Muztagh Ata who had lost seven fingers, and with it the ability to practise his profession, because he did not turn back while he still could. I did not want to make the same mistake of allowing frostbite to determine the rest of my life.

Four hours went by. Then five. Agonising over the right decision and praying for a sign, I kept going till it was 4am. Six hours had passed by. I had to decide *now* or forever bear the consequences.

At that moment, an extraordinary thing happened.

The sun began to rise. It was 4:15am. Of course at this altitude the sun *is* visible earlier. I just hadn't expected it *this* early.

As the sun rose, it warmed up the atmosphere and my extremities. I was saved from making a decision to turn back. The sunrise was the validation I had desperately sought as I prayed. I knew that only God had brought me this far safely, and he would see me through. It was one of the most emotional moments of my journey.

By 4:30am, the darkness was melting away by the minute. The sight before me was surreal — a landscape *below* me, filled with white, pointed peaks cascading into the distant horizon, a plain of rolling clouds at their feet, the curved horizon in the distance gilded with the golden tinge of sunrise.

When people ask me now what the most memorable moment of my expedition was, this sunrise was it. The Tibetan plateau spread out to my right, with Nepal to my left, under the imposing shadow of Everest. There was only colossal mountain and cloud, rock and sky to be seen; not a single sign was there of human existence. It was as though I was standing at the dawn of civilisation.

By that time, I was at such an altitude that I found myself looking *down* on the mighty Lhotse. Heavy as I was, each step laden, each gasping breath all I could hear reverberating around my oxygen mask, the dim knowledge that the end was close motivated me to keep pushing.

The bony spine of the Southeast Ridge was so narrow, it only allowed one climber (going up or down) to pass at any one time. The sides fell away sharply, plunging into oblivion. It was enough to give anyone vertigo. With dark humour, people joke that if you fall off the ridge on the right, or Tibetan side, you get to live a little longer as it is higher than the left, Nepal side.

From this vantage point, there was a clear view of the South Summit and, beyond that, the formidable, near-vertical stretch of solid rock and unstable snow that was the Hillary Step. The 12m rock face, so named after Sir Edmund Hillary, was just 60m from the summit.[11] Sir Edmund and Tenzing Norgay were the first to scale it in 1953 in their bid to reach the summit.

Even at that early hour I could already see a thin line of climbers snaking up and down the Hillary Step, and others waiting, anxiety in their body language.

The two-way traffic — some climbers were already returning from the summit — on a one-lane thread of a path, was harrowing. Manouevering past the climbers making their way down was a test of nerves. In order to let climbers past, we had to unclip ourselves from the fixed line for excruciatingly long periods. A slip of the foot and we could have been the next Everest fatality.

The Hillary Step as seen from the South Summit before the 2015 earthquake.

11 The 2015 earthquake that rocked Nepal, including Everest, demolished the iconic Hillary Step, fundamentally altering the landscape just below the summit. So purely by circumstance, I became the last Singaporean to climb the Hillary Step.

By the time I touched the Hillary Step — the only obstacle between a climber and the summit at this point — I was pretty wrecked. In the thin air, the exertion of simply moving forward now was so great that the universe had shrunk to a small window of focus: Clip, jumar, one foot, another foot, moving mechanically, heavily. All sound was reduced to the crunch of crampon on snow and my very lifeforce made tangible in every gasp of air. Colours were reduced to monochromatic rock grey and icescape white.

Other climbers were impatiently pushing my jumar out of the way, angered that I was not moving fast enough. Dawa, on the other hand, was moving as though he was at sea level, pointing out to me which ropes to grab.

This final stretch was far more difficult than I had expected. I was panting so hard when I reached the top of the Step that I had to turn up my O2 to 3L/minute just to catch my breath. I now understood what climbers meant when they cautioned that this was the crux of the climb — both physically and psychologically.

There was nothing now between me and the summit but my halting steps. It had been 12 hours of continuous climbing since I left camp. The fatigue was nothing I could ever have imagined. Sheer will power had to be dragged from somewhere within my depths. I pushed forward in a fog of pain, lightheaded from breathlessness.

I went onwards and upwards till there was nowhere else to go.

The path — and my far-reaching journey over years and distances — had finally come to an end.

It was 0655h (Nepal time), 26 May 2012, and I was on the summit of Everest.

+ + +

Finally, the summit of Everest at 6:55am on 26 May 2012 0655H.

26 May: Chocolate cake

Imagine nothing above you but sky and more sky.

The privilege of standing at an altitude of 8,850m, literally the top of the world, was surreal.

There are moments of human triumph that cannot wholly be attributed to human effort. And this was one of them.

In years to come, 2012 would go down as a nightmare year when the harsh weather allowed a summit window of only four days, compared to the average of 11 days. The unusually warm temperatures had also resulted in unstable snow. I recognised my summit as a blessing, a gift in the face of storms, avalanches and a myriad challenges seen and unforeseen. This was not just my proudest moment. It was also my humblest.

Dawa and I clapped each other on the shoulder in elation. He had tears in his eyes, becoming emotional as I thanked him and told him I could not have done it without him.

My walkie-talkie crackled to life: *"Congratulations! Now get the hell down as soon as possible."*

The narrow summit was covered with prayer flags. About a dozen other climbers were celebrating their triumph, some even without supplemental oxygen.

Far from the elation and satisfaction I had envisioned, I was in a daze, exhaustion threatening to overtake me. Pushing through my hazy consciousness was the knowledge that it was dangerous to stay too long. You only hit the halfway point at the summit — there was still a long journey ahead. The majority of fatalities happened on the descent, when motivation and energy easily ran out after a climber gave everything to set foot on the summit.

Quickly I got down to business, unfurling my Singapore flag, my sponsors' flags and my Scout flag, shooting some videos and photos, and only then taking a few quiet moments for myself.

It turned out that I was the only Singaporean who summited that year, the only doctor, and the only Singaporean who had climbed Everest for charity.

An overwhelming sense of gratitude washed over me. While it was my privilege to stand on top of the world, it had been a journey taken by many people — family members, sponsors, friends, supporters.

I knew then and there that this extraordinary community spirit should not end with me, should not end here, but be paid forward to new communities and new generations.

The sense of urgency was asserting itself, and I made haste to pack up and head down within 20 minutes. I would celebrate at Base Camp.

As I was descending below the South Summit at around 9 or 10am, the legendary Conrad Anker was ascending, just below the South Summit. He was without oxygen, didn't seem to be wearing much clothing and didn't even have a backpack with him, just a water bottle.

"Hi," I managed with awe.

"Hi!" came the reply. And then he was gone.

Ascending was arduous, descending was worse. It was all I could do, in my exhaustion, to give full concentration to each step. If I didn't, the consequences could be fatal. As we descended, the extraordinary vista of mountains was a sight to behold, the mighty Makalu (8,481m) standing out as a pyramid of ice and snow among a crowd of lesser, but no less formidable, peaks wreathed in cloud and mist.

Dawa kept urging me: "Just keep moving, just keep moving." So I used distant rocks as markers, pushing my heavy body from one rock to another. *Just keep moving.*

A full view of the immense Makalu ahead as climbers descend Everest.

I hadn't had a sip of water for hours and was severely dehydrated. Descending from C4 to C2, using one rock and then another as markers, I echoed: *Just keep moving. At C2 you can drink.* Tucked in my backpack was a thermos full of hot water from last night's camp. Stumbling forward, one step at a time, C2 finally came into sight. But when I opened up my thermos, the water was frozen solid. I had been carrying ice all the way.

My spirit just broke.

If not for Dawa, I might still be on that rock. He stopped every passing climber to beg for water, but nobody had any to spare. He gave me whatever he had and, when that wasn't enough, he collected snow in his hands and warmed it until it melted just enough for us to swallow. It was enough to keep us going.

When Dawa and I finally arrived at C2 at 7pm, I had my first real sip of water in more than half a day. I had pushed myself to the very brink of my being, dragging up every last ounce of energy and self control till there was utterly nothing left. Staggering to my tent, I dropped in exhaustion and dehydration. It had been a 23-hour summit push with no food and just a trace of water.

When I peed that night, I had a shock. There was blood in my urine. Only then did I realise that I had pushed my body so far that it had started breaking down my muscles in order to obtain energy. What I was seeing was a phenomenon known as myoglobinuria – where the red pigmented myoglobin from the muscles got excreted from the urine due to muscle breakdown as the body didn't have enough energy stores.

It wasn't a pretty sight, but medical experience told me this wasn't life threatening. What I needed for recovery was rest and nourishment.

The next day, somewhat refreshed, we trekked down to Base Camp as fast as we could, all the while praying that the late season's melting ice would not crumble above us as we passed.

As soon as our team arrived back at Base Camp, the IMG tent erupted with cheers and many claps on the back. I think it was only then that I allowed myself to celebrate, grinning from ear to ear … it had been an unbelievably gruelling two months on Everest, when I had to pull out every ounce of determination and strength I possessed. There were many moments when I wasn't sure I had what it took to carry on. It was finally sinking in that … I had done it!

That year, the fatalities would number 11, the highest at the time since 1996. I felt incredibly lucky to be alive.

Not everyone in our IMG team summited — the ones who did included the Latvian couple Olga and Vadim, an ex-NFL player in his 50s, Craig, who was my tentmate in C3, and Lars from Norway. Among the unfortunate teammates who were forced to turn back through illness was my C4 tentmate, the guide who had ticked everyone off.

That evening the Base Camp cooks produced their celebration dessert, a round chocolate cake that read:

"2012.5.27 … CONGRATULATIONS ALL SUMMITS EVEREST"!

It was the best cake I'd ever tasted and ever will.

+ + +

28 May: Reunion

On the morning of 28 May, after a glorious night's sleep at Base Camp, I woke up to a chorus of congratulatory pings on my phone. Evidently news of my summit had reached Singapore.

While almost everyone had chosen to stay on at Base Camp to rest, my journey was not done yet.

Gayathri was anxiously waiting for me in Phortse, so that we could head to Kathmandu together to meet up with my secondary

The congratulatory chocolate cake for the Everest summiteers back at BC.

school teacher, Mr Krishnan. Together, the three of us were expected in Gorkha, where we had promised the delivery of computers to the students in Aahale, the mountain village I had first visited at the age of 15.

I had been delayed because of the weather, and Mr Krishnan had already been kicking about in Kathmandu for too long. He had to leave for Gorkha without delay, or return to Singapore with the mission unfulfilled.

After sleeping over in Base Camp for a night, the next morning saw me hastening down the mountain all the way to Phortse within one day, half the time it normally took.

The son of the owners of the Phortse lodge Gayathri was staying at had been on a separate expedition with the same outfitter as I was, IMG. We had summited almost at the same time, and we returned to Phortse on the same day. His elated parents slaughtered a chicken for us in celebration — meat was only eaten on special occasions — and we enjoyed a home-cooked curry chicken meal at the lodge that evening.

Gayathri and I had been apart for two weeks since Pangboche. Relief that I had returned in one piece was written all over her face.

With Dawa Finjhok Sherpa on the day we parted from BC.

Our reunion was alternately bashful and stressful, as we needed to hurry down to Lukla the very next day to meet up with Mr Krishnan. It was an emotional farewell for Gayathri and the Phortse villagers, after she had spent two months living amongst their families.

+ + +

Making our way to Kathmandu was an adventure in itself. It was imperative that we arrive in Kathmandu the very next day as we were scheduled to leave Kathmandu for Gorkha the day after.

Wending our way down to Lukla on foot as fast as we could, we somehow lost our porter, who went missing for three hours in Namche Bazar. At 5pm, he was still nowhere to be found, even after we went knocking from door to door in Namche. We couldn't leave because he had all our equipment, and there was still a six-hour walk to Lukla.

After a frantic search, we found him chugging drinks with his buddies at a village carnival to welcome Sherpas home. For the rest of the journey, Gayathri and I walked with him sandwiched between us. We were dragging our feet in the dark now, each halo of village lights a false promise of our destination.

We didn't make it to Lukla — it was too late — but limped into the village of Phakding at midnight, completely frazzled. At 4am the next morning, we hurried to Lukla to catch our flight back to Kathmandu. But at Lukla, we found the weather so tempestuous that it was impossible for us to fly out in the regular twin otter planes. No plane had taken off from Lukla for three days. There was no choice — we had to fork out USD$600 each for a private helicopter instead, which choppered its way down to Kathmandu in a dizzying descent through fierce rain and wind.

In Kathmandu, we finally met up at the Tibet Guest House with Mr Krishnan and Mr Netra Mani Kattel, the former principal of the Shree Saraswoti higher secondary school in Gorkha. Together we were going to transport 20 computers and monitors with uninterrupted power supply adaptors (UPS) — industriously sourced by Mr Netra and Mr Krishnan from shops offering good value — to Aahale, where my enduring relationship with Nepal had actually begun.

Our happy reunion continued at the Fire and Ice Café in Thamel. (Incidentally also the café that was our first stop on our school trip in

Dinner at Fire and Ice Café in Thamel with Mr Krishnan (extreme right) and Mr Netra (2nd from right).

1999 with Mr Krishnan.) I had lost 12kg on Everest, and was ready to savour my first good "city food" in almost three months on the mountain. Salami and ham pizza never tasted so good.

+ + +

31 May: Back to where it all began

It was incredible how much had transpired in the 13 years since I had first set eyes on Everest from an airplane headed to Ghorka. I had been a greenhorn 15-year-old then — the same age as many of the children in the mountain village of Aahale.

Gayathri was eager to see in person what she had heard so much about from Mr Krishnan and me. I had described to her the embarrassingly effusive welcome we had been given in Aahale then, the village schoolchildren lining the road into the village to welcome us with shouts and garlands.

This time, I assured her, there would be no such thing — our little group of four surely would not justify any fanfare. But I had forgotten the extent of the villagers' hospitality.

We could hear the cheers from the schoolchildren bobbing up and down in excitement almost before we could see them. They had stopped lessons just to welcome us with showers of flower petals. Even though I was just as embarrassed as I was 13 years ago, their genuine delight to see us — especially their former headmaster — brought a lump to my throat.

Garlanded so profusely that we had to crane our necks to see above the red, pink and yellow blooms, we were ushered directly to the school assembly hall, where our gifts were accepted with speeches delivered amidst a sea of young faces.

Gayathri and I were overwhelmed by the welcome and the appreciation. Mr Netra related how I had first been to the village as a 15-year-old and was now back as a doctor after 13 years. (They seemed more impressed by that than by the fact that I had just summited Everest — an achievement not so uncommon in Nepal after all!)

The progress of the school since we last saw it was remarkable. Where there used to be a single-storey, dirt-floored building, with metal construction rods sprouting haphazardly from the roof, awaiting the funds needed to complete the next storey, there now was a spanking, double-storey school, complete with computer classes.

They were elated to see the 20 additional computers that Mr Netra and Mr Krishnan had purchased from Kathmandu, through the generosity of my title sponsor, Cerebos, who kept their promise to match the 10,000 likes on the Cerebos Facebook account with S$10,000. There were also more modest gifts of stationery packs and coloured photos which we had printed out for the children, recalling how they used to take delight in hoarding coloured labels.

The beaming faces and bright eyes of the children were a fresh reminder that one doesn't need much to be contented with life.

I couldn't have asked for a sweeter end to this expedition of a lifetime — starting out with running clinics for the Sherpas in the Khumbu Valley and ending with this poignant reunion in Aahale.

More and more, the Nepali people were becoming my second family.

+ + +

3 June: Home, finally

In the Silkair flight on the way home, the captain who welcomed all passengers on board over the PA system, added: *"A special welcome to Dr Kumaran Rasappan who is here with us. He has successfully scaled the summit of Mt Everest and raised money for charity in doing so. Congratulations, Dr Kumaran!"*

I sank into my seat with embarrassment as the passengers clapped. Ana Dhoraisingam had planned that little surprise. Gayathri and Mr Krishnan looked as if they were thoroughly enjoying the moment.

The three of us were the only ones disembarking in Singapore, the other passengers were flying onward to Australia, which I discovered later had a sizeable Nepali population.

Other than my family, I had not told anyone else about my arrival. So I was taken aback by the crowd that was gathered in the arrival hall near our airport belt.

My mother was the first to greet me outside the gate. She gave me a tight hug and a kiss on the cheek — something I only remembered her doing when I was a young child. Then the media engulfed us. My title sponsor, Cerebos, was here, as well as the alumni and current Scouts from the 01 Raffles Scout group. Pockets of friends waved from the fringes of the group and the rest of my family quietly stood back. But it was my family that I went to first.

This was just the start. The months that followed were filled with media interviews, photoshoots, emails from aspiring Everesters and lectures at schools, medical institutions, commercial enterprises and the Singapore prisons.

Today, I still give talks. And every time I share my passion, I feel like I am back on the mountains again.

My mother was the first to receive me at Changi Airport on 3 June 2012.

+ + +

3 June: New beginnings

There was one final chapter to this expedition.

In the airplane on the way home, I slipped my laptop to Gayathri and urged: "Look at my photo album."

"I've seen your summit photos," she replied, puzzled.

A warm welcome from the 01 Raffles Scouts at the airport.

"Not *all* of them," I said mysteriously.

So she opened my album, went through the photos one by one and … there was a new photo I had surreptitiously slipped in.

On a banner that I was holding up on the roof of the world, in the midst of whipping winds, were the words:

> Gayathri, it has been a long journey so far. I know this question is far overdue. Do you want to grow old together? Will you marry me?
>
> Yours truly, Kumz

It had been the plan all along to propose to Gayathri from the summit of Everest. Dawa, who had taken the photo, had been my happy accomplice.

Gayathri's face registered astonishment. Then came the squeal and the tears. And for the first time she was at a loss for words except two: "Of course!"

Mr Krishnan was so elated by the news that he started clapping. At that moment, the plane rode into turbulence, and the bemused passengers were wondering why these crazy Singaporeans were clapping in the midst of violent turbulence.

A year later, on the first anniversary of my Everest summit, Gayathri and I made our way to Hastings Beach on the British coast. It was a special place for Gayathri who, during her housemanship year at Conquest Hospital, Hastings, had often sat on this very beach, wistfully clasping a phone with me on the other end of the line. More often than not, I was thousands of metres up a mountain.

My marriage proposal to Gayathri from the summit of Everest.

"Come and visit me," she would plead. And I finally did.

Right on the beach, I got down on my knee properly, and produced a ring and a necklace that was set with jewels around a stone that was nondescript, except for the fact that it had been plucked from the summit of Everest for this very moment.

Incidentally, our parents had been rooting for this union almost from the day Gayathri and I were 17 and our families met at the SINDA Excellence Award ceremony. Gayathri's family had already heard of my dad as one of the pioneer Tamil teachers in Singapore. Not long after, when my parents discovered that my best buddy and classmate, Gayathri, would be going overseas for her medical studies, both my parents uncharacteristically told me how much they liked Gaya, and in case I missed their point, added plainly: "Why don't you marry her?"

The fact that I didn't marry her at the time was excusable — we were just 20!

Gayathri will tell you how well I illustrate the fact that "men are from Mars". Rather unromantically, I picked her up for our JC prom with my dad and sister in the car. To that tale, she often adds that she had wild hair then ("I hadn't discovered hair straighteners") and at our wedding, when my sister remarked in her speech that she had hoped, even from the day of our prom, that Gaya would be her sister-in-law, the thought that ran through Gaya's head on hearing that was: "Oh my god, how could she think that when my hair looked like a mess? Maybe they thought, okay, this girl is not vain, she doesn't care about appearances!"

Wild hair or not, suffice it to say that my beautiful bride and I tied the knot in the Sri Dhandayuthapani Hindu temple on 15 September 2013 to the overwhelming approval of friends and relatives. That she now loves the people and country of Nepal as much as I do, is the biggest bonus in our relationship.

On 21 September 2013, we had a lunch reception for friends and family in a wedding hall at Marina Bay Sands. To the amusement of our guests, I made my entrance wearing my orange mountaineering down suit carrying Gayathri in my sleeping bag over my shoulder. For the sake of our mothers, I did wear a tux and Gayathri a bridal gown, which we revealed when we unzipped ourselves out of the mountaineering gear.

Gaya says that Everest was our invisible matchmaker. Planning the Phortse clinics threw us together for many hours as we animatedly discussed how to go about our medical social work. The terror she felt when I was caught in the Cho Oyu earthquake and was climbing Everest in a dangerous season that took the lives of 11 people, were the moments she realised the depth of her feelings for us.

We weren't the only ones who took our relationship to "new heights". Remember Olga and Vadim, the Latvian couple who were my Everest teammates? They both made it to the summit as well, Olga becoming the first Latvian woman to summit Everest. On the summit, Vadim proposed to Olga. It was the second marriage for both of them, a romance born of their mutual love for the mountains. We kept in touch and, on a conference to Lithuania, I took a side trip to Riga in Latvia, where I met up with Olga seven years after our unforgettable Everest expedition. Gaya and I were happy that they actually attended our wedding in 2013. The bond between climbers transcends language and time, and we chatted far into the night, reminiscing about the mountains.

Walking down the aisle in my down suit, with Gayathri in a sleeping bag, at our wedding reception in September 2013.

Climbing and community work — who would have thought that my vastly different passions could come together so beautifully?

If you are reading this and wondering how to satisfy the sum of your parts, your passions, let me encourage you: If you can find a way to answer the call within you, you won't regret it. No matter how much work it takes and how many detours and rejections complicate your route.

And for me, along the way, I got my girl too. Something I could not have foreseen nor planned.

So Chomolungma, Goddess Mother of the World, became forever weaved into the deepest recesses of my heart.

CHAPTER 12

"Friends are the family we choose for ourselves."
Edna Buchanan

Saturday, 25 April 2015, will forever go down as a black day in the history of Nepal.

A magnitude 7.8 earthquake struck the seismically active country with devastating impact, flattening rural homes, crushing buildings into dustpiles and sending landslides pouring down the Himalayan mountains.

Nearly 9,000 people died, more than 22,000 were injured and thousands more were displaced. It was the deadliest earthquake in the region in 81 years. Thirty-nine of Nepal's 75 districts were affected — about a third of the national population of 27 million.

The epicentre was none other than Gorkha — a region especially dear to me, as that was the first destination I had ever visited in Nepal.

Gayathri and I did not hear the news of the quake until the next day, as we had been hosting our old junior college classmates for a happy and long-awaited reunion at our home on the evening of 25 April.

Unbeknownst to us, even as we were enjoying the lively company of our Singapore friends, disaster and death were befalling our Nepali friends.

The next day, the news was buzzing with reports of the calamitous quake. Gayathri and I were filled with dread. All day long we tried to reach our Nepali friends via Whatsapp and Facebook to make sure they were safe. The replies came in excruciatingly slowly.

They were safe, our friends said. But, for some of them, homes and livelihoods had been destroyed.

As we monitored the news, the true extent of the quake sank in. The death toll was rising by the hour and scenes of the devastation were appalling. News channel CNA and newspaper Tamil Murasu requested interviews with me, knowing my close ties with the country. I declined, as I felt that the information I had from the ground was, as yet, inadequate.

Later that evening I saw Dr Rahul Goswami being interviewed on CNA. Gayathri's supervisor for a spell at Changi General Hospital emergency department, Dr Rahul subspecialised in disaster medicine, and was one of the most credible sources of what was happening on the ground. He would become the lead doctor in a Mercy Relief medical rescue team to Kathmandau.

Bits and pieces of information were trickling in from our friends in Nepal. Some sent photos taken in Gorkha, the epicentre, where village homes had been flattened. I sent the photos to Tamil Murasu, which published them.

Gayathri and I knew that we needed to help one way or another. Our Nepal family was in crisis and our instinct was to leap into action.

Almost before the thought formed in our minds, Gayathri received a phonecall: *Will you come with us to Nepal to aid in disaster relief efforts?*

The call was from the Singapore Ministry of Health which was pulling together a medical team to fly into Nepal with a combined Singapore Armed Forces contingent. Without hesitation, she agreed.

The earthquake happened on a Saturday. We heard the news on Sunday. Gayathri was hastily placed on standby to fly to Nepal from Monday.

To my frustration, my efforts to go on the same team were thwarted — I was a junior doctor in an orthopaedics residency programme at the time. Taking leave of absence was difficult. It was no use going in a personal capacity either — others who had tried had had their planes turned away from landing. That was understandable. The one international airport in Kathmandu was unable to cope with the rush of foreign military planes and aid agencies trying to land on a single airstrip.

As I despaired of not being able to help my family in Nepal, good news arrived: Aid agency Mercy Relief International needed orthopaedic doctors. They would take me on their team.

+ + +

Gayathri's Singapore Armed Forces/Ministry of Health team left on 29 April on a C-130 military plane, together with a contingent of military personnel and government sanctioned doctors and nurses. The Kathmandu airport was in such chaos that their plane was forced to circle Kathmandu for hours before being redirected to Calcutta when the plane was dangerously low on fuel.

When they finally arrived in Kathmandu the turmoil on the ground was plain. Not only had buildings collapsed, services and communication had crumbled as well. The team was shuttled to a large open area just beside the airport, teeming with overseas medical contingents.

Gayathri could not believe her eyes. The charming city of meandering lanes lined with colourful eateries, trekking shops and rustic vegetable carts that we loved like our second home looked like a war zone. Piles of bricks, zinc, and wood lay in haphazard mounds where buildings used to be. The frontage of some shops had crumbled to reveal their ruined bowels. Military vehicles and ambulances blared their horns at the press of people wandering about, some purposeful, others distraught.

Concrete buildings that had withstood the tremors became makeshift hospitals where locals, sitting or lying on the ground with nothing but the clothes on their backs, were being treated for various injuries. Here and there, blue tarpaulins flimsily held up by bamboo sticks became tents sheltering families.

Aid was pouring in. The more organised NGOs had a system of distribution: Villagers, who had walked for two to three hours to get to Kathmandu, could carry off boxes of food and supplies like tarps, ropes, blankets and mosquito nets back to their villages. But many more shipments of internationally sponsored items could be seen sitting idle at the airport as a result of a breakdown in logistics.

Meanwhile, my Mercy Relief contingent was still in Singapore, gathering the equipment we needed to head into the disaster zone.

Dr Wayne Yap, a colleague from the same year as I was in the orthopaedic residency programme, was joining me on the team. Our head of department supported our taking urgent leave on short notice and our colleagues offered to chip in during our absence. We had a matter of days to round up donations from sympathetic colleagues from Tan Tock Seng Hospital and Changi General Hospital, as well as family and friends, which went into buying ortho equipment for the mission: Dressing sets, plaster of paris, fracture immobilisation equipment, gauze, bandages, wound cleansing equipment, disposable toilet and suture sets.

One hasty late night briefing and a flurry of equipment packing later, our team, too, found ourselves enroute to Kathmandu. On our commercial flight were a Singapore Civil Defence Force team deployed to do search-and-rescue, a few news reporters, and our Mercy Relief contingent.

Dr Rahul, who was leading Mercy Relief's medical efforts, had flown into Kathmandu on 2 May, with the Wave 1 Team that included Dr Jimmy Goh from Changi General Hospital and a team of nurses. Wayne and I were in the Wave 2 Team that landed on 3 May.

Donning our Mercy Relief jackets emblazoned with the Singapore flag, we were waved through customs without having to stop by the visa counter, and were met by Mercy Relief staff Mr Masahiro.

Amidst the bustle of the milling aid workers, there was a subdued air. Everyone felt the weight of being on the site of thousands of tragic deaths.

+ + +

So it ended up that Gayathri and I, while both in Nepal for the same mission of disaster medical relief, were in different locations with different rescue teams.

Like all other military personnel from around the world, Gayathri's Singapore Armed Forces team encamped in a small field just outside the airport.

I had fully expected to be sleeping in a tent as well. But my team was ushered to a small guest lodge instead — one of the hundreds

The devastation the earthquake left on the buildings in Kathmandu.

in Kathmandu normally used by trekkers and hikers. The lodge had survived almost intact, with only long cracks on the walls and some buckled floor tiles to show for the trauma.

When we walked through the streets, the devastation revealed itself, particularly in the ancient monuments — the old royal palace was decimated. Durbar Square, a UNESCO world heritage site with structures dating from the 15th to 18th century, saw temples reduced to rubble.

Every night, as we lay in our beds, aftershocks reverberated through the lodge. We were to discover that the 25 April earthquake would be followed by hundreds of aftershocks.

Because of the danger of gas leaks that could potentially cause fiery explosions, piped gas was shut off at the guest lodge. The cooks resorted to preparing meals with kerosene and bottled gas cannisters. Bizarrely, there was a club opposite our lodge, and every night loud, thumping disco music blared from across the street. I had no idea who would be patronising a club in the midst of all that was going on, but evidently there were enough patrons for the club to stay open for the duration of our stay.

Unlike some of the larger operations, our Mercy Relief team was small — just two orthopaedic doctors and two emergency doctors, three nurses, and three Mercy Relief support staff. This was intentional, as it meant that we could respond nimbly.

The support staff took care of meetings with government bodies and other NGOs, working with them to map out places where medical aid had yet to be reached. They coordinated and arranged the logistics so that the medical staff could focus on delivering medical care.

The day after we touched down in Kathmandu, we were deployed to Dhulekiel Hospital, a private facility about 40km east of Kathmandu. When the earthquake struck, much of the infrastructure in Kathmandu was affected and hospitals were struggling to operate. Dhulekiel was one of the few functioning hospitals in the periphery of Kathmandu, as a result of which patients were flooding in from around the region.

Though small, Dhulekiel Hospital's standard of care was so high, and the staff's rapport with patients so mindful, that many refused to go to Kathmandu for treatment even when the main hospitals were restored and fully functional. This added a tremendous burden to Dhulekiel. Yet, as far as I know, no patient was turned away.

The night our team arrived in Kathmandu, we gathered for a Mercy Relief briefing at our lodge under kerosene lamplight. There was no electricity. The next day, our first morning meeting at Dhulekiel saw the head of the hospital, as well as his team of heads for all medical and allied health departments, deep in discussion on problems raised, issues to be ironed out, and objectives to be fulfilled by the end of the day. There were a number of other foreign doctors present besides the Singapore team.

Dr Dipak Shresthra, the head of the orthopaedic department, came across as intimidatingly stern. (But we were to learn later, it was a sternness underlaid with genuine kindness). So strapped for time was he that our hurried introduction to him by Dr Rahul as "orthopaedic surgeons from Singapore" was done on the run, as he strode down the corridors to the operating theatre (OT).

Even as Wayne and I were trying to get oriented to our new surroundings as quickly as possible, Dr Dipak was wasting no time in handing us two X-rays — one featuring a shattered tibia and one of a shattered femur — asking us to pick a surgery each.

We were taken aback, and somewhat mortified. Wayne and I were only third-year residents, with little experience in handling trauma cases unsupervised. Clearing our throats nervously, we clarified: "Sir, we are residents, not surgeons yet", bracing ourselves for his displeasure at being sent such junior doctors to his OT.

To our surprise, he was delighted.

It turned out that he had more than enough consultant-level surgeons from international hospitals who wanted to run an OT in their particular way.

We witnessed first-hand how, in one incident, a senior consultant from a first-world country struggled through an orthopaedic surgery, taking three times longer than what the local team would have done, only to give up and have the local surgeons finally take over. The grace with which the local surgeons did so, not to mention their surgical skill, was immensely humbling.

Residents like Wayne and myself could help the surgeons to prepare the patients before complicated surgeries, start off the surgical approaches, and stitch and dress wounds after the surgeries, allowing the overextended local surgeons to catch a few minutes' break between cases.

Time and again we saw surgeons from first-world countries descending on this highly-regarded hospital in Nepal, armed with a hero mentality to "show how it's done". Little attempt was made to understand the socio-economic implications of treating patients who work off the land and live in harsh terrain, or to consider medical resources and techniques used in Nepal.

Yet the absolute courtesy with which the Nepali medical team handled these incidents was a lesson in hospitality and decency. It deeply affected the way I thought about practising medicine.

+ + +

Wayne and myself outside the operating theatre in Dhulekiel Hospital on our first day.

By the time we had set foot in Dhulekiel, it was 10 days after the devastation of the 25 April quake. Most life threatening cases had already been taken care of, leaving a trail of orthopaedic trauma cases — broken bones, open wounds.

The flood of patients streaming into the hospital meant that triage for the first week included sending everyone with only upper limb injuries home in a backslab or cast, with instructions to return in a week.

Lower limb injuries were of the highest priority. In a large part of Nepal, where villages were two to three hours walk to the nearest town centre and the hilly terrain made vehicular traffic prohibitive, villagers spent many hours each day on their feet. If they could not walk, they could not work nor go to school.

From the time the earthquake hit, it was clear to the local medical team that their services were going to be needed round the clock for a protracted period. So the first thing they did was head home, hastily throw together a bag of personal essentials and return to Dhulekiel, knowing they would not be seeing their home for a while.

By the time Wayne and I arrived at the hospital, some of the doctors had been staying in the hospital for a week-and-a-half straight. There were just too many cases for them to leave. They would start operating from 8am every day and continue well past midnight, grabbing a few hours of sleep at the hospital before waking up to resume the cycle every single day to clear the patient load.

We saw everyone chipping in to support each other — from the nurses and allied health team, to the radiographers, anaesthetists, operating theatre technicians, cleaners and surgeons — everyone did their best for each patient.

Then there were the local medical students. Their university classes were cancelled because of the crisis, and they were instead given schedules to help out at the various hospitals around Kathmandu. Not once did we hear a word of complaint despite the fact that their university fees were not being put into education and they were essentially working as volunteers. Instead, the level of determination and passion we saw in these youths, and the fulfilment they got out of helping their fellow countrymen in time of need, was admirable.

It was remarkable how the hospital functioned in a resource-limited setting. One X-ray machine was shared among five operating theatres, and surgeries had to be carefully scheduled so that the X-ray could travel from one OT to another as the need arose.

There were only one or two radiographers and anaesthetists shuttling among the five OTs, impelling the junior residents, orthopaedic residents and medical students to dash about chipping in to take X-rays and tweak the anaesthesia machines with instruction from the consultants. They also helped prepare surgical instruments when the scrub nurses were too busy. In Singapore, autoclaving, where used surgical instruments are cleaned and sterilised by steaming, is invisibly done offsite. But the surgeries here were so numerous that the scrub nurses had the autoclave machines running at full tilt 24/7 right on the OT floor. The resource sharing was incredible and everything ran like clockwork. It was pretty amazing to observe.

The traction table is a familiar device for orthopaedic surgeons. It is designed to pull on a patient's leg in order for the surgeon to operate on a fracture. As there was only one traction table to be shared among the OTs, there could only be one patient on the table at a time. But here, multiple surgeries had to take place concurrently. So the medical students became human traction tables, manually holding and pulling on the patient's limb throughout a two-hour surgery while the surgeon put in the metal plates and screws and rods to stabilise the bone.

They stoically performed any menial task required. In turn the consultants, exhausted though they must have been, made it worth the students' while by continuing to teach them during the course of the surgery. Both sides benefitted from the remarkable partnership.

The residents like Wayne and myself, as well as the medical students, were kept busy stitching up wounds and performing the smaller procedures so that the burnt-out surgeons could snatch a few moments of respite here and there.

What orthopaedic surgeons in a resource-rich hospital would do with multiple X-rays, these surgeons did with limited X-rays, yet they could guide the placement of plates and screws quickly, efficiently and accurately. This was how they had been trained, so used were they to sharing resources. Wayne and I were impressed by their high skill level.

And even then — with every possible healthcare professional jumping in to do whatever needed to be done to keep the surgeries going — there was not enough personnel to take care of the patients. So, patients' relatives stepped in.

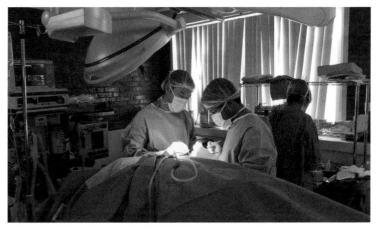

Operating almost round-the-clock with the local surgeons.

They were the human "ambulances", bodily carrying in patients on home-made stretchers made out of planks and bamboo. We saw men, women and children with open wounds and visible fractures, some with external fixation devices (temporary skeletal stabilisation rods) sticking out of their limbs while more urgent injuries were seen to.

There was no waiting room in the hospital. The injured, and their relatives, stood under the hot sun outside the hospital, waiting patiently for treatment.

The "human ambulances" turned into nursing aides once their relatives were warded, helping the patients to the bathroom, feeding them and bathing them.

Through the haze of frenetic activity, I was incredibly moved by these stalwart people who never had much and never asked for more than they were given.

+ + +

Up at 6am, a quick breakfast and on the way to Dhulekiel by 6:30, starting surgery by 8am and carrying on till we arrived back in our Kathmandu lodge at 10pm for dinner and bed. Wayne and I were getting used to the daily routine, tiring as it was.

After six or seven days in Dhulekiel, the ground staff of Mercy Relief appeared at our Kathmandu guest house. The cases in Dhulekiel were now manageable, they said; we should head out to the outskirts of Kathmandu, where the more remote villages were still waiting for medical help.

Piling into four-wheel drive vehicles that could handle the rugged terrain, we made our way for several hours to villages where roads had just been cleared of boulders, trees and mudslides after the quake. A local hospital linked up with us to provide primary healthcare services to the villagers who had been waiting for more than two weeks for medical attention. Travelling past the villages, we saw many mud houses flattened by the quake, leaving villagers homeless.

At our first village, the school building, which was the sturdiest structure around, became our makeshift clinic, and long queues formed quickly, snaking all the way around the hillside.

Another village did not have any shelters big enough for the medical team and volunteers, and we had to set up an open-air table with pen and paper for consultations out on the hilltop.

Local schoolchildren with their classroom-acquired knowledge of basic English, volunteered to be translators, standing beside the doctors from 8 or 9am when we started the clinic, to 5 or 6pm when we wrapped up. Small as they were, they were stout of heart and eager to help in whatever way they could.

In one case, a five-year-old child had gone missing after the quake and the mother, who had been working in the field at the time of

Seeing patients at the make-shift outdoor clinic.

the earthquake, had searched frantically for 12 hours before she heard crying and found her child trapped under a collapsed roof, alive but badly injured. Since then they had received no medical help because the roads had been closed. By the time we arrived, the little girl was limping. She had a pain in her hip and swelling and cuts on her fingers. Her injuries were serious enough to warrant making arrangements to transport her to the nearest hospital where scans could be done to ascertain if she had infection in the joints or fractures that had to be set.

The hospital provided free transport and we would gather the more seriously injured villagers. Twice a day there would be 10 to 15 villagers who needed hospitalisation and they would wait for this hospital shuttle service.

Another villager had his forefoot spontaneously amputated when a heavy object fell on it during the quake. Without immediate medical attention, the foot had become infected. He, too, was shuttled to the hospital.

Backaches, shoulder pain, knee injuries, even hernias and varicocele (fluid collection in the testes of young males) — we were kept busy examining patients, stitching up wounds, bandaging and prescribing medication, even for non-earthquake related conditions, as there was no medical facility in the area for the villagers. Without fancy lab tests and X-ray machines, it was back to the basics of using physical examination and history taking for our diagnoses. Our basic clinical acumen was put to the test.

Far from being morose, the villagers actually said they were lucky that the earthquake happened in the afternoon when many of them were out in the fields farming. Had it occured in the middle of the night, while they were sleeping in their homes, there would almost certainly have been more fatalities .

Occasionally we would sleep in the village school overnight. In the dead of night, we would be awakened by the rattling of the zinc roof. Aftershocks came one after another. The first aftershock was severe enough for Wayne, myself and some of the nurses to run out of the school in alarm, for fear that the building would collapse. Most nights we would feel the aftershocks reverberating through the stone floor.

Everest taught me what it meant to be bone tired. Now, I was learning about a different kind of exhaustion. Every day started early, and the pace at which the clinics ran did not let up till the end of the night when we would make plans for the next day, pack our equipment and drop like a stone for a few hours of sleep before the cycle began all over again the next day.

Despite the calamity, there was little time for any emotional response. Snaking queues made it necessary for us to limit our consultation time to five minutes per patient, during which time we had to hear them out, examine, diagnose and treat them, as well as prescribe medication.

It was only in our last two days in Nepal, when consultations were tailing off and Mercy Relief was preparing to extricate from Nepal that Wayne and I managed to share a beer in a Kathmandu café and reflect on some of the stories we had heard from our patients.

Only then did we have a moment to mourn with the Nepali people for their terrible losses — job and security, house and home, even life and limb.

With this brief breather, came the opportunity for me to personally connect with my Nepali friends — Jamling, Tenzing, Mr Netra Sir, Ang Jangbu. I met up with them face-to-face in Kathmandu, and one of these meetings changed the course of my life.

+ + +

When Mr Netra retired as principal after his long and accomplished leadership of Saraswoti Secondary School in Gorkha, he moved to Kathmandu with his wife, son and daughter. Sadly, his wife passed on shortly, even before my reunion with him after my Everest climb in 2012. His daughter had married and moved out of the family home, and his son was working in Australia.

So when the earthquake hit in 2015, Mr Netra was alone in his Kathmandu flat. When the tremors shook his flat, he had fallen and injured his back and knee. Struggling to recover, he still suffered from headaches and high blood pressure days after the earthquake. But when he heard that I was in town with Mercy Relief, he was determined to meet us at our lodge despite his ailments. As he told us about the plight of the villagers in Gorkha, some of the Mercy Relief staff were moved to tears.

Mr Netra related how, even though Gorkha was the epicentre of the quake, much of the attention was on Kathmandu, where most of the international relief work was focused. The country's institutional chaos meant that equipment, medication and food were mostly stuck in Kathmandu and help was not filtering to the rest of the country, which was left to fend for itself.

Gorkha, the epicentre of the quake, was especially hard hit. In Mr Netra's home village of Kattel Danda, 90% of the homes had been destroyed. The school, too, had suffered damage. But instead of closing school, the teachers had kept the classes going by conducting lessons in the field under tarpaulin canvases.

With their homes in shambles, villagers were sleeping outside in the livestock pens with their farm animals. There was no electricity and no gas available. They were in limbo, unable to sleep under their own roof and, at the same time, unable to repair their homes as they had been promised compensation by government authorities who needed to inspect the damage. No compensation had been forthcoming after weeks of waiting. They subsisted on whatever they could scrounge up and cook on kerosene and charcoal stoves in the open.

Urgent help was needed, as the June monsoon season was almost upon them. Without a roof over their heads, the villagers would not survive.

The Nepali people are nothing if not resilient, and in my many encounters with them, not once have they actually asked for any kind of help. But, for the first time in the almost 20 years that I'd known him, Mr Netra, looking embarrassed, asked our Mercy Relief team for whatever help we could give to his fellow countrymen. Much as he

Decimated homes in Kattel Danda.

wanted to up stakes and head to Gorkha to help, he knew he was in no state to do much.

Understanding the humility in Mr Netra's request, the Mercy Relief team very much wanted to help. But we had been commissioned to base our relief mission in Kathmandu; our hands were tied.

Listening to Mr Netra pour his heart out, I knew that short medical missions like the one I was on was only a stop-gap measure for the heaving country. Rehabilitation and recovery of the crippled nation would go on for years to come.

That day, a small seed of resolve was planted in my soul. There were no words yet to describe it. But it would eventually have a name: *Project Aasha*.

+ + +

As soon as I could arrange it, I met up with Ang Jangbu, the IMG expedition head I had come to know and respect during my Cho Oyu and Everest expeditions.

Ang Jangbu was at the Everest Base Camp (EBC) when the earthquake struck, making him a witness to one of the deadliest disasters in Everest history. The massive earthquake shook the very foundations of Pumori, which unleashed an avalanche that slammed into a segment of the EBC, sweeping 22 unsuspecting climbers to their deaths.

The ghastly death toll surpassed the 16 Khumbu Icefall fatalities of 2014.

Team Singapura was actually at EBC, intending to climb Everest to celebrate Singapore's 50th anniversary, and had narrowly missed being buried in the avalanche.

Singapore-based climber George Foulsham, who was at EBC, told AFP news agency that he was knocked off his feet by a "50-storey building of white".

"I ran and it just flattened me. I tried to get up and it flattened me again. I couldn't breathe, I thought I was dead," he said, adding that he could hardly believe that he survived.

Everest Base Camp was not known to be dangerous until that day.

Ironically, climbers who were at the Icefall and C1 and 2, historically far more dangerous than Base Camp, eventually made it down safely. The ill-fated people at Base Camp who were in their tents during the tragedy, were a grim illustration of being at the wrong place at the wrong time.

National Geographic reported horrifying eyewitness accounts of Base Camp casualties resulting from the immense air blast generated by the avalanche. American mountaineer, Dr Jon Kedrowski, who estimated that 40 to 50% of Base Camp was destroyed, related soberly: "People that took refuge in tents turned out to be the unlucky ones … only a few feet away, if a person hid behind a rock or an ice bank, they escaped unharmed."

The six helicopters which reportedly reached Lukla airport hours after the quake, were prevented by bad weather and poor visibility from reaching EBC until the day after.

Approximately 60 survivors were evacuated to Kathmandu. But some who got on the helicopters never made it.

American Ben Ayers, the executive director of the Dzi Foundation who was in Lukla at the time of the earthquake, described the overwhelming trauma: "There were lots of broken bones, broken backs, broken pelvises", adding that 4 patients appeared to have died en route to Kathmandu.

Meanwhile chaos erupted up and down the mountain as aftershocks set off more slides in the area.

"Horrible here in Camp 1," tweeted American guide Dan Mazur. "Avalanches on 3 sides. [Camp 1] a tiny island. We worry about icefall team below … Alive?"

Alan Arnette sent an audio dispatch from Camp 2 saying: "That aftershock has created more damage in the Khumbu Icefall, thus those people that were valiantly trying to repair the route have deemed the icefall … impassable."

I knew Ang Jangbu to be a patient and stoic man — necessary qualities for a leader who needed to make life-and-death decisions for his Sherpas and clients on a daily basis during expeditions. But, as he related to me the scene of chaos and calamity he had witnessed at EBC after the earthquake, he was choked with emotion.

IMG had the largest camp site on Base Camp at the time, with good-sized kitchen tents. It became the chief medical facility as the tragedy unfolded. Doctors conducted triage among the expedition leaders, guides and climbers, placing the injured — and the dead — in different IMG tents.

The kitchen tents became consultation/triage/observation units. Whatever treatments could be meted out with limited resources were done so.

Trauma, both physical and emotional, was high. Shuttling between the IMG tents to help in whatever way he could, Ang Jangbu saw climbers in pain and distress, waiting in vain for rescue to arrive. But rescue was excruciatingly slow because of bad weather and because of the sheer number of rescues that were taking place all over the Khumbu Valley.

He comforted climbers trying desperately to cling to life, even as their heart rate slowed and their breathing weakened until death overtook them and they had to be transferred to the tent where the other dead bodies were kept.

This was a man who had pretty much seen it all after decades of high-risk expeditions. But he was deeply affected by all that he was witnessing — friends, associates, the climbing fraternity injured, dying or dead. And, all the while, his churning mind wondered: "What is to become of my people?"

My former climbing guide, Jamling, also came to meet me at my lodgings on his motorbike. He was almost in tears as he related how his beloved Kathmandu, which he had loved photographing when he was not on expeditions, was in shambles, including the UNESCO world heritage site, Durbar Square. He was afraid he had post-traumatic syndrome, as every rumble and sound made him jittery and fearful.

It was clear that, even though my friends were (thankfully) physically unscathed, they were deeply affected by the earthquake, with homes damaged, livelihoods lost and all that was familiar to them crumbled.

+ + +

When Gayathri and I reunited in Singapore, our minds were reeling from all we had seen and heard in Nepal.

We talked long into the night about our separate medical missions but, more importantly, about our friends — Mr Netra, Ang Jangbu, Jamling, the Gorkha schoolchildren — and the ordeal they were suffering.

Mr Netra's plea for help — the only help he had ever asked — was still ringing in my ears. We knew our brief medical mission in Kathmandu could not be the extent of our involvement. There had to be more we could do.

Back in Singapore, Mr Krishnan was anxiously awaiting our updates. When we recounted our sobering experiences, consternation was written all over his face.

That was enough to seal my resolve. We would help the villagers buy the zinc roofs they needed. *Before* the monsoon arrived.

The next weeks were a blur of activity and serendipity. Together, the three of us unabashedly called up family, friends and colleagues who might be willing to donate towards the cause. A friend had asked me to give a talk at the Rotary Club of Raffles City, Singapore, and I'd never had the time. Now I made time.

The Rotarians responded with great altruism, donating $15,000.

Separately, we spread the word and, within three weeks of our return from Nepal, we had raised $40,000 in total.

What made everyone's generosity remarkable was that I was no charitable organisation. As an individual, I had no IPC status and could not offer the donors a tax deduction. Their trust touched me greatly.

It made Gayathri and myself more determined than ever to keep meticulous accounts in order to be accountable to the donors.

There was yet one big hurdle to clear — Gayathri and I were in a medical residency programme and we had wiped out all our annual leave by going on the earthquake relief trips in April. Much as we wanted to, there was no way for us to personally deliver the funds and the zinc sheets to the villagers.

In stepped Mr Krishnan and Mr Netra to do the groundwork.

When Gayathri and I were in Kathmandu, one of the things we noticed was that some of the big NGOs were flying in their CEOs and lodging them in fancy accommodations with expensive food, presumably at donors' cost.

Logistics and planning was sometimes lacking as well, with stacks of donated food and other aid items languishing at the airport. When Gayathri and I finally made it back to Kathmandu in the winter of 2015 with Project Aasha, we saw crates and crates at the airport, still undelivered.

On the other hand, one Singapore school principal, Mr Krishnan, set off to Kathmandu with wads of cash comically stuffed in his pockets, backpack, luggage and shoes. With the help of Mr Netra in Kathmandu, they managed to change the Singapore dollars to Nepali rupee at the best bank rates.

The two of them were able to buy zinc sheets in the market at local prices, unlike foreigners who paid a premium for goods. And they arranged for delivery at local rates to the villages of Gorkha. Every last cent of donors' funds was used to maximum effect.

Together they meticulously documented every cost and had the families who received the sheets state their name and sign off on the manifest. Photo evidence was also taken. Accountability was topmost on our minds. And donors appreciated seeing the faces of the villagers whom their donations had helped.

In all, 700 families in Kattel Danda and the neighbouring Aum Danda — which Mr Netra said was even poorer — were provided with zinc sheets before the great monsoon arrived. Once again, Mr Krishnan saw firsthand the grace of the Kattel Danda villagers who, upon receiving their sheets, urged Mr Krishnan and Mr Netra to give the rest of the sheets to their neighbour, even if they could have used one or two more sheets for their homes.

The gratitude of each and every villager for the simple gift had Mr Krishnan and Mr Netra tearing many times.

Even though Gayathri and I could not be there personally, it was one of the most satisfying things we had ever been involved in. We could not have done it without the dedication and drive of Mr Krishnan and Mr Netra.

+ + +

In a BBC interview, young Syrian architect, Marwa al-Sabouni, author of *The Battle for Home* and *Building for Hope*, related how, in 2015, in the midst of war-torn Homs, Syria, she and her husband, Ghassan Jansiz, decided to open a bookshop.

The neighbours, cowering from the fierce fighting, were astonished. The narrow Oxford and Cambridge English bookshop appeared almost ludicrous as war continued to rage, as did anti-foreign sentiment.

But soon the city's residents began telling the architect couple that the bookshop stood as a symbol of hope in the neighbourhood — hope

Mr Krishnan and Mr Netra issuing the zinc sheets to households in Kattel Danda and Aum Danda.

The villagers starting to rebuild their roofs with zinc sheets.

for better days to come, perhaps days when normalcy would look like sitting at home with an open book in a peaceful city.

Hope is a powerful life force. Especially among beleaguered people who have little control over their circumstances or the fate of their generations.

So when Gayathri and I thought of a name for a long-term service project in our beloved Nepal, we settled for Project Aasha — *aasha* being hope in the Nepali language.

The earthquake of 2015 was the impetus for us to launch Project Aasha. Serendipitously a student from Nanyang Technological University's Lee Kong Chian School of Medicine, Melvin Lim, had approached me around this time to lead their OCIP (overseas community involvement programme). He was interested in Nepal in particular and had read about my climbs and community work there.

We pulled together a team of eight medical students for our first trip at the end of 2015. Gayathri's and my aim was to set up a community programme that was sustainable and have continuity even when it came to the point that we had to bow out and allow the students to run it.

It was the first time I was taking students to Nepal, in the same way that Mr Krishnan had taken me in 1999 when I was a student. Everything seemed to have come full circle.

I wanted these students to experience what I had, and so I invited Mr Krishnan to join us to be a co-mentor to the students. Mr Krishnan took along his wife and daughter, as the last time he had been to Nepal with his wife was many years ago on their honeymoon. He had long dreamt of returning to Nepal with his wife and daughter. It was a very special trip indeed.

The first Project Aasha trip saw us making connections in Kathmandu to set up sustainable community work. We also returned to Kattel Danda to find out how the villagers were doing since the earthquake in April.

When we returned to Aahale to revisit Shree Saraswoti Secondary School, the schoolchildren once again lined the road to shower us with flower petals and garland us with sweetly scented blooms. The generous welcome for Mr Krishnan and me was nostalgic (if no less embarrassing).

We bought some building materials to repair damaged parts of the school. To our delight, the computer room we had helped set up all

The first batch of Project Aasha students with the orthopaedic department staff at Dhulekiel Hospital, December 2015.

My homestay family and their house in Kattel Danda where I had stayed back in 1999.

those years ago was still functioning. But the staff room had fallen into disrepair when the earthquake happened.

The village had arranged a celebration for us at their central community area and this time, instead of schoolchildren waiting for us, it was the elderly men and women of the village who were lining the mud road to throw flower petals at us. We felt bad that they were waiting in the winter cold, but we understood that this was their way of thanking us.

They started singing songs of praise for our team. Mr Netra was present to translate the song of how we, their foreign friends, had rendered them help in their time of need during the earthquake. It was an incredibly touching moment, to realise that they had specially penned poems and songs for us.

We tried to meet up with different NGOs to find out more about the needs on the ground. One of them directed us to the village of Bung in Solukhumbu District in north-eastern Nepal, where the maternal and neonatal mortality rates were high.

When we returned to Singapore and debriefed, we narrowed down two potential community projects: 1) Working with Pokhara's Himalayan Eye Hospital on cataract camps in Ghorka, and 2) decreasing the neonatal and maternal mortality rate in Bung.

The following year when we returned, it was with two teams for the dual projects. Dr Rupesh Agrawal, an ophthalmologist from Tan Tock Seng Hospital, led the Himalayan Eye Hospital team, which identified elderly villagers who could not make it to the hospital for cataract

The villagers of Kattel Danda singing and dancing in appreciation of our help during the earthquake.

surgery. The team performed cataract surgeries and worked with the local ophtalmologists in the region.

Subsequently we would team up with Birat Nagar Eye Hospital for continued cataract camps that included training blind students in first aid and physiotherapy.

The second team headed for the remote village of Bung.

Edmund Hillary had set foot in Bung when he climbed Makalu in the 1950s. In the old days, mountaineers had to make their way to Darjeeling, India, and trek westwards towards Bung and Jiri Bazar in order to climb Makalu and Everest. But when the Lukla airport was constructed, all traffic was redirected and these lower villages were bypassed and fell into disrepair.

The team that made for Bung — myself and three medical students including Melvin — intended to recce the area, find out about the current state of health in the village and conduct a survey about current practices and beliefs of maternal healthcare and delivery.

To get to Bung was an adventure in itself. It was so remote that, from Kathmandu, it was a bone-rattling 10-hour jeep ride to Salleri, the district headquarters of Solukhumbu, followed by a six- to eight-hour off-track ride to Dudh Koshi river, where the road abruptly ended. The river was especially fast-flowing in the summer, fed by meltwater from Everest, and we had to cross on foot, carrying on with a two-day hike to the village (one night of which was spent in an animal shed).

"Road" was too kind a description for the pot-holed, mud-covered trail littered with gravel and boulders. In the dark of night, our jeep hit a rock which broke the axle. We found ourselves out in the open at 3am in -5°C winter temperatures as our driver tried to repair the axle.

Even when we could continue on our journey, the road remained treacherous. (The state of this road was no better the following year, when the jeep got stuck in loose sand and we had to get out and push it uphill.)

Once we reached the river, we started on our two-day hike to Bung. As our path passed through Sotang, where a regional healthcare centre was located, we dropped in to meet with Mr Shreedoj Rai, a respected healthcare worker at the outpost. Mr Rai had kindly assisted us with our arrangements in Bung.

As we visited with Mr Rai, a harried father came rushing in with his five-year-old son who was so malnourished he looked more like three.

The child had had a bad fall and appeared to have broken his forearm. The health workers at the outpost excitedly exclaimed that I was an orthopaedic surgeon and it was lucky that I was on hand to help.

We took an X-ray in an ancient dark room using wet washing techniques I'd only read about in my orthopaedic textbooks. Sure enough, there was a complete displaced fracture of both the radius and ulnar bones of the forearm. Without surgical fixation, the outcome would be poor.

There was just one problem: The father was too poor to take his son to Kathmandu where surgery could be performed. The desolate man was the sole caregiver of the young boy, as he had lost his wife a few years ago. The family had never even set foot in the capital.

Putting our heads together, we came up with a plan: Our medical team would carry on to Bung and conduct our programme as planned. On the way back to Kathmandu, we would give a ride to the father and son, dropping them off at a hospital which would do the surgery without charge.

I explained to Mr Rai that I would give his son a backslab (a half-casting technique used to stabilise a fracture) using POP (plaster of paris) to tide the boy over till we returned in three days.

This conversation, overheard by a Year 1 student on my NTU team, made no sense to him. Bewildered, he thought I'd said: "We need to give the boy a back slap (pat on the back) until it 'popped'." Wondering how on earth that would help the child's fracture, my student kept mum about his bemusement until much later. We cracked up when he finally confessed his misinterpretation. Till today, it remains one of Project Aasha's most memorable jokes.

After three days, we wrapped up our recce work in Bung and returned to Sotang as we'd promised. The father and son were ready to go. They literally had nothing with them except some water and food in an old, tattered bag. They did not know anyone in Kathmandu and could not speak English. I secretly worried about how they would survive the confusion of Kathmandu.

On the way to Kathmandu, we enquired at the A&E departments of the bigger paediatric hospitals if they would do the boy's surgery pro bono. The answer was consistently 'no'. We knew there was only one option left for free or subsidised treatment: The main hospital in Kathmandu itself.

We arrived in Kathmandu close to midnight. The driver stopped us at a busy bus terminal. Our plan was to break into small groups and take taxis back to our lodgings. We did not know the father's plans but he assured us that he knew the hospital in question.

A multitude of taxi drivers swarmed around us, haggling over prices, pushing us to take their fare. It was dark; we were all cold, hungry and tired after our long and uncomfortable journey. Father and son alighted from the jeep; the father turned to talk to the driver for just a minute and when he turned back, his boy had disappeared. We were aghast. No-one had seen what happened.

Frantically we spread out to look for the boy, the father ashen with fear. After 10 minutes, we saw in the distance two men holding the hand of the small boy, leading him into the alleyway. Racing up to them, we confronted the men and wrested the boy from them. There was a high incidence of child trafficking in Kathmandu, with criminals targetting naïve, first-time visitors to the busy capital. We had almost seen the unsuspecting boy kidnapped from under our very noses. Shaken, we felt very lucky to have found the little fellow, who had a tearful reunion with his father.

Before we parted, we arranged for transport to the hospital for the father and son. I pushed S$50 in rupee into the father's hand, worried about how they would fare in this rough city, have the surgery done, and return safely to Sotang. The Singaporeans were sober as we made our way to our lodgings, the father and son still on our minds.

The following year, 2017, the Project Aasha team, including Prof Tham, returned to work with the eye hospital in Ghorka, as well as to Bung where we conducted educational clinics on sterile delivery techniques to lower the risk of sepsis among neonates, and worked with local staff to distribute birthing kits and medications to decrease postpartum haemorrhage.

On the way to Bung, we once again stopped at the Sotang health post. To our delight, we learnt that the father and son had made it back safe and sound. The boy had successfully undergone surgery to this radius and ulnar. In fact, they had heard of our visit and came to greet us in a joyful reunion.

Despite this happy ending, the whole incident caused me to reflect deeply on what the plight of the boy might have been had we not serendipitously been in Sotang precisely at the right moment. He may have had a malunited fracture and lost partial function of his arm. This was the plight of many an impoverished villager in the poorest areas of Nepal.

The healthcare workers said the boy was lucky to have stumbled upon us that day. But I felt lucky to have had the opportunity to help someone who truly needed it.

The Bung project carried on for three more years. Our aim was to augment the existing system and facilities so that they would become self sufficient. Each year we returned, we saw that the road to Bung was built further and further, so that finally in 2018 there was a road all the way from Kathmandu to Bung (although it was another pot-holed one).

On our second visit to Bung, we noticed many locals coming to see us with musculoskeletal ailments. The medication and aid we could offer on our short visits provided only temporary relief. So the next time we returned, it was with physiotherapy students from the Singapore Institute of Technology. They handed out useful pamphlets and taught the patients exercises that would alleviate knee pain and back aches, much to the bewilderment of the locals who retorted that they had enough exercise walking up and down the hill on a daily basis. We had to explain that it was not the same as the strengthening and stretching exercises we were advocating for their back and knee health.

Dr Rupesh and team continued to conduct cataract surgeries in Biratnagar in eastern Nepal, working to reduce the rate of diabetic retinopathy that can cause premature blindness. Together with Gayathri and myself, he continues to be a mentor in Project Aasha. When COVID-19 prevented us from conducting clinics in the Himalayas, the students in the Project met up with the elderly living alone in one-room flats in Singapore to conduct physiotherapy exercises, assess their medical situation and refer those who needed further assistance to medical facilities.

The students who journeyed with us came on board with the innocence of youth and a save-the-world passion that was endearing. Gayathri and I, a few degrees more jaded, having worked through years of exhausting on-calls and occasionally puzzling politics, hoped to encourage the youths' exuberant zeal as they learnt about obstacles to medical community work. We hoped that through experiential learning, they would develop perspectives of community work founded on values like integrity as much as efficacy.

As our own mentors, both from school and work, had equipped us with the kind of wise counsel not found in textbooks, we hoped to do the same, growing the students' leadership so that they could in turn pass on valuable lessons to generations to come.

The spark that Mr Krishnan lit in me on my first trip to Nepal at 15 had never been extinguished. And my hope was that it would catch and multiply. For that reason, Gayathri and I have returned to Nepal for community work every year since the launch of Project Aasha until COVID-19 put a halt to travel.

It bears saying that Project Aasha blossomed not by Gayathri's and my efforts alone. The students, our mentors such as Dr Rupesh and Dr Tham Kum Ying (the consultant who encouraged me to go for my mountain in 2012 when others were not as approving), and donors big and small, have played a role in knitting the operations together and allowing more medication, more equipment, and more education to be spread in Nepal than we ever thought possible.

In one incident, a stranger, Mrs Hendricks, contacted us after reading about how we were taking a team of students to Nepal to render aid after the earthquake. It seemed she and her husband were involved in logistics shipping and, while they had made it a point to include medical goods for needy communities, the goods were often unused and discarded. Since then, she has supplied us with the unused medicines and equipment for Nepal every year.

If there's one lesson Gayathri and I have learnt from our community work in Nepal, it's that there are more good-hearted people among all of us than we know.

CHAPTER 13

"K2 is a savage mountain that tries to kill you."
George Bell

On 16 January 2021, 10 Nepali mountaineers achieved what Outside Magazine called "the greatest unclaimed feat in mountaineering": The first winter summit of K2.

The history-making feat was significant on two levels: One, immense national pride broke out over the accomplishment of the all-Nepali group, an indigenous people whose expertise has remained largely in the shadow as spotlights shone on the climbing firsts of foreigners.

The 10 climbers were actually from three different Nepali teams led by Mingma Gyabu (Mingma G) Sherpa, Nirmal "Nims" Purja and Sona Sherpa. Toiling their way up the punishing inclines at intervals, the 10 men regrouped 10m from the summit. Then, singing Nepal's national anthem, they made the final strides to the summit in unison.

Those of us who count our Himalayan teammates as personal friends cheered almost as loudly as our Nepali comrades.

The Sherpa race, from which Mingma Gyabu and Sona hail, has long been synonymous with Himalayan expeditions. Scientists have found that Sherpas are physiologically adapted to living at high altitude. This, together with their fortitude and experience, have made them the heroes of the Himalayas.

Nirmal "Nims" Purja, from the Magar race, was remarkably raised in the flatlands of Nepal. He had followed in his father and brothers' footsteps to join the Gurkhas at the age of 18, and only climbed his first mountain, Lobuche (6,119m), in 2012. In 2019, however, the supreme athlete distinguished himself by climbing all 14 "death zone" mountains in six months and six days in what he dubbed Project Possible, even conducting four rescue missions during the time, three of them above 8,400m. His story has been immortalised in the popular Netflix documentary, *14 Peaks: Nothing is Impossible.* Nims was the only one of the 10 who summited K2 without supplemental oxygen in January 2021.

In a Facebook post prior to their ascent, Nims wrote: "I promise the hardest, the last, and the greatest mountaineering feat #k2winter will belong to the Nepali climbing community. All 13×8000 peaks have been climbed in winter by our international climbing community so it would be a great feat for the Nepali climbing community to make history. I will not leave the basecamp until the mission is accomplished."

He kept his promise.

The second reason that winter summit was so extraordinary was that it was, well, K2.

Up until this 2021 achievement, K2 was the last 8,000m peak yet to be summited in winter.

A behemoth at 8,611m, K2 is the second highest mountain on earth, only 237m lower than Everest.

It is notoriously perilous, even in ideal weather conditions. From 2000 to 2010, it had a higher fatality ratio than Everest, with 6.52 deaths for every 100 ascents compared to 1.37 on Everest.

In tragic proof of its extreme danger level, just three weeks after the Nepali team's successful winter summit, three climbers from a different expedition perished on K2. Muhammad Ali Sadpara, 45, of Pakistan, John Snorri, 47, of Iceland, and Juan Pablo Mohr, 33, of Chile, were last seen just 300m short of the summit.

The news hit home personally. John Snorri was on my own K2 team in 2017, when he became the first Icelander to summit K2 that summer. A friendly, outgoing chap with a big laugh, Snorri's strength and fitness exceeded most climbers'. As a result, we didn't climb together much, as he would be way ahead of me. I do remember, though, how he had happily announced at dinner one evening that his wife had just discovered the gender of their soon-to-be born sixth child — it was a boy. Sadly, his son must have been just three years old when his father's body was found in August 2021 after he went missing in February in his attempt to make a winter ascent of K2.

Mingma Gyabu Sherpa, one of the 10 Nepali climbers to summit, gave an idea of the hazards the team faced when he described in an Instagram post how the journey had seemed impossible at points.

Winds whipped "at typhoon speed … more than 30-40 knots on a good day". Temperatures plummeted to -50°C. Air pressure dived dangerously low. Even after the disappearance of the Nepali group's tents with essential supplies, the men persisted onward in a journey that would have been impossible had it not been for the collective determination of the group.

To climbers, K2 is one of *the* ultimate tests of skill and endurance and, as National Geographic puts it, "the graveyard of many [climbers'] ambitions". In 2008, 11 climbers died climbing K2, in the worst accident in its notorious history. That was the year two Singaporeans — Edwin Siew and Robert Goh — also made a first attempt at K2. (Their Sherpa guide was Jamling, my guide in Ama Dablam in 2011.) The summit success rate was so low, only 10 to 20 people climbed it every year, and years could go by without a single person summiting, or even making an attempt.

+ + +

In 2012, just before my Everest climb, Khoo Swee Chiow had invited me to climb K2 with him immediately after Everest.

I was sorely tempted. After all I would be at my physical prime and acclimatised from the Everest expedition. It seemed like a no-brainer.

But I couldn't do it.

I had promised not to put my family through another ordeal so soon after Everest. I was also due back at work in July 2012.

I could not break my word.

Swee Chiow went on to climb K2 and, on 31 July 2012, became the first Southeast Asian to summit K2.

In the years that followed, K2 never left my mind. It was like a distant star with a irresistibly magnetic pull. I knew I had to climb it one day.

It was five years later, in 2017, that the possibility became real for me again.

By that time I was in Year 4 of my orthopaedic surgical residency, with far heavier responsibilities than I had when I climbed Everest in 2012. Work-wise, it was far from ideal in terms of timing. But Gayathri and I had started planning a family by this time and I believed that, if I wanted to gun for K2, it was now or never. I couldn't see myself climbing another 8,000er once I became a father. Like my Everest teammate Amin, I did not want to risk leaving my child fatherless.

Yet doubt starting setting in. To take on one of the world's most formidable climbs after not climbing for five years seemed like madness.

I spent time reflecting and praying over the decision. It was not easy to leave my family once more and add another year to my residency. Honestly, this was a harder decision than even Everest. My family and friends were full of misgivings. To this day, I appreciate them for loving me enough to release me to this life goal that mattered deeply to me.

So for the next six months, I found myself in the familiar grind of working fulltime while scrambling for sponsorship, sorting out permits, equipment and logistics and, in between all of it, grabbing pockets of training between long shifts at the hospital in preparation to face another 8,000er.

This time, I took the opportunity to raise funds, through my climb, for the Home Nursing Foundation (in particular to support respite care for caregivers) and the Singapore National Stroke Association.

Mr Shanmugam from Gayathri Restaurant once again backed me with his sponsorship. Also supporting me for K2 was Dr Matthew Cheng, a brilliant orthopaedic surgeon who was a visiting consultant at Tan Tock Seng Hospital when I was a senior resident doing a tumour posting. An adventurer himself, Dr Cheng was part of the Tan Tock Seng Hospital group with whom I had made an EBC trek in 2016.

As he handed me a cheque, he quipped: "Promise me you'll come back alive. Don't let me face Gayathri asking why I gave you money to kill yourself."

One of the biggest hurdles for me was getting a visa to Pakistan. From what I'd heard, the delicate political situation between Pakistan and India meant that rarely was an Indian national given a permit to climb any mountain in Pakistan. Even though I am Singaporean, my race was a liability here.

After multiple applications which were turned down "for security reasons" (they went so far as to ask my grandfather's birth place in India), I appealed to the Ambassador of Pakistan in Singapore who in turn appealed to Islamabad. Finally, barely a few weeks before I was to leave, my visa arrived. It was for 66 days — exactly the time I needed to climb K2. There was zero margin for unforeseen circumstances.

On 14 June 2017, I arrived in Islamabad, the capital city of Pakistan, where I met my small K2 expedition team: Americans Vanessa and Hari, Icelanders John and his videographer, Kári, who was along to chronicle the first Icelandic ascent of K2; and Chinese nationals Ah Jung, Cheng Xue and Zhang Lian, who were on their third attempt at K2 (all competing to be the first Chinese national to complete all 14 of the 8,000ers). Our support team included 9 Sherpas, 4 Pakistani high-altitude climbers and five cooks.

These would be our comrades for the next two months.

My personal Sherpa was Kami, from Pangboche in Nepal. It was the first time I was climbing with him, but his reputation preceded

Kami (extreme left) and his family at his home in Pangboche enroute to Everest BC in April 2012.

him. On Singapore's first successful team ascent of Everest in 1998, a number of Sherpas were fundamental in taking the Singaporeans to the summit. Kami was one of them.

In appreciation, some of our pioneer climbers, including Robert Goh, Edwin Siew, Lulin Reuters and Dr Mok Ying Jang, created the Khumbu Education Fund to help put the children of Sherpa families through primary and secondary school. Eventually more climbers chipped in and we were able to fund some through university as well, one of whom was Kami's son, Mingma, who is now working as a hydroelectric engineer in Thame.

Kami's youngest daughter, Karma, is studying nursing with a view to community care and, last I heard, she was helping to administer COVID-19 vaccinations and provide other care during the pandemic. Two of the youth beneficiaries, Kami and Mingma, later joined Project Aasha as our translators.

The local Balti people, who are of central Asian origin, have the physique but, by and large, lack the finesse of Sherpas, as the climbing culture in Pakistan is not as developed as in Nepal. So our team preferred to invite the Sherpas to join our K2 team.

At 53, Kami was the oldest and most experienced of the Sherpas on the team. This was his fourth K2 climb; he had summited once with the well-known mountaineering writer Alan Arnette, who incidentally was the oldest American to summit K2 at the age of 58 in 2014.

Our onward flight on 16 June took us straight to Skardu (2,230m), in the northernmost territory of Gilgit-Baltistan in Pakistan. This was lucky, because most teams take a two-day drive up the Karakoram Highway, passing the Chilas area notorious as being a terrorist hangout. In 2013, Taliban terrorists carrying AK47s had brutally attacked a camp of mountaineers in Nanga Parbat, the world's ninth highest mountain and ironically dubbed "The Killer Mountain" for its 20% fatality rate. The terrorists, targeting foreigners, shot dead three Ukrainians, two Slovaks, a Nepali, a Lithuanian, two Chinese and a Chinese-US dual national.

Remarkably, a Chinese climber who happened to be Swee Chiow's friend managed to escape the assailants. Taken by the terrorists, he was already on his knees with his hands tied, about to be executed when, in a moment of inattention, his assailants looked away. The climber made a mad dash on the glacier, zigzagging to avoid the bullets that were

Hari and I in the C130 aircraft flying from Islamabad to Skardu.

With Kami at the mouth of the Indus river enroute from Skardu to Askole.

flying at him and jumped into a ditch where he hid the night until he was rescued. This Chinese climber must have had nine lives, because just the previous year, Swee Chiow was climbing K2 when he saw the same climber and his teammates tumbling off the mountain. Horrified, Swee Chiow thought they were dead for sure. But astonishingly, they survived by landing on flat ground just metres from the mountain's edge. The next year this same climber survived the terrorist attack.

In any case, my team was flying over, rather than driving through, the dangerous Nanga Parbat area. This was thanks to Vanessa, our American teammate who was well connected enough to book us all on a C-130 military plane to Skardu.

We spent three days in Skardu restocking our food items, repacking and sorting out our permits. Skardu was the last place with readily available wifi and mobile reception before we started out for K2.

Tomorrow we would begin our jeep ride to Askole (3,300m) at the foothills of the Baltoro Glacier, followed by a six-day journey on foot to the K2 Base Camp (5,150m).

+ + +

The Karakoram mountain range of Pakistan, which adjoins the Himalayas, is home to five of the world's fourteen 8,000m peaks, including its crown jewel — K2 (8,611m). The greatest concentration of high mountains in the world and the longest glaciers outside the high latitudes lie here, in an austerely rugged landscape.

So remote is K2, that there is no consensus of a local name because there simply are no villages within 120km of the mountain. Hence the surveyor's notation of K2 (the second peak in the Karakoram range to be surveyed) stuck.

From 2018 to 2019, the number of trekkers registered to enter this Central Karakoram National Park was 1,300, compared to over 30,000 people making the EBC trek every year, reported Lonely Planet in 2021.

All chopper rescues at K2 were carried out (at exhorbitant cost) via the Pakistan Air Force because of the sensitive political location.

Our jeep ride from Skardu to Askole took seven hours. Along the way, landslides had to be manually cleared and our narrow route wound past cliff edges with boulders perched so precariously they were on the verge of causing a landslide at any moment. And this was a two-way road.

Arriving in Askole meant the start of our long hike. The loads — barrels of water, sacks of food, oxygen tanks, climbing paraphernalia

The division of loads between the porters in Askole before we started our trek to K2 BC.

— were divided into 25kg packs for each porter to carry. Our campsite teemed with jostling local porters vying for a job. It took police presence to prevent events from escalating.

The trekking route took us on a rocky trail past some of the tallest peaks in the world, including Nanga Parbat. We would not set eyes on K2 until we were five or six days into the trek. Our route: Askole (3,100m) to Jhola (3,200m), then Paju (3,400m) to Urdukas (4,150m), and Goro II (4,300m) to Broad Peak Base Camp (4,800m), and finally to the K2 Base Camp (4,980m).

This route was heavily militarised as it was so close to the Indian border. The tension was palpable, and each time my passport was examined at checkpoints every few kilometres, I braced myself to be turned back. Every now and then, in the silence, we could hear artillery fire.

I could understand neither Hindi nor Urdu, the national language of Pakistan, but mostly the Baltis thought I was one of the expedition's military liaison officers (though they did wonder why there were two instead of the usual one). When they spoke to me, I had no clue what they were saying and would just smile and nod. Our liaison officer was a cool guy who took it upon himself to helpfully add that I was mute. The porters played along and only when I overheard them telling the locals that I was mute did I realise why everyone subsequently left me alone.

This was the longest and most rugged trekking I had ever experienced. The imposing western face of G4 dominated the landscape

The awe inspiring Baltoro glacier, alongside the highest concentration of the world's tallest mountains.

from Urdukas all the way to Concordia (4,690m). Dubbed the "throne room of the gods", Concordia is at the confluence of the Baltoro and Godwin Austen glaciers and is famous for its amphitheatre view of the sky-scraping Gasherbrum giants.

Six days of trekking across 65km of the Baltoro Glacier took us past the serrated summits of 7,000 and 8,000m peaks rising skyward in brutal beauty.

Along the way, we could see dead mules, bones exposed — it was so arid and cold in these harsh surrounds that the bodies did not full decompose. Streams that were small and languid in the morning turned into torrential rivers by the afternoon, fed by melting ice. We crossed when we could — stripping off our boots to wade through 2°C water that froze our feet numb.

Yet during the day, the sun beat down fiercely, and I sweat so much that a fine "powder" of salt crystals covered my face when the sweat dried.

While the glacier looked solid, meltwater was audibly flowing in an invisible tunnel underneath. An unsuspecting footfall on weak ice could send you tumbling straight into the underground river where it was all but impossible to get a grip on the ice. The torrent could take you 20km down. As a result, climbers on K2 have been known to die by drowning.

All along the way, unforgiving rain, hail and snow pelted down as we carefully navigated our way up and down the glacier.

It was not an easy trek. But one of the most stunning I have ever made.

Walking among the highest concentration of tallest peaks in the world was humbling, daunting, and as far from the cityscape of my Singapore home as imaginable. I felt like I was in a dream, long treasured.

After five days of hard walking, we turned a corner from the Baltoro Glacier onto the Goodwin Austin Glacier and, instantly, there she was infront of us — K2 in all her notorious magnificence. I had not seen K2 in person until now.

Almost always shrouded in cloud, K2 was exposed in her glory that cloudless day.

More than awe-inspiring, K2 was prayer-inspiring.

Our first sight of the mighty K2 from Concordia.

At the sight of her, Kami, walking beside me, started muttering prayers. In 2015, Kami had been climbing near C1 when falling rock had smashed into his helmet, knocking him unconscious, dislocating his shoulder and fracturing his arm and finger. If not for the fact that he was jumaring up the fixed line, he would have fallen to his death. He had to be evacuated for surgery, and ended up foregoing the rest of the season.

As I gazed on K2, I tried to decipher the different routes climbers had historically taken: The Abruzzi Ridge, Cessan Route, central rib, magic line, western ridge. None guaranteed success. None guaranteed that climbers would leave with their lives intact.

In 2015 and 2016 no one had summited. My teammate, Vanessa, had been there both years.

+ + +

Unlike EBC, almost carnival-like with its profusion of tents and coloured prayer flags, the K2 Base Camp was a stark, windswept area of earth and ice, rudely marked by a pile of rocks.

On Everest, the nearest local village to Base Camp (Gorek Shep) was just 1½ hours' walk away. That meant that the comforts of a warm lodge, hot food, wifi and mobile reception were never too far away. Even in 2012 there was the option of hailing a helicopter from here to Kathmandu if one so needed (and could afford).

There was no such luxury in K2. The nearest village, Askole, was six days' walk from Base Camp. Unlike other 8,000m peaks, K2 was so remote that it was not visible from any inhabited place. There was no mobile reception or wifi, and chopper rescues were few and far between due to military control.

We were so far from civilisation that we had to bring with us all our supplies as we trekked to Base Camp, including a few goats and chickens, the numbers of which slowly depleted in the course of the trek.

One particular fluffy goat patiently made its way up the Baltoro Glacier with us. By day it was led along the same path we took. When we stopped to make camp, the goat's tether was simply wound around its horns. How that kept the goat from straying I would never understand. Sadly for the goat, which was actually the most sure-footed among us, it would meet its end in a cooking pot in the weeks to come.

We rested for four days at Base Camp, waiting for a good weather window to start our acclimatisation climbs. The Sherpas had fixed ropes to C1 but there was too much snow to make further progress up the mountain.

Making an attempt from the Abruzzi Ridge that year were 28 climbers — Pakistanis, porters, Sherpas and international climbers. Attempting the Cessan Route were 32 climbers.

Our group, with the whimsical name of Dreamer's Destination, was the biggest expedition team heading up Abruzzi. On the Cessan side, Russel Brice's Himex team was the largest. We would be fixing our routes independently, with a plan to combine efforts above C4 where the two routes met.

As we started our rotations, it soon became clear how K2 had earned its formidable reputation.

In short, K2 is a beast.

Its deadliness is the result of a combination of violent, unpredictable weather plus avalanche and rockfall-prone terrain. The topography is punishing. Whereas on Everest, there are steep portions and portions

The national flags of all the clients in our team at K2.

that level out, K2 offers very little by way of a break. The only respite from the steep climb is a shoulder about 7,300m up.

Little wonder that years can go by without a single climber summiting K2.

Getting to ABC from BC took us 2½ hours of traversing eastwards across the Godwin Austin Glacier.

And then we hit the icefall.

Though not as extensive as Everest's Khumbu Icefall, this one had its unique challenges. Uneven slabs of slippery snow and ice crusted the steep flanks, making navigation slow and tricky. Crampons were not normally used. Melting ice and route changes happened without warning.

Past these falls, it was a short, rocky climb before ABC revealed itself at 5,300m. "Camp" was perhaps a deceptive description. The site was so small, it could accommodate no more than three to four tents. It was, in fact, more often used as a storage and staging point where crampons were donned before hitting the Abruzzi Ridge.

Luckily, or unluckily, I did have the chance to spend a night at ABC during my first rotation before heading upwards to C1 the next day. It was precariously located below huge ice chunks from a previous avalance. If another avalanche were to hit, we would have been right in its path of deadly debris. We were also near a stream, which worried Kami as warm weather sometimes saw a surge of meltwater which could wash away the tents.

At the doorstep of ABC, the Abruzzi Ridge rose in wordless challenge. From the moment we set foot on its flanks, the onslaught began. There was no flat ground the entire way, with the mildest incline being 40°.

I had been warned about avalanches and rockfall before we started out. But I did not expect the avalanches to be *this* frequent. The moment we hit the slope, shouts of "AVALANCHE, AVALANCHE!" filled the air.

We had to scramble to the left and flatten ourselves against the rocks to avoid being dragged down with the snow. The avalanche cry came with increasing frequency. Some were small, rolling puffs but others were huge, wiping out the tracks with great chunks of ice, making the incline even more difficult to scale.

It was exhausting just to stay alive, and I was left with not much left in the tank to keep climbing upwards.

But if I thought the avalanches were the worst kind of threat, the rockfall soon changed my mind. More insidious than avalanches, loose rock that fell without warning could be the end of you.

As I was climbing on the fixed lines, a low rumble reverberated through the air. Looking down, I saw a great rock, bigger than a kitchen tent, shearing off from the side of the mountain with a groan. It slipped on to the track and started hurtling downwards, yanking up the fixed lines I was attached to and dragging me down. Desperately I tried to unhook myself but, in the next instant, I felt a give and was released from the drag. The falling rock must have snapped the ropes, or torn up an anchor. Either way, I was fortunate to be alive.

The ashen face of Kami said it all. If I had been three minutes slower on the trail, the rock would have smashed into me. If there had been any climber below me — I happened to be the last one that day — he or she would have perished. "We could have died," he said flatly.

There was no time to recover emotionally. When I peered up shakily, I could see an enormous rock tower looming above. The longer we stood still, the greater the chance that another rockfall would prove fatal. We had to keep moving. I kept God in mind as I inched upwards — only he could protect me now.

The slog to C1 did not let up for seven hours. The snow could reach thigh high and trails were often buried by debris from strong winds and avalanches. By the time I made it to C1 at 6,070m, I was so exhausted that even the precarious camp looked like a haven.

C1 was perched on an area so bare that the tent lines were simply wound around any rocky protuberances to be found. It was crazy to think that these jumbled and chaotic lines were all that kept our four tents from being blown away in the high winds … and us with them. Crawling into a tent, I was vaguely aware that I was perched at the very edge of the rocky ledge. But, in truth, I was too tired to care.

Kami and the other Sherpas warned that the climb from C1 to C2 was shorter but even harder. I had learnt to add one to two hours to whatever timing the Sherpas gave. So if they said it was "hard", we could be sure that was another understatement.

True enough, the climb from C1 to C2 was relentless. We were trudging in crampons on inclines that started around 50°, and got gradually steeper until we were climbing with the ground close to our noses. There was no flat spot to put down our backpacks and we had to eat and drink cautiously as any water bottles not clipped on the lines would have slipped all the way to oblivion.

The difficulty of the route soon intensified. The closer we got to C2, the more vertically inclined the rock face. Every step had to be carefully planned and kicked hard into the solid seam of blue ice.

Unlike the Lhotse face on Everest, where you could follow in the steps of climbers ahead of you, here we had to kick in and create our own steps. Climbing K2 meant climbing in bad weather with low visibility *all the time.* Whiteouts, winds, storms, snow — everything the weather could throw at you, it did.

Our group decided to place C2 just below the whimsically dubbed House's Chimney, named after American Bob House who free-climbed the chimney in 1939. This 30m crack in a brown rock wall, a shoulder-width couloir just wide enough to allow passage to a single person, has been compared to the Hillary Step of Everest. But, though lower in altitude than the Hillary Step, it is higher in difficulty level. Climbers have rated it a 5.6 in difficulty without aid. But as Alan Arnette quipped, "at 21,500 feet (6,550m) it is a challenge regardless of the rating, or aid".

Just getting to the foot of the chimney was an ordeal. "The lower section was a serious obstacle of thin ice over 45 degree angled rock with an anchor half way up the 30 foot ice rink," describes Arnette. Anchors and fixed lines usually lay on the ground, but the ones here were above our head; you had to pull down on them.

Steadying my breathing, I looked up the chimney. Inside was a spider web of tangled old ropes and a flexible ladder, wobbling almost as much as the ropes with every gust of wind. The coating of slick ice on the ladder made every foothold and handhold a challenge. But rung by rung, hand over hand, a blur of crampons, jumar, carabinar ... and finally I emerged from the chimney to be buffeted by whorls of snow in the whipping wind.

The final steep 60m to C2 was a crawl through winds bearing down on us. In 2013, a New Zealand-American father and son pair had perished here from an avalanche. As a result of the original C2 commonly being wiped out, we placed our C2 somewhere below.

C2 was like a tent graveyard, with the wind relentlessly ripping at the abandoned tents. Fighting the blasting winds, we inched our way to the upper C2, hoping to carry on to C3. We made it halfway up C3

House's Chimney with ropes and aluminum ladders from previous expeditions.

Climbing past C2 with Broad Peak over our shoulder.

to the point just before the Black Pyramid at 6,800m. But the harsh winds won out and we were forced to turn back and hole up at lower C2 before making the long descent back to BC the following day.

We rested three days in BC, our minds focused on one thing: The elusive summit window. Weather predictions put that in three days on 22 July. Before that, bad weather would make summiting impossible.

Waiting for the summit window was a crazy backwards-and-forwards dance of science, instinct and experience. In the end, whatever illusion of control we nursed returned to remind us that we were not in charge, Nature was.

After two rotations, weather predictions shifted the summit gauge to 27th, then 28th, and subsequently 26th. We grew used to the predictions changing daily.

For any 8,000er the weather plays an immense role in predicting summit success. But on K2, it is everything.

The capricious winds and tearing blizzards can put up such a mighty resistance that tents, and people, can be blown clear off the mountain.

We finally set our summit date for 27 July, which happened to be Gayathri's birthday. That meant setting out from BC on 23 July. I was not taking chances, I would head out one day earlier with Kami on the 22nd and join the others along the way. This was it. After 1½ strenuous months on this mountain of mythical proportions, the outcome of all our efforts would be revealed in one week.

At the back of my mind was another worry — a bad throat infection had caused me to lose my voice. I was coughing up blood-stained mucus and my throat was painfully dry. On top of that, conjunctivitis had set in, a mild condition in normal circumstances, but dangerous on the mountain. Wearing contact lenses over my conjunctivitis would inflame my eyes further, but I had no choice as I could not wear spectacles because of my goggles.

+ + +

As Kami and I started out towards ABC on 22 July, I couldn't believe my eyes. Much of the icefall had dissolved and melted so that our route was totally unrecognisable. The ropes that had been painstakingly threaded through the ice by the Sherpas on our earlier two rotations now lay limp, and the trail towards ABC had completely disappeared.

Kami and I stood in the middle of the icefall, bemused. We spent the next hour figuring out and constructing a new path through the remaining icefall. What used to be hoary ice frozen into striking blue towers were randomly collapsing in lethal showers of ice shards.

I could see the worry on Kami's face. But recceing a new route, he set up temporary fixed lines and managed to get us past the technical segments to ABC. This late in the year, the melting snow and ice put us in mortal danger of falling through thin ice and being buried in avalanches. My heart was hammering in my chest the entire time, in fight-or-flight mode.

The "easiest" segment of the summit push turned out to be a challenge.

That night, exhausted and with self doubt running through my mind, I wondered if I should carry on. The constant rumble of distant avalanches had Kami looking out of the tent often. Our unappetising dinner of instant noodles was swallowed in a haze of worry.

After a restless night at ABC, we struck out early for C1 on the 23rd, not sorry to leave the cold and bare camp that was frightfully exposed to the wild elements.

Immediately on leaving ABC, the weather turned foreboding. While I felt stronger than I did during the first two rotations, the punishing 40° incline and inclement weather made progress excruciatingly slow.

Historically, late July has seen the best weather for summiting K2. But not this year. From the get go it was snowing heavily and, halfway through our climb to C1, the winds started picking up as well. By the time we staggered into C1, the snow had reached blizzard proportions.

Notwithstanding the current snow dump, previous days of warmer weather had melted the snow beneath our tents so that the tents were either lopsided lumps or were sliding down the slope.

There was no help for it but to try to stand our ground in the howling winds and pelting snow storm to carve out meagre foundations for our tents and re-pitch each one. Finally collapsing in our tents, we were drained of energy from our battle with the elements. Through my mental haze, I wondered how our team was going to make it to C2 if this punishing weather continued.

Vanessa, Zhang Lian and I stayed on in C1 for the night. But, to my surprise, Hari, John, Ah Jung and Cheng Xue determinedly decided to proceed straight to C2.

The next day we awoke to a cold but clear day. It was such a contrast to the day before, we felt like we had been transported to a different mountain. On the spot, our expedition leader, Mingma G, decided to take advantage of this window of splendid weather to have the C1 climbers head directly to C3, bypassing C2. This would put us on track with the group who had headed to C2 the previous night.

But our optimism soon turned to dismay as the sky turned grey again and the winds picked up almost immediately after we left the relative security of the tents. Visibility grew murky as a shroud of cold fog settled over the mountain. The clouds, which had been heavy with the portent of further snow, released its load and soon I could not see anything beyond 20m of my fingers. Footprints of the climbers five minutes ahead of me were obliterated in seconds as snow filled their tracks.

By this time in the season, the top seam of snow on the steep inclines had melted away, exposing blue ice. You needed solid boots to kick in, and mine were the wrong size, causing me to waste energy. Imagine the slipperiness of walking on an ice rink. Now imagine that ice rink is tilted at a 40° angle and scattered with loose rock. The surface was nearly impossible to grip, either by hand or foot. We had to take extreme care not to step on or touch a loose rock. In fact, every foothold and handhold had to be carefully placed or we would either slip and tread air, or send a dangerous shower of rocks down on the climbers beneath us. Each step took a hard kick into the virgin ice. The fact that this was our second time here made zero difference.

Most of us were spent by the time we arrived at C2. Zhang Lian was the only one who decided to carry on to C3 in this dreadful weather. Vanessa and I chose to stay in C2 to recover. As I rolled into my tent, I was surprised to see our friendly teammate, Hari, in a sleeping bag. He had been in the previous day's party that had left for C3 instead of overnighting at C1. But he had taken ill with gastroenteritis and was coughing badly. Resting here in C2 for the night, he would attempt C3 with the rest of us the next day.

Hari was the fittest among us, a marathon runner who had trained in the Andes and in Bolivia before coming on this K2 climb. If anyone could summit, it was Hari.

We woke up on the 25th to weather that was even worse than the day before. Winds 50kmh rattled the tents so violently, I thought they would rip right apart. The snow was whipping past in blinding horizontal streaks. All the weather reports were being contradicted.

Expedition leader Mingma all but gave up on any data we had gathered.

We were at a crossroads. Not proceeding to C3 would cost us the summit. Yet to go on in this blizzard would be to stumble on blindly. On a mountain like K2, such a decision had danger written all over it.

Hari decided to turn back. Vanessa, on the other hand, summoned up every ounce of grit to turn her feet towards C3. It would likely take her eight hours in this wicked weather. She had spent almost a year in BC trying for the summit three times and she wasn't about to give up now.

The four Austrian/German climbers from Furtenbach Adventures turned back from C2. We heard that all the Himex climbers on the Cessan route also decided to turn around. The two Mexicans, a husband and wife pair, were still in BC waiting for clear weather to set off — they had not yet started on their summit bid. The Polish, too, were still stuck in BC. That left our team, a Swedish climber and a Mongolian climber some way behind him on the Abruzzi Route.

A million thoughts were running through my mind: The weather predictions were no longer in unison with weather reports, which put the summit day on 27 July in question.

If, against the odds, we made it to the summit, the weather on the 28th looked like it would be horrific, making the descent dangerous.

To make matters worse, the fixed lines betwen C3 and C4 had been swept away by a huge avalanche. It was possible that our stash of oxygen and other climbing equipment we had stowed above C3 had also been swept away.

Even the hardy Sherpas were unable, in this weather, to ferry further loads up to C4. It was impossible for them to check the state of the fixed lines and equipment above C3. The high winds expected on the 26th would make it unlikely for them to repair the fixed lines up to C4 by our summit try on 27th.

I had to face the facts: My chances of summiting were low to zero and the risks were high. My fitness and health were not at their peak, and my reserves at this point were thin. Any event out of the ordinary on the way up or down and I knew I would struggle. Worse, I would be a burden to my team.

To be honest, I'm not sure I would have chosen to turn back if this had been my first or second climb. But over the years I had learnt to respect the mountain, respect my team and respect my limitations.

It was still a difficult decision to turn around and head back. But I was at peace with it.

I would push as far as I could with Kami, then peel off from the rest of the team to return to BC.

The 26th dawned without sun but with fog. Visibility was so poor, we could not make out anything but the tent infront of us. There did not seem any point in heading up. Rapelling and trekking our way down to ABC, we descended into the rolling sea of fog, feeling for rock and crag for a steady foothold or handhold. The icefall had reinvented itself once again, even since we had passed it on the way up.

By the afternoon, we had made it back to BC.

Some time during the journey, an unusual incident occurred. A climber had hired two Balti guides, who did not quite have the expertise of Sherpa guides. One of them broke his crampons. Another heard I was a doctor and came to consult me as he said he had stomach pains. From what he described, it was possible he had appendicitis. Vomiting and feeling poorly, he asked if he should turn back. I told him appendicitis could be serious. He decided to turn back. When the climber heard about his guides' decision, he was livid. He suspected that his two guides were just making excuses to leave and threatened to sue me for advising his guide to turn back. It struck me as bizarre that, during my years in medical practice, I had never been threatened with a lawsuit, but it happened on K2. I gave the climber my professional details as he demanded, but curiously, I didn't hear from him subsequently.

Descending from C2 after our decision to turn back from the summit push.

+ + +

In the coming weeks, I followed the fortunes of my teammates with interest.

Vanessa fought the bad weather to reach C3 on the 25th, joining the three Chinese and John. The five of them pushed upwards from C3 to C4 (7,600m) in thick fog and wild winds on the 26th. The weather made the going slow and, despite climbing till about 7pm, they could not find the true C4 site and decided to pitch camp where they were. The freshly fallen snow was so thick around them that they had to dig away 1.5m of snow and ice in order to construct their tents. The next morning, they woke up to find that they had drifted way off path and, had they ventured further in the darkness, would have fallen to their deaths.

The team realised they were not going to make the summit on the 27th, and decided to aim for the 28th instead. With oxygen tanks on, the climbers rested in C4 for the whole of the 27th, gathering their strength for the final push. But the Sherpas braved the elements to fix the lines above C4. Deep snow prevented them from going further than just below the Bottle Neck.

This was the most dangerous part of the climb. No one knew if the serac would collapse and, if it did, they were dead. Even if it didn't, the way ahead was complex. You'd have to go under the serac, then snare the rope past the serac to proceed. Below was a sheer drop.

In 2008, a group of climbers who successfully summited were returning when the serac collapsed and tore away their fixed lines. To descend would basically mean rockclimbing down at 8,000m without any safety lines. They were in the death zone where their oxygen and water had run out. Their options were cruel: Descend and possibly die from a fall, or stay put and most certainly die. There was no choice but to descend, and true enough some of the climbers fell and were found dead many metres below the Bottle Neck.

At 10pm on the 27th, the team set off for the summit, pushing against high winds. The plan was to turn back at noon on the 28th, regardless of the outcome of the climb. It was a matter of life and death, as the weather was set to turn extremely bad after noon the next day.

From 9am on the 28th, the Sherpas started fixing ropes past the Bottle Neck, with their clients following closely behind. Again the winds defied the weather reports, but this time to the climbers' advantage. The high winds predicted for the afternoon calmed down instead.

Mingma took a chance and had the group push on, banking on the morning's report of calmer skies in the afternoon. Even with this gift of good weather, the group needed to push through, at times, waist deep snow, less than ideal visibility and winds that picked up as the afternoon wore on. After 17 hours, the team was close to the summit when — a miracle — the weather cleared up brilliantly, allowing the team to summit K2 at 1535h on 28 July.

Together with their Sherpa guides, they were the only five clients to summit K2 that year.

By 8pm, they had made it back to C4. On the evening of the 29th, they had returned to Base Camp, some straggling in as late as 11pm.

This was Vanessa, Cheng Xie and Jang Ga's third attempt at K2. John had set his sights on being the first Icelander to summit K2. Zhang Liang was on a quest to complete all 14 peaks over 8,000m.

I was chuffed for all of them — they had pushed themselves to the limit and taken risks which paid off. Together with the Sherpas, who had led them all the way to the top, they deserved all the accolades for summiting in such a difficult and unpredictable season. My congratulations to them was heartfelt.

That year also saw two records by Pakistani guides: Amin was the fourth Pakistani to complete five of the 8,000m peaks in Pakistan with his successful summit of Broad Peak. Fadzeel became the first Pakistani to climb K2 twice successfully and is, I belive, the first Pakistani to do so twice without supplemental oxygen.

The wonderful weather window on 28 July saw Fadzeel and our team's five clients and six Sherpas summiting K2 for the first time. Mingma summited for the second time, and would go on to be one of the 10 Nepali men completing the first-ever winter ascent in January 2021 with Nims Purja.

Was I disappointed in my decision to turn back on the 25th? I would be lying if I said I wasn't.

K2 was the toughest expedition of all for me. I was not as fit as I could have been, I fell ill, and I was wishing I could have been with Gayathri as she took her emergency medicine specialist exit exams. Worst of all, my grandma passed away while I was here, just after my first rotation. She'd suffered a massive stroke and was hospitalised when I left. Not wanting to break my focus, my family only told me over a crackling satellite phone line when I was back in BC. I was devastated that I had not been around during her last rites.

In turning back, I made a decision I could live with.

Now, when I look back on K2, I am grateful to have even had the opportunity to climb (and survive) this legendary peak.

After all, many haven't.

CHAPTER 14

"Thousands of tired, nerve-shaken, over-civilized people are beginning to find out that going to the mountains is going home; that wildness is a necessity."

John Muir

In every ER (emergency room) in the world, doctors save lives.

But in a tragic twist of fate, on 26 April 2015, it was the ER doctor who died.

American Marisa Eve Girawong, 28, was volunteering as a camp doctor at the Everest Base Camp ER when a massive avalanche triggered by a 7.8 earthquake engulfed the camp.

Eyewitnesses say the 21 fatalities at BC died as a result of the explosive air blast generated by the avalanche.

"The compressed air that the chunks of snow and ice created in the bowl adjacent to the Glacier had to be released somewhere," Dr Jon Kedrowski, a Colorado mountaineer who was at BC at the time of the earthquake, told National Geographic.

"People in tents were wrapped up in them, lifted by the force of the blast and then slammed down onto rocks, glacial moraine and ice on the glacier."

Ironically, the climbers who were up in C1 and C2 during the calamitous quake were physically unharmed, though significant aftershocks were still reverberating around them.

The tragic news shook Gayathri and me.

Just three years ago, in 2012, we were standing in that very Everest ER tent, talking to American Dr Luanne Freer.

It was Dr Freer who, in 2003, had set up the world's highest ER at 5,380m. The director of medicine at Yellowstone National Park, she had envisioned providing timely, basic medical intervention for the thousands of expedition climbers pushing their bodies to extreme limits every Everest/Lhotse season.

This high-altitude facility, with its eye-catching red Everest ER logo on its side, is no more than a plain, cylindrical tent with the capacity for a handful of camp beds and an assemblage of mostly donated medical supplies, transported by yak or porter. Still, the ER tent is one of the most solid structures at Base Camp.

Run by the Himalayan Rescue Association and staffed by volunteer doctors from around the world including Nepal, international clients are charged for consultation and medication while Sherpas received free care.

Common ailments appearing in the medical tent include fractures, hypothermia and respiratory tract infections like the notorious "Khumbu cough". This is a cough triggered by cold, dry air that is so violent, it has been known to break ribs. Scores more come down with gastrointestinal problems, which affect climbing ability. Others fall prey to AMS when they push themselves too far too quickly.

And then there are the accidents.

Snowstorms, hailstorms and high winds buffet the tents at EBC, a "pop up metropolis" set at the foot of the Khumbu Glacier. Occasional earthquakes and avalanches dial up the danger.

In a BBC article, Dr Freer told of an Italian climber who was hit on the head by a falling ice chunk. In a daring rescue by 50 climbers, the injured man was strapped to a sled and transported gingerly over the dangerous glacier to EBC, where he was heli-evacuated to Kathmandu.

"Climbers tend to get a bad rap for being a selfish group, wanting to bag a peak and not being team players," Dr Freer told BBC News.

"In fact what we got to see was an extraordinary example of people pulling together for the benefit of someone that nobody even knew.

"Everyone was absolutely committed to getting him down safely and it was really quite inspiring."

At the time we met Dr Freer, I had just completed a month at the Phortse clinic, and Gayathri was about to take over the community work. Already, we felt a sense of belonging here in the Khumbu, and the idea of one day joining Dr Freer and other doctors volunteering at the Everest ER was hugely appealing to me.

But I wasn't qualified yet.

Dr Freer, a member of the Wilderness Medical Society for medical professionals working in extreme environments, urged me to first get trained in mountain medicine.

I never forgot that.

In November 2017, I found myself back in Nepal, first to climb K2 and Makalu, and then to lead a Project Aasha trip to Bung. In between, I would take my Diploma in Mountain Medicine.

+ + +

You could say the Diploma in Mountain Medicine (DiMM) is the Bear Grylls of medical qualifications.

Combining fieldwork, skills training and classroom teaching DiMM has been designed to train doctors and nurses in mountain medicine and rescue.

In Dr Freer's words: "It's really very satisfying to take a situation — an illness or an injury that would make many doctors throw their hands up and say, 'I don't have my nurses, I don't have my hospital' — and make it work in a really hostile and austere environment."

I got to see for myself what she meant during the DiMM course.

My 20 or so classmates in Nepal turned out to be a fascinating bunch from the US, Ireland, Australia, Lithuania, UK, Nepal, Iceland and Canada. They were around my age and were mostly residents in anaesthesia and emergency medicine who were taking the diploma as part of their residency programmes. One of the Canadians was, impressively, both a certified climbing guide and an anaesthesia resident. I was the only orthopaedic resident. The local participants were young medical graduates sent by the Mountain Medicine Society of Nepal, which was keen to boost participation of local doctors in the Everest ER.

The faculty was an equally global group hailing from the US, Canada, UK and Switzerland, mostly emergency specialists, some of whom had published papers on high-altitude medicine. Scottish orthopaedic surgeon, Dr John McCall, was not just an accomplished physician but also a leading name in the climbing community.

Tenzeeng, one of the local instructors who would teach us climbing techniques, was a familiar face. I had met him on my first trek to EBC and Island Peak in 2009 with a group of friends from MIR, and we have been friends ever since. Lean and wiry, with a mild-mannered personality, Tenzeeng's tenacity, humility and good humour gave me my first glimpse into the capability and warmth of the Sherpa people. It's rare to find anyone anywhere whom you feel you can totally count on, and I found that in Tenzeeng.

By 2017, Tenzeeng had been certified by the International Federation of Mountain Guides Association (IFMGA), the highest level of credential attainable by a professional mountain guide, recognised in more than 20 international IFMGA member countries. Very few climbers in Nepal had these credentials, which made him well respected in the climbing community.

DiMM classes started out with lectures on mountain medicine. Briton Dr Suzy Stokes managed our medical syllabus. Not only was she an emergency medicine physician, she had been at the Everest ER in 2014 when 16 Sherpas died in one of the worst accidents in the history of Everest. They were victims of an avalanche that suddenly fell from the hanging glaciers along the west shoulder, burying the Sherpas in the "popcorn field" or sweeping them into the crevasses of the Khumbu Icefall.

Suzy was shaken as Sherpas were rushed into EBC needing triage. She and the other volunteer physicians had to compose themselves to treat fractures and open wounds, and immobilise those who had spinal fractures, preparing them to be heli-evacuated to Kathmandu, praying all the while that they would stay alive. There was only so much that could be done in the basic Everest Base Camp ER. One by one the worst cases died from their injuries. The Sherpas she saw remained stoic till the end, she said.

After her tale, we were even more motivated to pick up any medical skills that could be of critical help in the mountains. There was no way to treat major health conditions at EBC, but in those environments even minor conditions can turn life threatening. So we went through the minor procedures, including sedation, incision and drainage of abscesses, toileting (cleansing a wound), immobilising fractures with splints, treating heat exhaustion and sunburn.

When I was on my expeditions, it was rare to find another doctor on the team. Now, I was surrounded by doctors who climbed. It was a novel and refreshing experience.

Fascinating as the coursework was, it was the instructors' personal sharing that really made an impact on me.

The Swiss instructor, an emergency physician, related how he was once on a climb and was thinking about home and his wife and kids. In the middle of the night, he woke up with an inexplicably sharp pain in his upper thigh. He was unable to identify the cause, and remained uneasy. The next day, he phoned home and his wife asked: "How did you know I was just about to pick up the phone to call you?"

It turned out that their son had been diagnosed with a pathological fracture of the femur, a benign bone tumour, and the exact time his son felt a stab of pain was also the time his father, over 7,000km away, was woken up by pain in the same anatomical area.

Our instructor did not attempt to explain this extraordinary incident. But here he was, a scientifically trained physician, relating this phenomenon to a roomful of other scientifically trained physicians. And the odd thing was, we all knew what he meant. There are some things in this universe that cannot be explained away by science and hard facts.

While our classes were in Kathmandu, I was staying at the Manaslu Hotel, near Thamel. It was climbing season again, and many of my friends were in town. So after classes during the day, I'd rendezvous with them in the evenings, when we'd regale each other with our adventures, or misadventures, together.

Rollicking reunions included dinners with Ang Jangbu, his friend Ang Rita (who had connected me with medical institutions in Bung for Project Aasha), Jamling, Tenzeeng and Pasang. It had been five to seven years since I'd seen most of them but, to my delight, they hadn't changed much. We ate a lot at the hipster café with a dance floor just beside my hotel, as I caught up with their lives.

Ang Jangbu was my first guide ever in 2009 as our MIR group trekked to EBC and climbed Island Peak together with Tenzeeng and his friends Pasang and Kabit. He was now based in the US with his Nepali wife and was working with an American climbing outfitter.

Tenzeeng and Pasang had started a mountaineering equipment company, Everest Outfit, and were still jovial and fun-loving. When they came to Singapore in 2018 to publicise their company, they had stayed in my home. Tenzeeng had a baby boy then, and now has two kids.

They were all still guiding, with Jamling continuing to take on the big mountains. Here they were not my Sherpa guides, they were my friends — in fact, my oldest friends in Nepal. There is something about the friends I've made in this raw, rough-and-tumble, wild country that I can't help but warm to.

Other reunions included catching up with Esther Tan, with whom I had climbed Chola, and Mr Netra who updated me on his beloved Aahale.

After two weeks in our Kathmandu classroom, it was time for our DiMM class to make our way to our "outdoor classroom" for the field component.

The outdoor half of DiMM was a great adventure. From Kathmandu, our van travelling on a paved road to Besishahar gave way to a four-wheel-drive bumping along on a rougher track to Chame rural municipality, whereupon we ditched the wheels totally for a three-day hike to Manang (3,500m) which was to be our base for the next two weeks.

Scenarios were thrown up even during our three-day hike, and there was plenty of interactive problem-solving. We were split into different teams — some in the forest, some on the mountain. Once an instructor told two teammates to hide, just to see how long it took before the other teammates noticed their absence and how they would organise a search-and-rescue.

Our lodge in Manang, where we would stay for two weeks, was perched on the edge of the circular Annapurna range. It was one of the last few villages before the Thorong La Pass connecting the eastern and western parts of the Annapurna Circuit. Temperatures were falling as winter approached, and every night a stray cat would come to my sleeping bag to take refuge.

Early in the morning, we would head out to learn how to create a lightweight stretcher out of our own backpack; improvise a makeshift harness out of ropes; assign rescue duties and call for help; signal a heli and evacuate the sick. There were navigation exercises with a compass and map. Dr Ken Zafren, a doctor from Anchorage, Alaska, gave us lectures on frostbite.

Dr Zafren had been a famous climber in the 1980s and was also known for his textbooks on frostbite and other emergency medicine topics. He was one of the remarkable people I met who would show me that it was possible to be both a fine physician and pursue a passion outside of medicine to a high level.

After two weeks at the lodge, we went even higher, camping out in tents on the Kang La Pass (5,320m), where temperatures dropped to -20°C at night. Our final week's "classroom" was on the Kang La Glacier.

Up to this point, we'd been given mostly high-altitude medical training. Now the physical portion kicked in. The physicians switched out with mountaineers like Tenzeeng, who became our new instructors.

We went from low-altitude rock climbing in Kathmandu to high-altitude rescue operations on the Kang La Glacier, learning how to tie ourselves safely in an improvised self belay, how to clip on to a rescue heli, how to fasten ice screws on the ice and conduct a rescue on a vertical ice wall.

It was so cold on the glacier that I had to wear the down suit I used when climbing 8,000m mountains.

Before my classmates and I parted ways after this unforgettable month, there was a party where we had to, yup *improvise*, our costumes. (I was Batman.)

DiMM had not been all fun and games — in fact, it was quite an undertaking that spanned over 1½ years, including assignments and assessments before and after this one month in Kathmandu and Kang La.

But, like everything I'd done related to climbing, delving into mountain medicine deeply fulfilled the part of me that loved the physical challenge, loved expanding my horizons by meeting different people with eye-opening stories, and loved knowing I had learnt something that could somehow, some day, be of help to others.

+ + +

Training on the use of the gammow bag in Manang.

Improvising high altitude casualty rescue.

The 2017 Nepalese DiMM course participants and instructors during the helicopter rescue training session.

With Tenzeeng, my DiMM instructor and good friend, against the backdrop of the Annapurna range.

In the six-month window I'd taken off from work, I'd set my sights on climbing K2 and Makalu, spending one month on DiMM, followed by two weeks in Bung with Project Aasha.

Makalu (8,485m), the world's fifth highest mountain, was the final 8,000er I was compelled to climb before retiring from death zone peaks.

Sir Edmund Hillary himself had mentioned this remote and beautiful massif: "While on top of Everest, I looked across the valley towards the great peak Makalu and mentally worked out a route about how it could be climbed.

"It showed me that even though I was standing on top of the world, it wasn't the end of everything. I was still looking beyond to other interesting challenges. "

Makalu looms large in the eye of every Everester descending the south-east ridge. It was on my Everest climb that I first set eyes on Makalu and knew I had to climb her one day. Amidst a sea of incredible peaks, Makalu still stood out in size and stature, hence its name in the local dialect: Kumba Karna, or Giant.

Jamling Bhote, my guide in Ama Dablam in 2011, would be my Sherpa on Makalu.

Jamling had started life in a humble village in the Sankhuwasabha district at the foothills of Makalu. With Makalu in his backyard, he had always wanted to climb it but had never had the chance.

Married as a teenager and a father soon after, Jamling had started as a humble mess tent boy helping the camp cook. Bit by bit, he rose up the ranks to be a cook, then a porter, then even further to be a Sherpa. Eventually the enterprising young man set up his own climbing company, Everquest. My Ama Dablam climb was the first-ever expedition organised by Everquest. So it proved to be historic, not just for our team, but for his, too.

The first time I heard of Jamling, I was still in NUS MIR. He was already a Himalayan superstar whose fitness was reputed to be on another level. At the time he was only the second person in the world who had summited K2 twice, once with Khoo Swee Chiow and the other with Lien Choong Luen.

Like many Sherpas, the jovial, happy-go-lucky Jamling had no formal education but picked up languages like English through his years of guiding. Through the earnings from his guiding, he managed to put all three of his children through university.

The Sherpas' relationship with the mountains is ambivalent. While many of them do not want their children to face the dangers of guiding, Sherpa friends tell me that the profession provides them with the only means to give their children a better future. Many Sherpas start off in humble circumstances but become superstars in the climbing community because of the mountains. In one lifetime, the fortunes of their families can change. Many go on to own guest lodges.

It is not an easy decision for them to leave the mountains, despite the danger.

+ + +

My 33rd birthday on 7 September 2017 saw Jamling and me making our way to Lukla. We were lucky to get on this flight to Lukla — for 12 days before this, all flights had been cancelled because of horrendous weather.

Soon after the plane took off, however, we weren't feeling so lucky.

By now I'd taken multiple flights to and from the "world's most dangerous airport". But this flight turned out to be the most harrowing yet.

There was so much turbulence, I feared that the wings of the plane would break off at any moment. No one, probably not even the pilot, could make out the airport. The runway was completely enveloped in thick cloud. One moment it was invisible, and the next moment — through a break in the cloud — the runway appeared directly below us. I was certain that it was too late to land on the notoriously short runway. But, no, the pilot descended the plane with such alacrity, it felt for an instant like we were free falling. Before we could panic, he landed the plane safely, to everyone's great relief.

The timing was fortunate. It turned out that we would be the last flight that day as the weather took a turn for the worse.

We overnighted in Phakding (2,610m), a rustic village set in the lush Dudh Kosi river valley just north of Lukla that, by virtue of its traditional Himalayan charm, is a Unesco World Heritage site. Then it was on to Namche (3,440m). The overcast skies and pelting monsoon rain lingered unseasonally, driving away tourists and leaving the usually lively Namche a soggy ghost town.

The next day we headed to Thame (3,800m) on an idyllic trek across swinging bridges, up and down earth paths and past an unbelievably stunning panorama of mountain ranges only seen in the Himalayas.

Before Phortse held the record of being home to the highest number of superstar Sherpas, there was Thame. In the 1980s and 90s, Thame was home to many a famous Sherpa, including Apa Sherpa, nicknamed "Super Sherpa", who held the world record for summiting Everest 21 times until he was surpassed in 2018 by fellow Thame resident, Kami Rita Sherpa, who has since summited Everest an astounding 25 times as of May 2021. No doubt they were inspired by the original Everester, Tenzing Norgay, who also had his childhood home in Thame.

At 5,360m, and about 1,500m above Thame, Sunder Peak is described by Lonely Planet as "the toughest of all the viewpoints (to reach) in the Khumbu" thanks to its steep paths. But an unhampered view from the peak of Sunder which took in almost the whole of the Khumbu valley, promised to be worth the effort.

As soon as we hit Thame from Namche, we took off for Sunder Peak, preparing ourselves mentally for the 2km increase in vertical elevation within a single day. Perhaps it was the knowledge that Makalu would be my final 8,000m climb, or perhaps the earth and green scrub beneath my feet and the brilliant blue of the sky, with wisps of cloud blowing in, made me feel like I was walking heaven's path.

Whatever it was, this turned out to be the kind of trek that fed my soul. From time to time, the clouds parted to give us glimpses of the snow-cloaked Thamserku and Kongde ranges. Our path was well trodden, and there was just a slight scramble up some big boulders close to the summit.

After 4 hours and 15 minutes, we made it to the False Summit, just below 5,000m. Darkness was quickly descending and we decided to make our way down before the going got unsafe, keeping in mind that our objective was just acclimatisation. Within 1 hour and 45 minutes we were back in our warm Thame lodge.

The nine-hour trek had been exhausting. But it did a lot to boost my confidence. I was feeling fitter and faster than when I'd trekked K2 just weeks before.

Waking up refreshed, we refilled our rations, packed lightly, and headed west towards Rolwaling village. This part of the valley was off the beaten Everest trek and we didn't pass a single other trekker. At 4,800m, we hit the High Camp, expecting to pitch our tents.

To our pleasant surprise, we found a new wood-and-stone shelter built. It felt like a resort to us. That night, we sipped hot tea in our sleeping bags as we watched *Fast & Furious* on Jamling's phone. (Climbers watch a lot of movies to pass the evenings.) Even dinner — the ubiquitous instant noodles — tasted perfect. (Our other meal of choice was peanut butter sandwiches, which were sweet, nutritious and easy to chew.)

As I lay in my familiar sleeping bag, with the patter of raindrops on the shelter's zinc roof drumming a soothing tattoo, I couldn't help smiling as my eyelids drifted shut. It had been a long time since I had felt this sense of well-being. All I possessed at the moment could be carried on my back. But it was all I needed.

This stone shelter was a stark contrast to where I was a month ago, on the harsh Baltoro Glacier in Pakistan.

Here in the eastern Himalayas, everything was gentler. I was in a familiar setting with familiar faces. I was in the company of a trusted friend and climber, Jamling, who enlivened each moment with his cheerfulness and simple outlook in life. Despite the nip of the cold mountain air, the satisfaction of the moment kept me nice and warm.

Jamling and I hit the Tashi Lapsa Glacier quickly the next day. It was a relatively challenging climb, with no flat ground on which to rest. The slip and slide on the ice reminded me of the endless days I'd spent on the Baltoro Glacier. Numerous rockfalls and scrambles up loose rocks and scree took us to an altitude of 5,500m, where Jamling made the decision to set up camp under a sheer vertical cliff, just 100-200m from the top of the pass.

Despite the danger, the day's climb had been satisfying and, as the night passed, we were glad there were no signs of AMS. Mentally as well as physically, I was feeling ready for Makalu as we walked back to Namche the next day and to Lukla the day after.

We had gone from 1,300m in Kathmandu to 5,500m on the Tashi Lapsa Pass in five days. It was a pretty taxing acclimatisation schedule. But, luckily for me, bits of altitude memory lingered and I hoped this acclimatisation and the experience of K2 would bode well for Makalu.

+ + +

On 14 September, Jamling and I took a chopper straight to the Makalu Base Camp (5,700m). As the chopper flew low towards Makalu, we were treated to close-up views of the soaring Ama Dablam and Island Peak as we crossed the saddle between Num Ri on the left and Baruntse on the right.

Looming right ahead was Makalu, its sheer size inspiring awe. The Makalu Barun Conservation Area alone is about 1,500 sq km — that's more than double Singapore's total area of 720 sq km.

Profound snow, dizzying drop-offs and extreme weather conditions make Makalu an 8,000er with a low summit success rate. Which might have accounted for the fact that our team was the only one on Makalu this autumn.

Our compact team from climbing outfitter Sherpa Shepherds consisted of six foreign climbers, including myself, as well as just seven Sherpas to set the lines, transport equipment, break trails and personally guide us.

The clients included French team leader François, who worked in telecoms in France, and fellow Frenchman Meidi, who worked in Gabon, Africa. They lived life as a series of adventures, climbing, skiing and paragliding around the world. Their comfort food was wine, cheese and prosciutto, which they toted up the mountain to the benefit of the rest of us who got a taste after our acclimatisation climbs.

Their friends were compatriots David, an older but fit guy with an academic forehead, and Pasçal who was more prim and proper.

There was also a female from China who didn't speak English. An uber fit climber, she was attempting Makalu without oxygen.

Our small, but colourful, team included Sherpas Dukchung, who was Jamling's cousin, and Dhakipa, who had had a role in the movie *Everest,* which he went to Europe to film. Nima was unusually tall for a Sherpa and super strong, easily spotted by his trademark grey cap and yellow jacket. Kami, with his high cheekbones, reminded me of Mike Tyson.

Pempa (whom the rest nicknamed "Speed") and Nurbu made up the rest of the Sherpa team.

The most remarkable person in the support team was a slight fellow in his early 20s whom the Sherpas dubbed "Rescue". In his nondescript grey beanie and red suit, he would regularly wend his way up and down the extremely rough trail to the Yak Lodge for supplies.

From Base Camp, we could see him, head down and a basket strapped to his forehead, making his way down into the ravine shod only in sandals. After we lost sight of him, it would still be several hours' trek to the Yak Lodge and back.

I never found out why his nickname was Rescue, but it could well be because he regularly "rescued" them with supplies of fortifying Khukri Rum. Arguments would sometimes break out at the Sherpa

The trek from BC to Yak Lodge.

Our Makalu BC on the Southwest route.

camp after a round or two of the rum, but the next day they would be none the worse for it.

The monsoon season would normally have been tapering off when we started our climb in September. But we were to discover the fickle nature of Makalu weather.

After the puja day, my first day of acclimatisation had me touching C1 (6,150m) and coming back to BC on the same day. The four Frenchmen arrived on 18 September by helicopter. Seasoned climbers all, they were, like the Chinese climber, attempting to summit Makalu without oxygen.

The plan for my next four-day rotation was to sleep at C1, then spend a night at C2 (6,400m), carry on the next day to climb as high above C2 as possible and return to C2, making my way down to BC the following day.

But the weather turned dreadful from the start. Without crampons till C1, I was using my axe to chip at the hoary ice to make steps upwards. The sky was dumping snow when we hit C1 at about 2pm and it continued a heavy onslaught through the next two days. We made it to C2 under poor visibility, digging into the snow just to pitch our tents. But we were forced to descend to BC in knee-deep snow the next day as the snow dump had heightened avalanche risk.

This second rotation was meant to be our final rotation as the summit weather window was approaching. There would not be another cycle. My nerves were on edge. Was I acclimatised enough for the summit push?

We were following the weather forecast closely. September 30 and October 1 looked like good days to leave for the summit push. During our rest days, some of the Sherpas took turns to lay fixed lines. For two days, they did the fixing from C2 and came within 200m shy of C3 before returning to BC for a brief rest in preparation for the summit bid. That left the terrain after C3 largely unknown.

From the team, only the muscular Kami had summited Makalu. Norbu had reached C3 in past expeditions. The rest of us were new to Makalu, and depended heavily on Kami to lead the way.

A day's rest at the Yak Hotel on the southeast ridge BC (4,700m) would make for a good break. Or so we thought.

That trek proved to be one of the worst treks I'd done to date. The way was littered with boulders and marked with icy, swift-flowing rivers which we had to cross in order to get to the other side. It was far

The view of Makalu from Yak Kharka, the last lodge along the Makalu Barun trek.

from the easy climb we had envisioned. Making our way on slopes of slippery scree and moraine the size of motorbikes was exhausting.

On 27 September, we decided to start out from BC on our summit push. There were two teams: The first team included myself, the female Chinese climber Jiandan, Frenchmen Meidi and David, and a team of Sherpas comprising Jamling, Nima, Kami, Dhakipa and Duk Chung. A day earlier, Kami, Dhakipa and Duk Chung had left to finish fixing the lines to C3. The plan was for them to join our team when they hit C2.

The second team, who would follow two days behind, included the other two French climber, Pascal and Francois, as well as Sherpas Pemba, Kanchi Maya and Nurbu.

We left BC with the goal of making it straight to C2. Skipping C1 would be a first for me. To be honest, I wasn't feeling hopeful. Despite being at my fittest, self-doubt weighed me down and I felt as though I was taking on an 8,000m peak for the first time.

The trail from BC (5,700m) to C1 (6,150m) was not a trail at all but a huge expanse of loose moraine of various sizes, some as big as boulders, that had us scrambling on all fours at times. There was some straightforward, though near vertical, rock climbing and a crossing over a rapidly flowing stream before we could walk to the massive glacier flowing from the southern ridge of Makalu.

The glacier, tucked in a valley surrounded by the high head walls of the ridgeline, was a relatively straightforward walk on a sustained gentle slope all the way to C1.

From C1, our crampons and fixed lines made it relatively easy-going to reach the southwest ridge, where the glacier evened out to the level of the moraine.

The weather at C1 was similar to that of the Western Cwm on Everest. The three walls of the ridgeline angled the sun's rays into the centre of the glacier where C1 sat, warming it like a microwave oven.

I felt strong as we left BC and was leading the team all the way to the crampon point. Only the French had stashed their crampons in a duffle bag at the crampon point, allowing them to easily mount the glacier and quickly be on their way to C1.

Jamling and I had left our crampons in C1. Getting onto the glacier with no harness or crampons was too dangerous. So we made a tediously slow scramble up the loose moraine until we found a suitable spot to safely climb onto the glacier.

Heavy snow from a storm the previous week had melted away to form an icy crust. Every few steps, our feet would break through the crust and sink knee-deep into the slushy mix of ice and snow beneath. It was a slow, draining slog to C1 that took four hours.

Each time the sun beat down on us, I wished for the shadow of cloud cover; each time a passing cloud obscured the sun, the cold crept into our bones. The fluctuating temperature didn't do much to help us regain lost energy. Too tired to make a fire to cook lunch, we downed a few bites of canned sardines, boiled egg and chocolate at C1 (6,150m), before starting out for C2 (6,400m).

Almost immediately the steep wall of an ice ridge bore down on us. After about 200m of vertical jummaring, the slope flattened out, exposing an enormous expanse of snow all around.

As the trail turned southwards, we passed impressive crevasses before turning north again, this time over a gentle slope of pristine snow, till we reached C2 at the foot of the massive face of Makalu II (7,678m).

The Frenchmen had reached C1 an hour before we did, heading towards C2 an hour before Jamling and I even left C1. The two of us were the last in the team to ascend.

In the absolute silence, with the towering mountains standing guard over this snowy landscape as they have since time immemorial, it was as though we were in a land before time. I relished the solitude. Apart from Jamling, there was just me with these mountains, my thoughts, and God.

Knowing this was the last 8,000m peak that I would climb made the moment achingly poignant.

+ + +

A big advantage of Makalu's low traffic was being able to clear the fixed lines relatively quickly. We had a 3½-hour slog up the deep snow drifts to C2. Still, it was faster than our timing during the previous rotation.

We made it to C2 about nine hours after leaving BC. I had overcome the first day of my mental barrier: Fearing the long climb from BC to C2.

Kami, Dhakiapa and Duk Chung, who had left a day earlier than we did, had just finished fixing all the lines to C3, and had returned to C2 for the night.

What a relief to know that the lines to C3 had finally been established.

By reputation, the toughest stretch of the climb was right ahead of us: From C2 (6,400m) to C3 (7,500m).

After one night in C2, the next day a gradual 250m slope took us to the base of the wall leading to Makalu La on the southwest ridge. Here, at 6,650m, the second set of fixed lines started.

It was a technical mixed-climb up rock, ice and snow for about 900 vertical metres on this vast eastern wall, until the trail flattened out at Makalu La, where C3 was sited. This kind of terrain was familiar to me as it was similar to C1 to C2 on K2.

C3 saddled the summit of Makalu (8,463m) on the south and Malaku II (7,678m) on the north. Technically, Makalu La formed the border between Nepal and Tibet, which meant that reaching C3 would place one officially in Tibet. It was much easier crossing the border into Tibet this time — no passports needed — than when I was making my way to Cho Oyu!

We left later than the rest of the team and, once again, were at the rear. I didn't mind; it gave me the privilege of solitude.

The fixed lines started again at the bottom of the eastern wall leading to Makalu La. This time the technicalities stymied me. Every time I thought we had arrived at C3, there was another slope. Without oxygen, I was exhausted at the seemingly endless, steep climb without any flat ground to stop for a break. But Kami kept saying that we were guaranteed the summit if we reached C3, and that motivated me to keep going, knowing that I was tackling the toughest part.

Jamling had had the foresight to ask Duk Chung to standby an oxygen bottle for me, in case I was too slow on this segment. But, surprisingly, I was able to keep up with the rest of the team ahead and didn't need the oxygen. Most parts of this segment were actually steeper than the slopes of K2, but were easier to climb. The weather was perfect.

Jamling was right behind me and called out encouragingly that my pace was strong. We made sure we didn't lag too much behind the rest of the team.

But as we approached the pass, my steps slowed excruciatingly. I felt like I was on the moon — progress was at a snail's pace. I was incredibly winded.

Forcing myself to keep moving forward, the slope finally flattened out at Makalu La. At this point, C3 was just about 100m away, yet it took me another 15 mins to get there.

I staggered into C3 totally spent. The climb from C2 to C3 had taken nine hours. But the reward was sublime.

The views of Everest and Lhotse were pristine. From this angle the two were inseparable.

Chomo Lonzo (7,804m) loomed to the north, and the entire Tibetan plateau spread out before us. This was the highest I had ever been without supplemental oxygen — my personal record. It was an incredibly proud moment for me.

Before Jamling and I arrived at C3, the other Sherpas had recced the trail above the camp, returning with a report of deep snow all the way to C4. It might be impossible to break trail to C4, came the sobering news.

Nevertheless they would try. So the next day turned out to be a rest day for Meidi, David, Jiandan and me, as the Sherpas tried breaking trail to C4 and fixing lines above that.

Summit day was pushed back by a day. That meant we would be short of food on summit day; if the weather changed and we were unable to get down the mountain, that situation could turn disastrous.

But we would take it a step at a time. That night, I was a happy camper, as I slept comfortably with oxygen. But Duk Chung wasn't so lucky. During the night he came down with a headache and popped some paracetamol. Unfortunately he developed an allergic reaction, which left him itching away the entire night. He woke up sick the next morning. By midday, he had lost his motivation to continue and planned to go down the mountain the following day.

It was a big blow to our team's morale. The small support team of five Sherpas become even smaller.

After our unplanned rest day at C3 on 29 September, we set off for C4 on the 30th knowing that the route had been painstakingly broken by the four brave Sherpas without oxygen the day before.

From C3, a largely flat, but extensively snowed-in trail stretched eastwards, further into Tibet, until the trail reached the icy, steeper slopes just below the summit.

Some climbers had been known to skip C4, making straight for the summit from C3, as the 150m elevation gain was minimal. Other expeditions had been forced to turn back from C3 as a result of deep snow, unstable conditions and risk of avalanche. We could not know which we would be until we stepped out of C3.

The weather was perfectly clear as we made our way from C3 (7,500m) to C4 (7,650m). Everest and Lhotse towered over the trail in the background, dwarfing us as we inched our way forward.

Both Jamling and I used oxygen, while the rest of the team went without. It was an easy trek (thanks to the work of the Sherpas), which saw us making it to C4 in 2½ hours. From C4, we could clearly see Kanchenjunga towards the east.

The view of Everest (right) and Lhotse (left) from the trail between C3 to C4 Makalu.

The placement of the C4 camp had to be done with care. If pitched too close to the ice slopes, there was a risk of avalanche from above.

After setting up C4 on an angled slope of knee-deep snow, Nima, Kami and Dhakipa went ahead to recce and fix lines above C4. By then, we had run out of hot food and were mainly sustaining ourselves on liquids, sugary drinks and energy bars.

The three stalwart Sherpas returned at 6pm after about six hours. There was good news. They reported that the terrain above C4 was sound and that they had fixed lines all the way to just below the French Couloir.

Despite the exhaustion they must have felt, they were in high spirits as they believed that there was a high chance of summit success. The rest of us were extremely encouraged by this news and crawled into our sleeping bags knowing that D-Day would dawn in just a few hours.

We set off from C4 on 1 October at about 0030h. Oxygen made a huge difference, allowing Jamling and myself to advance way ahead of the rest who were climbing without oxygen.

At that hour, the sharp cold almost took over our senses. And this was not yet winter. In an interview with Simone Moro and Denis Urubko who made the first winter ascent of Makalu in February of 2009, they described to the reporter the brutal conditions in the coldest part of winter: "The cold was indescribable … Up there there was a real battle against the wind. Between 90 and 100 km/h the gusts slapped us unexpectedly, stunned us and slammed us onto the ground. Often we remained gripped to our ice axes so as not to fly away."

The route from C4 (7,650m) to the summit (8,463m) began with about 200m of a gradual slant that became progressively steeper, leading to an immense expanse of blue ice. This required some technical climbing until the trail opened up at about 8,000m to a sloping field of snow. This was the point where there was a high risk of avalanche danger.

Above on the left, there were two wide seracs that had to be passed by way of climbing up the thick snow just adjacent. Once above the seracs, the trail veered left towards the bottom of the French Couloir (8,350m). There were broken ice rocks sprawled across the field indicating a recent avalanche. If another avalanche occurred, one of these hefty rocks could come sliding down on us.

But the knowledge that we were inching closer to the summit drove us on. This was the last technical part of the climb before hitting the summit ridge. Turning right, the trail struck out in the southwest direction to the False Summit and, once we passed that, the true pyramid summit could be steps away.

Jamling led strongly, I followed, with the rest trailing behind. We were on form, starting off from C4 with a rhythm of 30 steps at a time and, as we went higher, were keeping to a rhythm of about 20 steps.

The Frenchmen had slowed down considerably and were drained, as they had spent two nights at 7,500m without oxygen. For much of the time, Jamling and I ended up waiting for the rest of the team; there was no point moving too far ahead.

As the Sherpas had reported, the terrain was indeed good. The slope here was gradual, and the snow only knee-deep. Even when we hit the blue ice, we found that snow had covered most parts, making it easy for us to use crampons.

The three Sherpas were ready to continue fixing lines above the point they had stopped the previous day. I had no idea how the three of them had managed to fix the lines so high up the previous day and still have the strength to push for the summit with only a few hours of rest.

Jamling and I made it to the point where the fixed lines ended about 8,100m (well below the French Couloir at 8,350m), then hit this relatively flat segment above 8,000m — the only one since C4 — at about 0530h. We sat waiting in the numbing cold till the rest arrived.

The sunrise was silent and stirring, a faint peach glow growing in a slow, creeping time lapse. This was only my second time above 8,000m, the only other time being Everest; all my other attempts had stopped before the 8,000m mark. The significance of the moment moved me deeply. We could see Kangenjunga clearly to the east. The whole of Tibet stretched out sleepily, softly covered with a thick duvet of cloud.

While waiting for the rest of the team, I took off my oxygen mask for two to three minutes, just to see if I could tell the difference with and without oxygen in this death zone. Almost instantly an uneasiness and agitation came over me; I was breathing but could not get a full breath in, even while resting. Movement slowed to a crawl. I felt a certain loss of focus, like a creeping madness. I understood now why climbers who died without oxygen hallucinate.

In a medical situation, when patients come in with low oxygen, doctors call this a "combative stage" as thrashing patients try to pull off their oxygen mask and IV lines. It is a low consciousness stage. Sitting at over 8,000m in Makalu, I had a sudden insight into what these patients go through.

+ + +

By the time everyone arrived and caught their breath, it was 0630h and, at this elevation, the sky was now completely bright. Only then did we look up to see how avalanche-prone the area above was — enormous blocks of ice had broken off and were scattered over the snow field towards our right. We also realised that we were still far below the French Couloir.

Nima was determined to carry on despite the risks. Kami and Dhakipa, too, took the ropes and wordlessly began to break trail. There was not a chance we could have made it even this far without these solid fellows.

But, as we struck out, it was clear that we had underestimated the depth of the snow. Each step we took had us helplessly sinking deep in. The toil was immense, with little result.

David and Meidi proceeded at a painfully slow pace until, finally, they knew they did not have enough energy to plough through snow that grew increasingly deeper. They finally decided to turn back, Dhakipa turning back with them.

It was down to just five of us and the trail seemed impossible to break. Nima was leading, dragging the last coil of Korean cord[12] we had, ready to fix it along the way if necessary.

As we cleared the slope leading to the trail above the two huge seracs, Kami made the decision to turn back. This was a big blow to the team as he was the only one among us who had summited Makalu.

So it was just down to the four of us now: Jamling, myself, Nima and Jiandan. The French Couloir was just metres away, but each step we took broke the crust of ice and we would sink waist deep into the snow. There had been a huge snowstorm a few weeks before and there had not been enough time for the deep snow to compact. The unexpected struggle at this final stretch hit us hard.

---

12 Korean cord is a thin, lightweight nylon rope. Kernmantle rope is what is normally used as it is more durable and heavy.

Jiandan was fast for someone without oxygen, but was still straggling behind Jamling and myself.

The time was already close to 1400h but, with oxygen, I knew I could spend the whole day in the "death zone" if need be.

I worried about Nima and Jiandan, though Nima appeared to be stronger than any of us, even without oxygen.

As the slope angled steeply upwards, we crept along at such a painful pace that Nima was obliged to start fixing our final length of rope to just below the French Couloir.

While the three of us were jumaring up, Nima went ahead by himself to recce the area above the couloir. Just as we arrived at the start of the couloir, Nima returned with bad news: There was no way to make it to the summit, he said.

Nima had proven himself to be tremendously strong, with a determination so stout that he almost single handedly led us from 8,000m to 8,350m in the toughest of terrains.

When someone like Nima said it was not possible, I had to believe it.

The snow was too profound and, what's more, we had run out of rope. In milder conditions in spring, the summit ridge did not usually require many fixed lines. But the heavy snow storm of a week ago had likely left the summit in this dismal condition.

By that time, it was already 1530h. We were only 150m from the summit. Our tiny corps of climbers had pulled out everything we had to make it to this point. But it was not to be.

Jamling and I literally teared as we turned our backs to the summit. This was Jamling's backyard, his chance to summit the mountain he had seen from childhood.

Jiandan and Nima stayed awhile longer to consider every conceivable way of summiting. In the end they, too, turned back.

As we approached C4 2½ hours later, we caught sight of Pemba and Maya with Francois and Pascal from the second team. A long discussion followed but, in the end, everyone made the decision to head down the mountain the next day.

Even though we didn't reach the summit, our friends at C4 congratulated us, knowing the effort it had taken to go as far as we did. That night I was very cold and very sleepy and somehow I fell asleep in a dream state, not realising I had forgotten to put back my oxygen mask after eating. Falling into a deep sleep, I awoke gasping for air, to Jamling's consternation.

That was the end of the season on Makalu for everyone.

+ + +

Somewhere between C4 and C3 as we headed down, Jamling and I stopped to take a photo I still hold dear. In it we are standing in the snowy wilderness, smiling through tiredness and disappointment. This climb had cemented our friendship.

The emotions churning within me were mixed. Yes, the disappointment of being so close to the summit and yet so far cut deep. Yet this was also one of my proudest climbing moments. We had achieved the near impossible by making it so far in a season of poor probability, and with a small team of 14 (six foreign climbers and seven Sherpas). In fact, we were down to four people near the summit.

It was an honour to climb with my fellow teammates, and getting this close to the summit would never have been possible without the courageous Sherpas.

They had worked hard as a team to set the fixed ropes nearly all the way to the start of the French Couloir. I had nothing but the utmost respect and awe for their determination and strength.

With Jamling at C4 after turning back from the summit.

The brave Autumn 2017 Makalu expedition team.

It was not just the Sherpas who had my respect, it was also the humble kitchen staff, particularly Rescue, who regularly trekked from our Base Camp on the southwest ridge to Yak Lodge on the southeast ridge for supplies.

I had walked this trail myself on one of my rest days during the acclimatisation rotations. It had taken me four hours in descent and seven hours in ascent on the loose moraine and scree. One trek on this route and everyone in the team agreed they never wanted to walk the trail ever again. But Rescue made this walk, without complaint, almost every day. And in sandals.

Rescue reminded Jamling of how he, too, had started as a mess tent boy. Respecting the youthful Rescue for his fitness and fortitude, Jamling hired him for an expedition the following year with his trekking company, Everquest.

Perhaps it was because I was aware that this would be my last 8,000er, but my Makalu expedition had a poignancy like no other.

What a privilege for me to have made it to, not one, but 4 of earth's 8,000m mountains.

There is a simple, black Casio Pro-trek watch that I still wear to work today. Gayathri had given it to me in 2011 at the start of Climb Everest 2012. I have used it on every single climb since.

One moment is memorialised on the watch: 4:06pm, the moment I made it to 8,300m, the highest point I reached on Makalu on 1 October 2017.

Nobody knows it, but every time I strap on this watch, I feel like a different person. I feel like I am in my beloved mountains again.

EPILOGUE

"What you get by achieving your goals is not as important as what you become by achieving your goals."
Henry David Thoreau

For the first 26 years of my life, I would not have dreamt of being in a life-or-death situation. Within two weeks of turning 27, I narrowly survived the earthquake on Cho Oyu.

That was just the beginning of my Climb Everest 2012 expedition. In the course of the year, I would witness death close up: Fallen climbers who ran out of oxygen and became forever entombed in their beloved mountains; a dangling corpse hanging on a frosty serac; a half-buried blue hand in a tattered down suit, a frozen cadaver laid to rest under her national flag. The sobering fact was: *It could have been me.* With one small misstep, or if I'd let my mind wander, or if I had been at the wrong place at the wrong time.

Coming so close to death changed me. When I descended the mountains and returned to the familiarities of daily life, I found myself appreciating the fundamental life-giving things: The sounds of home, the sunrise, breath.

In short, facing death taught me to live.

I'm not at all recommending that we put ourselves in danger as a prerequisite to feeling alive. What I am saying is that the mountains brought into sharp focus for me what is important and what is not.

Growing up, I naively believed in the supremacy of cause-and-effect. I believed I was in control of my circumstances — if I worked hard, I would succeed, if I didn't I failed. A simple equation. Though that may be true for many things, overlaying that fact is another fact: There are forces completely beyond human control.

Nowhere is that clearer than on the mountains. When you are cowering in a flimsy tent as an earthquake heaves you towards the edge of an 8,000m mountain, when you sidestep a crashing boulder that could have instantly killed you if you had been one second too slow, when the liquid gold rays of a rising sun tint the world as far as eye can see, you believe. Our lives are not in our hands. Ego gives way to awe.

Knowing this has helped me to hold things a little lighter. I will do everything within my means to achieve what is important to me. But if I don't, I won't let it eat me up. The mountains taught me that.

The very unpredictability of the mountains is its beauty. Perhaps in the end that's why mountaineers climb.

+ + +

The people who became my friends from the Diploma in Mountain Medicine course opened my eyes too.

Coming from Asia, where a life path is often defined and unswerving, I was fascinated to learn about their meandering journeys. My Canadian roommate, Josh, started out in the construction industry, went on to become an IFGMA mountain guide, and only in his late 30s decided to study medicine, eventually becoming an anaesthetist.

Dee, an Irish lady in her 50s was a doctor in the Everest ER and travelled to remote corners of the world to do community work. The last I heard, she was a doctor in an Antarctic camp.

Her Irish compatriot, Jemima, had started out as a surgical scrub nurse, but decided to become a doctor. After DiMM, she went on to do an anaesthesia residency.

Ryan and Eric, an American and a Canadian, were emergency physicians who pursued all kinds of extreme sports, juggling their professions with adventure and community work.

Closer to home, Dr Mathew Cheng, the orthopaedic tumour surgeon who had supported my bid for K2, had been a medical officer in the Singapore Armed Forces (SAF) Commandos. He would later serve in war zones with the SAF where he used his surgical skills to treat locals with severe limb conditions. World reknowned in his specialty, he still managed the time to fly his own plane, maintain a helicopter licence, and go trekking and kayaking around Asia.

Each opened my eyes to the fact that it is possible to have a thriving, purposeful career while allowing room for other pursuits that feed the soul.

I was considered an outlier for taking temporary detours from my career path; it meant getting out of step with my peers.

But it made me a fuller and more fulfilled person, which in turn inspired me to be better at what I do and who I am as a husband, father, son, friend and surgeon.

+ + +

Asholkumat s/o Anbualagan was a young man whom I first met when he was incarcerated in the former Kaki Bukit Prison. At the time, I was invited by the Hindu Centre's Mitra programme to share with the young offenders my Climb Everest 2012 dream.

Yashodhara Dhoraisingam, the co-chair of the Mitra programme, said in a Singapore Youth Award 2014 video: "When Kumaran shared with these young offenders this dream he had, we saw immediately how they resonated because, as young offenders, they have many dreams and goals. And they worry, 'Does this time in incarceration mean that I can never achieve these dreams and goals?'"

Asholk added: "He came to each and every one of us, reached out his hand, gave a handshake, and went to take a seat and introduced himself as not 'Dr Kumaran', but 'Kumaran' only."

I had no idea till then the significance of a simple handshake or personal introduction.

Unbeknownst to me, even as I was in the mountains facing the dangerous aftermath of the Cho Oyu earthquake, Asholk was slogging to prepare to take the 'O' level exams in prison. I was alone with my fears of failure and death. He alone could make or break his exams. We both felt alone, and were both struggling.

When I returned to the prison to meet the boys again after Cho Oyu, uppermost on my mind was how to face them after two failed summit attempts on Mustagh Ata and now Cho Oyu. It came as a moving surprise to me that the boys were rooting for me even harder. After all, these boys with hard pasts knew what it was like to fail.

The best news of all was that Asholk had aced his 'O' levels against all odds, becoming Singapore's top scoring private candidate that year. In the Singapore Youth Awards video, he said: "I take it to myself that every day I'm climbing Mt Everest. So I will face obstacles, I will face challenges. If Kumaran can do it, why not me?"

Yashodhara added in the video: "Dr Kumaran's story revived in him that he had much potential and he should never give up on his potentiality."

But it wasn't only Asholk who was revived. At the time when I heard his good news, I was still struggling against all odds to find sponsors and train for Everest in the midst of long hours and overnight shifts at work. Physically and emotionally, I was drained. I honestly did not know if Everest would even happen. Asholk's affirmation was like a shot of adrenaline to my soul. I knew I wouldn't, couldn't, give up trying.

When I received the Singapore Youth Award 2014 at the Istana by then Deputy Prime Minister Tharman Shanmugaratnam, I invited Asholk as my guest. Some years later, he invited me to his wedding.

While Asholk and I met at just the right time for both of us, there were others in my life who had had my back for years. They were my safe place in a sea of naysayers.

Chasing a high (I seem to have taken that literally) is one thing. But my parents, who lived quietly and simply, taught me not to underestimate the value of being faithful in the small, mundane things of life. They embodied for me the Nepali saying that the mountain is not held up by the summit, but by the sides.

My sister and I used to fight like crazy when we were little. Six years older than I, her blissful existence as an only child got rudely interrupted when I arrived. As children, our age difference meant I was too young for her to confide in. But as I grew into a somewhat less annoying teen, she left for the UK where she studied and worked for the next 10 years. Without her, I felt like an only child and missed my sibling more than I expected. From the moment she returned we got on famously. Till today, she is the heart of the family, the calm, rational one who solves everyone's problems with love and sacrifice. She's the thread that holds and binds everyone in the family together.

My family and Gayathri, colleagues, Scout friends, the youth in prison, as well as the individual sponsors who dug into their pockets to support a dream that nobody, not even I, could guarantee, were the sides of my mountain that carried me all the way up to the summit.

Whatever your dream, believe in yourself and surround yourself with believers.

+ + +

The climbers who made the greatest impact on me were not the ones who single-mindedly went for the goal at all costs, but the ones who held all the precious parts of their life in judicious tension.

On my K2 team were three Chinese nationals who had attempted to summit Nanga Parbat (8,126m) — nicknamed "Killer Mountain" for its high fatality rate — just before our K2 expedition. During their summit push, they got lost and ended up running out of oxygen and food for 30 hours above 7,800m. Together with their guide, Mingma, they ended up with frostbite but, miraculously, they survived.

After our K2 expedition, one of the Chinese climbers, Zheng Lian, and Mingma decided to try for Nanga Parbat once again, to the climbing community's astonishment. By then it was way too late in the season for the journey to be undertaken safely — the ice was melting and the chances of avalanche and rockfall were significantly increased. Despite having recently survived Nanga Parbat, they were putting their lives in danger once again.

In a second miracle, they managed to summit.

Relieved as I was that they survived the dramatic ordeal, this was to me a gamblers move. Everything in their lives — including family and future — were slid across the cosmic roulette table and placed as an all-or-nothing bet.

On the other hand, there was Heidi.

The German sculptor in her 50s, who was a mother of three and a colorectal cancer survivor, was my teammate in Cho Oyu and Everest. Despite her hurdles, Heidi was the fastest of us all, male or female, even those of us in our 20s and 30s. I had secretly prided myself in being at my peak fitness. And Heidi was streaks ahead of me. I thought I had pushed myself to my absolute limit in getting this far. Heidi made me question the boundaries I had set for myself.

If I had kept to comfortable climbs, I would never have crushed my own mental limits.

I was reminded of the sports legend, Roger Bannister, the first man to break the four-minute barrier for running one mile. His 3:59.4 record on 6 May 1954, is often cited as "one of the seminal moments in the world of sports", according to Runners World.

"It has become a symbol of human achievement on the same level as the conquest of Mount Everest the previous year (29 May 1953).

"Four minutes was regarded as 'the impossible barrier', beyond human reach."

The 25-year-old medical student had constantly visualised the achievement "to create a sense of certainty in his mind and body".

It is said that once Bannister crashed through that barrier, the rest of the world believed in the possibility, and the record that had stood for nine years went on to be broken regularly.

As the saying goes: *Your comfort zone is a beautiful place, but nothing grows there.*

+ + +

Not long after my return from K2, I was hired by Dr Mark Puhaindran to join the musculoskeletal oncology division of the National University Hospital orthopaedic surgery department.

To my surprise, Dr Puhaindran, the head of the division, told me he had been more willing to offer me the job after he'd heard — not just that I had climbed K2 — but that I had turned my back to the summit and returned alive. In fact, he joked that if I had actually summited K2, he might not have offered me the job.

He extrapolated the decisions I made on K2 to surgical life, saying that my decision to turn back from the summit revealed that I knew my limitations and would request for help when needed instead of stubbornly pushing through despite safety concerns. In surgery, insight into one's own ability and humility to draw the line are essential, he reflected.

Dr Puhaindran saw my apparent failure as a success.

He showed me that there are different definitions of success. The one I hold most closely to is this dictionary definition:

"Success is the favourable or prosperous termination of attempts or endeavours."

It reminds me that my definition of success is a choice, a decision, a mindset. Success is personal, not determined by others or by any one outcome.

Through climbing, I have found that my decision-making has gained greater clarity. My empathy for my patients has grown. I am more composed and circumspect in my responses.

I did not expect these bonus benefits. And it highlighted the fact that all skills are transferrable to day-to-day life.

Climbing has made me appreciate life more, allowed me to understand myself more. I left for the mountains a jaded and tired doctor, and returned with renewed vigour for medicine.

My daily successes now come from the students I am able to teach, the patients I am able to treat, the camaraderie I am able to encourage within my team members. My fulfillment is not from the time I spent on the mountains but the time I have spent away from it.

Whenever I feel lost, I recall those nights in the mountains where you realise how small you are in the world, alone with just the stars, the mountains and the cold air — and I have clarity.

I wouldn't be the same person or doctor if I had not climbed.

When I was in a guesthouse in Gokyo, I chance upon a page from a National Geographic magazine with this quote:

"Had Mt Everest been climbed at the first attempt, the achievement would have been hailed as notable and then quickly forgotten. It was ironically repeated failures which gave the mountain real stature." (Walt Unsworth)

Success and failure are not mutually exclusive..

+ + +

When I returned from K2 and Makalu, nobody really spoke to me about my expeditions. Perhaps they thought I would be embarrassed that I had not summited either.

On the contrary, they were two of my proudest climbs. In the mountaineering world, both of these peaks are considered mammoths for their remoteness and technical difficulty. To go as far as my teams did and, in the case of Makalu, with only a handful of members, made these peaks high points in my climbing career.

Lesser known than Everest to the average person, the two peaks and their challenges were also less understood. In reality the difficulty level of K2 and Makalu posed a far greater challenge than Everest.

It made me aware of being sensitive to the challenges of others. We may not understand the extent of the difficulties they go through, but our perception does not invalidate their reality.

On the opposite end, success can also be an illusion.

In the K2 Base Camp one evening, a teammate related to me how he had summited the infamous Nanga Parbat twice, a mark of achievement in the climbing community. But his passion for the mountains had come at a cost. His wife had left him and his only child did not talk to him except when he needed money, which his father continued to oblige because it was his only contact with his son. He related all this with deep regret.

Beneath his public persona of success were unseen failures.

In the end our successes and our failures are defined by ourselves, not by others.

When I returned from Everest, the most common question asked of me was: "Now that you have summited the highest point in the world, what is there left for you?"

My reply was: "I'll just have to aim for something higher."

+ + +

It was Sir Edmund Hillary who said:

"It is not the mountain we conquer but ourselves."

Stepping on a summit did not make me a conqueror. I never conquered a mountain; I only conquered my fears and insecurities.

I think of the sole breadwinner, the exhausted caregiver, those struggling to make good after some bad decisions. Challenging as

Everest was to me, their mountains are higher, steeper, longer. But their summit can be even sweeter.

What is your Everest? What beckons your heart and fills your dreams?

Whatever you name, remember this: The destination is that which is defined by you.

ABOUT THE AUTHORS

Kumaran Rasappan is an Associate Consultant with the Department of Orthopaedic Surgery at the National University Hospital (NUH).

He is the first Singapore doctor to summit Mt Everest, and the first Singaporean to climb the world's highest peaks for charity. Dr Kumaran won the Singapore Youth Award and the ASEAN Youth Award in 2014 for his achievements.

Kumaran and his wife, Dr Gayathri Devi Nadarajan, return to Nepal annually, leading Singaporean medical students and doctors to provide humanitarian aid to various rural communities in Nepal, which has now become their second home.

Juleen Shaw is Managing Editor at Salt&Light. She hails from the newsrooms of Singapore Press Holdings and MediaCorp Publishing and is a veteran journalist. She is also co-author with Belinda Lee of *Larger than Life: Celebrating the Human Spirit*.

To view snippets of original videos and blog posts from Kumaran's previous climbs, Gayathri's blog posts on medical community work and to learn more about Project Aasha, please go to:

Kumaran's climbing YouTube channel:
youtube.com/user/koolmaran/videos

Kumaran's climbing blog:
climbeverest2012.wordpress.com

Gayathri's blog:
gaya3ramblings.blogspot.com

Project Aasha:
Website: projaasha.wixsite.com/blog
Instagram: instagram.com/lkc.projectaasha/
Facebook: facebook.com/lkcmed.projectaasha